Supermarket USA

SUPERMARKET USA

FOOD AND POWER IN THE COLD WAR FARMS RACE

SHANE HAMILTON

Yale

UNIVERSITY PRESS

New Haven and London

Yale University Press books may be purchased in quantity for educational, business, or promotional use. For information, please e-mail sales. press@yale.edu (U.S. office) or sales@yaleup.co.uk (U.K. office).

Set in Gotham and Adobe Garamond types by IDS Infotech Ltd., Chandigarh, India.
Printed in the United States of America.

Library of Congress Control Number: 2017963802
ISBN 978-0-300-23269-1 (hardcover : alk. paper)

A catalogue record for this book is available from the British Library.
This paper meets the requirements of ANSI/NISO Z39.48-1992 (Permanence of Paper).

10 9 8 7 6 5 4 3 2 1

For my family

Contents

Contents

Acknowledgments

The debts incurred in researching and writing this book are many. I am particularly grateful for research funding provided by the Rockefeller Archive Center; the National Science Foundation (Scholar's Award 0646662); the Willson Center for Humanities and Arts; the Hagley Center for the History of Business, Technology, and Society; the British Academy; and the Virginia Mary Macagnoni Prize for Innovative Research. Archivists and librarians at several institutions deserve more thanks than I can properly express here, including the staff at the Open Society Archives in Budapest, the USDA's National Agricultural Library, U.S. National Archives II, Richard B. Russell Library for Political Research and Studies (especially Jill Severn), Hagley Museum and Library, Baker Library at Harvard Business School, the Franklin D. Roosevelt Presidential Library, the Harry S Truman Library, the Library of Congress, the Museum of English Rural Life, and the Sainsbury Archive at the Museum of London Docklands.

I am grateful to the many colleagues at the University of Georgia and the University of York whose insights and conversations have helped improve this book, including Steve Berry, Lawrence Black, Jim Cobb, Bill Cooke, Chris Corker, Teresa da Silva Lopes, Beatrice D'Ippolito, Bob Doherty, Ben Ehlers, Peter Hoffer, Matthew Hollow, Timothy Johnson, Arun Kumar, Hilda Kurtz, Stephen Mihm, Simon Mollan, Bethany Moreton, Kathi Nehls, Tom Okie, Tore Olsson,

Akela Reason, Dan Rood, Claudio Saunt, Paul Sutter, Kevin Tennent, Levi Van Sant, and Pamela Voekel. I have been exceedingly fortunate to have received advice and support from several scholars whose generosity seems to know no bounds: Brian Balogh, Deborah Fitzgerald, Walter Friedman, Andrew C. Godley, Jonathan Harwood, Roger Horowitz, Meg Jacobs, Nelson Lichtenstein, Sarah Phillips, Merritt Roe Smith, and Julian Zelizer. Especially helpful critiques have been provided along the way by Paulina Bren, Nick Cullather, David Danbom, Tracey Deutsch, Bart Elmore, Mary Furner, Louis Hyman, Richard John, Mel Leffler, Marc Levinson, April Merleaux, Alice O'Connor, Patrick Hyder Patterson, Gabriel Rosenberg, Tiago Saraiva, James C. Scott, Elizabeth Tandy Shermer, Benjamin Siegel, Jenny Leigh Smith, and John Soluri.

The team at Yale University Press has been wonderfully supportive of this project. Thanks are especially due to Adina Popescu Berk and Susan Laity for their encouragement and support.

Spending years traveling to archives in faraway places to write a quixotic book requires a great deal of love and forbearance from one's family. Fortunately, Chloe, Finley, and Iris have provided both in great quantities. I can only hope that completing this book is an adequate expression of my profound gratitude.

Introduction

An absurd scene appears three minutes into the 1955 propaganda film *America's Distribution of Wealth*. Intended to introduce high school students to the moral and economic superiority of American capitalism, the film begins with a claim that the "wealth produced within American capitalism is widely distributed throughout our population." To illustrate the point, a pipe-smoking English socialist, wearing a salt-and-pepper tweed flat hat, walks through an American supermarket. "Who," he bluntly demands, "could possibly afford to buy things in a place such as this?" Stunned to learn that ordinary citizens can cram their shopping carts to the brim with packaged brand-name foods, the Brit's socialist proclivities apparently collapse on the spot, overwhelmed by the visible abundance that confirms the voiceover narrator's declaration that only American-style capitalism "provides a high degree of economic freedom."[1]

Twenty years later, a remarkably similar film produced by the supermarket chain Piggly Wiggly Southern sums up the supermarket as an ideal representation of "the American system, the American way of life." As images of farm fields and ranchlands scroll across the screen, a Piggly Wiggly manager declares that his store is a place where, "in dramatic contrast with the methods of government-dominated countries, where long queues line up for whatever is offered, the American system matches supply with demand, making available the best, and the most, for the least."[2] Supermarkets, as these propaganda films recognized, could serve as powerful tools in the Cold War ideological battle with communism, manifestly demonstrating the agricultural productivity and consumer abundance produced by American "free enterprise."

In this book I look at how American supermarkets came to be enrolled as weapons in the American economic arsenal of the Cold War. I base my analysis on two premises. The first is that the American supermarket should be understood not just as a retail space but as the endpoint of a supply chain dependent upon industrialized agriculture. Existing literature on the historical development of supermarkets prioritizes the experience of consumers and the culture and politics of a mass-consumption economy, but in this book I break down the artificial division between production and consumption. "Goods load up with meaning as they are moved from producers to purchasers," as the historian Victoria de Grazia has argued. Analyzing the supply chain of American supermarkets shows the ways in which U.S. agricultural productivity took on political as well as economic significance during the Cold War. Most important, the agricultural system that enabled the rise of the American supermarket was far from an embodiment of "free enterprise"; it was a product of powerful state investment in the science and technology required to maintain the abundance on display in mid-twentieth-century supermarkets.[3]

And yet, as the propaganda films suggest, supermarkets were upheld at that time as physical and metaphorical embodiments of free market capitalism, retail outlets in which consumers were sovereign and exceptional beneficiaries of free enterprise. Investigating how supermarket propagandists arrived at such assumptions led me to the second premise of the book: if supermarkets were understood as physical and symbolic bearers of American-style "economic freedom," there must have been consequences when they were shipped around the world as instruments of Cold War anticommunist campaigns. But what surprised me most, as I investigated such explicitly anticommunist efforts as Nelson Rockefeller's supermarkets in Venezuela in the late 1940s and the Supermarket USA exhibit in Yugoslavia in 1957, was how often supermarkets were referred to as "weapons." In 1953, for instance, the chair of the board of the Consolidated Grocers Corporation informed a group of European businessmen that "food has proved to be the most effective weapon in the cold war," a statement that was duly reported in the *New York Times* with nary a word of skepticism.[4]

It was at this point that I realized the need to coin a phrase. In what I call the Cold War Farms Race, certain key business leaders and policy makers both in the United States and abroad recognized the international agricultural implications of a supermarket-driven food economy. If supermarkets were weapons, it was because farms emerged as crucial battlegrounds in the economic contest between the United States and the Soviet Union. As the noted modernization theorist Walt Rostow explained in *Harper's* magazine in 1955, U.S. models of industrial agriculture could "shatter the belief in Communism as the unique method for rapid development."[5] Such thinking lay at the heart of the Farms Race, as American foreign policy makers developed strategies in which American-style food abundance operated as anticommunist propaganda, as a tool for counterrevolutionary economic development, and as a morally justifiable model for flexing American might on the world stage.

From the first premise flow two caveats about what this book is not. It is not a firm-level or industry-level business history of supermarkets; it is a history of capitalism that uses supermarkets as a lens into the workings of industrial agriculture. Very good studies are available of supermarkets as retail forms, of supermarkets and gender roles, of the place of supermarkets in the contest between small and big business, and of the contribution of supermarkets to mass consumer culture. Where appropriate I draw on these studies, but always to advance a fundamentally new understanding of supermarkets as endpoints on a supply chain, to think outside the box of the retail space of the American supermarket. Yet if I emphasize industrial agricultural production as a precondition for supermarket-style mass food distribution, I do not do so in a traditional history of agriculture that focuses solely on farms, farmers, or farm policy. By analyzing the agricultural supply chain of the supermarket-anchored food system, I hope to bring attention to the inherently intertwined politics of food production and consumption.[6]

The second premise, likewise, requires a word about what is not included here. This is not a military or diplomatic history of the Cold War, nor is it a study focused on cultural diplomacy or psychological warfare. I do, however, build upon recent historical studies that suggest the Cold War should be understood as, at heart, an economic contest, fought in realms from the cultural and intellectual to the political and material. The book is furthermore not framed primarily by questions of the "Americanization" of international consumer culture or business practices, although the global reach of American supermarkets was sometimes spurred by force, at other times adopted and adapted "by invitation," and at still other times met with outright (sometimes violent) resistance. Supermarkets were invented in the United States, and I shall explore how, from the 1940s on, they made their way around the world, often explicitly to bring American-style economic culture in their wake. But even if supermarkets did sometimes contribute to forms of "Americanization," I critically assess what that meant for the farmers, consumers, business leaders, and government agents both in the United States and abroad. In other words, rather than assume that supermarkets necessarily embodied American consumer capitalism, I explain how they came to be understood that way.[7]

American supermarkets were machines for selling goods as well as ideas, for enabling as well as constraining the choices made by food producers and consumers. As such, they were instruments of power. Supermarkets did not emerge from some inherent logic of capitalist "free enterprise," nor were they predetermined to become "weapons" in a Cold War Farms Race. Nonetheless, it somehow did not seem absurd for propagandists in the 1950s to imagine overseas socialists tearing up their Party membership cards upon entering the aisles of an American-style supermarket. And although supermarkets were not weapons in the same sense as nuclear warheads atop intercontinental ballistic missiles, the fact that such a strange and disturbing analogy was so widely accepted during the Cold War demands a book-length investigation. Let us begin in the central buying offices of the mid-twentieth-century world's largest retailer, A&P.

1

Machines for Selling

In November 1947, *Fortune* magazine detailed the workings of
the Great Atlantic & Pacific Tea Company, at the time the world's
largest supermarket chain. "One of the mightiest single distributive
organizations in the world," according to *Fortune*, A&P represented a
"distinctly American phenomenon." The mind-boggling volume of
foodstuffs that moved through A&P's distribution channels accounted for one aspect of its exceptionally American nature. In just one year
the company sold, among many other food items, 835 million pounds
of meat, 300 million loaves of bread, and 600 million doughnuts. Its
total sales volume, accounting for one-tenth of all U.S. retail food
sales at the time, was enough to "feed a country the size of Poland, if
Poland were eating as well as the U.S. these days." Dietary abundance,
in other words, was a mark of American distinctiveness, a stark contrast to the painful scarcity faced by postwar socialist consumers. But
what also marked A&P as especially American, according to *Fortune*,
was the powerful political message embedded in the machinery of its
operations. With a mere 1.6 percent return on sales in 1946, A&P's
profit margin was "so thin as to be practically socialism." Technologies
of mass distribution made a wide range of food available to American
consumers at low prices, demonstrating the inherent strength of capitalist free enterprise. "Indeed," declared *Fortune*, "A & P can show
socialism how to work."[1]

A&P was not the first chain supermarket by any means, but as of the mid-twentieth century it was the primary pacesetter in the American grocery field. Its business practices were widely mimicked as well as challenged by competitors including Safeway and Kroger in ways that helped permanently transform the American system of food distribution. At the time of the *Fortune* article's publication, A&P was embroiled in a federal antitrust investigation, accused by the U.S. Department of Justice of constraining competition. The firm's defenders, in both courts of law and public opinion, insisted that the chain supermarket was not only a product of highly competitive free enterprise but also a producer of unprecedented consumer access to a range of affordable foods. What both sides could clearly agree upon was that in the late 1940s, A&P and other national supermarket chains exercised extraordinary power within the American economic scene. The nature of that power is the central theme of this chapter. Contrary to A&P's public claims, the power of a midcentury supermarket chain was not a simple product of "free enterprise" but emerged in tandem with a state-supported process of industrializing agriculture. Even as the Department of Justice was calling supermarket chains to task for alleged anticompetitive practices, other arms of government—particularly the Department of Agriculture—were actively aiding and abetting the supermarket business model. It was indeed accurate for *Fortune* to uphold A&P as a "distinctly American phenomenon," but in many ways what made the supermarket chain so "American" was its tight integration into a technological system of agricultural production utterly dependent upon state-supported scientific research. Perhaps A&P could "show socialism how to work" at the height of the Cold War, but doing so would have required revealing that the American system of food abundance was no mere product of free enterprise.

———————

Before about 1910, the term "chain store" would have made little sense to most Americans. Wholesalers and manufacturers, not retailers, pursued vertical and horizontal integration in the late nineteenth century, seeking economies of scale by coordinating production and distribution or by merging with or acquiring their competitors. In the retail field there were important exceptions to the dominance of wholesalers and manufacturers, including mail-order firms such as Sears, Roebuck and urban department stores like Wanamaker's and Marshall Field's. Yet for many everyday goods, the retail landscape remained fragmented in the early twentieth century. Small, family-owned enterprises served as the primary liaison between individual consumers and the lengthy and complicated supply networks that provided them with food, medicines, and hardware. Yet by 1930, chain stores—that is, multiple retail enterprises with the same name operating under centralized management or ownership—were omnipresent in the American economy, accounting for approximately one out of every five dollars transacted in the nation's retail business. The Great Atlantic & Pacific Tea Company, along with a host of other grocery, drugstore, and hardware firms, developed techniques for standardizing, centralizing, and expanding operations to minimize transaction costs and make impressive profits off of high-volume, thin-margin sales. A&P was the most visibly successful grocery firm following the chain-store model, so much so that for forty-three years (until 1963), A&P was the largest retailer (measured by sales) of any type in the United States. In ascending to a position of retail prominence, however, chain-store firms such as A&P came under systematic attack in state legislatures beginning in the 1920s. In 1927 Maryland became the first state to levy a special tax on chain stores, and by 1939 twenty-seven states had enacted similar taxes.[2]

Those who deemed taxes on chain stores a necessity saw centralized retailer-distributors as a menace to competitive enterprise. Yet despite claims that chains were bent upon destroying small Mom-and-Pop corner retailers, usually it was wholesalers whose economic position was most threatened by the rise of chains. Before the 1920s, wholesale grocers served as crucial conduits between producers and retailers. Over the course of the 1920s, however, chains increasingly bypassed wholesalers, purchasing direct from suppliers. Between 1922 and 1928, the proportion of chain-store direct purchases from manufacturers increased from 76.5 percent to 81.2 percent of total purchases. But for all the understandable hostility wholesalers expressed toward the chains, both pursued at core a similar business strategy. Wholesalers as well as chain retailers aimed to gather up a wide array of goods from an economically and geographically dispersed economic world populated by many sellers, large and small, and position themselves as inescapable funnels through which those goods had to pass in order to reach a similarly widespread world of consumers. The economist Joan Robinson, surveying the marked rise of such forms of centralized purchasing systems in a wide variety of industries, became convinced that this form of economic consolidation was substantially different from monopoly power (in which a single seller dominates the market for a particular good or service). In her 1933 classic, *The Economics of Imperfect Competition*, Robinson introduced *monopsony* to the English-speaking world's economic lexicon. Though far less evocative than *menace*, Robinson's new term for concentrated buying power nonetheless sought to capture the sense of populist mistrust of big buyers expressed by consumers, small business owners, and politicians.[3]

Wholesale grocers put the problem of monopsony onto the federal legislative agenda in 1935 when they petitioned Congress for a nationwide rebuke to chain-store buying power. Finding opportunistic allies in Senator Joseph Robinson of Arkansas and the populist Texas representative Wright Patman, wholesale grocers were delighted when in 1936 Congress passed the Robinson-Patman Act. The law made the United States the first (and only) Western country with a statutory limitation on concentrated retail buying power. The passage of the Robinson-Patman Act marked the high tide of anti-monopsony politics, yet it did not lead to a dramatic turn of fortunes for chain stores. The Federal Trade Commission (FTC), charged with enforcing the act, permitted retailer-distributors to demand special discounts from sellers if done so in a "good faith" attempt to compete with other retailers on price. Large-scale buyers thus responded to the legislation by developing sophisticated accounting methods for cost analysis to justify discounts received from suppliers. Smaller firms, generally unable to afford the expense of such scrupulous accounting, often bore the brunt of FTC investigations under Robinson-Patman. And although the wholesale grocers who lobbied for the legislation successfully convinced many southerners and midwesterners that chain stores were a menace, FTC investigations in the 1930s suggested that concentrated buying power was not in and of itself the primary reason for the chain stores' success. Only about 15 percent of chains' low retail prices, according to one FTC study, could be attributed to centralized buying practices. More important was the chains' ability to sell high volumes of goods at low margins, thus reducing per-unit costs of sales.[4]

The problem of monopsony was politically salient during the Great Depression, but was often exaggerated and almost always misunderstood. Centralized purchasing was a necessary but not sufficient condition for the chain-store business model. The core determinant of chain-store profitability and competitive advantage was stock turnover—that is, how many items could be sold in a given time period. The longer inventory sat on shelves, the higher the cost of all goods sold. Time is money in retailing, and a high rate of stock turnover is the surest means of garnering reliable profits, particularly when a retailer's business model is geared toward selling low-margin goods. A&P pursued various techniques for boosting stock turnover, often with astonishing success. A 1929 FTC investigation discovered that in its largest store A&P turned over its stock sixty-three times in one year, while on average the company's stores turned over stock twenty-five times. Moving large inventories so quickly enabled efficient chain stores to reduce labor expenses by increasing annual sales per employee. A Department of Agriculture study undertaken in 1923 found that retail shops with annual sales per employee below ten thousand dollars incurred labor costs of 15.6 to 16.6 percent of total sales prices, while in stores with more than twenty thousand dollars in sales, per-employee labor costs took up only 8.25 percent of sales. In-store labor costs, in other words, accounted for the single largest percentage difference between small and large retailers in the expense of goods sold. It would have taken truly extraordinary discount structures for centralized purchasing to have such a degree of impact on consumer prices or retailer profitability. Yet centralized purchasing was undoubtedly a crucial component of the chain-store strategy of increasing stock turn. Having reliable supplies of standardized goods on the shelves when consumers were ready to buy was a necessary precondition for boosting average sales per employee. Furthermore, chains undoubtedly leveraged volume discounts into increased profitability; one study suggested that as of 1929, one-fourth of A&P pre-tax profits were accounted for by so-called allowances or discounts conceded by manufacturers to the retailer. But contrary to the Robinson-Patman Act's declarations, consolidated purchasing power was far from the only source of chain stores' competitive advantage over independent retailers.[5]

Self-service retailing, pursued by both independent and chain grocers, offered one potent means of reducing labor costs. Before 1916, when Clarence Saunders ballyhooed his opening of an entirely self-service Piggly Wiggly grocery store in Memphis, Tennessee, customers could expect every grocery purchase to entail an elaborate social ritual with a (usually male) clerk physically positioned between the buyer and the goods. Clerks sized up a buyer's social status and ability to pay before suggesting a particular brand of, say, canned coffee. Haggling over price might then ensue, with both the clerk and the shopper fully aware of the customer's credit history. Racial or ethnic prejudices might serve either to benefit or harm the customer's negotiating power. Retail food shopping before the self-service system thus could be understood as a form of "moral economy," with social norms, communal obligations, and unequal power relations of race, gender, and class embedded in every act of exchange. Saunders and every grocer who followed his lead in introducing the self-service format sought to depersonalize the moment of exchange, putting authority over transactions firmly in the hands of the store manager rather than those of either the clerk or the shopper. Transactions moved from the socially contested space of the store aisles to the more abstract regions of sales ledgers and inventory-control systems.

In the original Piggly Wiggly, this architecture of paternalistic control was starkly emphasized by a strict one-way routing of the store's aisles. "This circuitous path must be traversed by every purchaser who enters the salesroom," explained Saunders in his 1917 U.S. patent application for the self-service store. The layout not only enabled the merchant to "dispense with the employment of many clerks who are usually engaged to wait upon the customers" but also, according to Saunders, dramatically increased—"by three or four times"—the volume of sales per square foot of retail space. Many chain-store operators, as well as many independent grocers, immediately recognized the potential for profits and seized upon the self-serve model. Among national chains, A&P was comparatively slow in adopting the system, preferring to rely throughout the 1920s on its centralized purchasing and tight inventory management to keep margins low. But in the 1930s A&P switched to the self-service approach.[6]

One reason A&P executives felt compelled to adopt self-service in their stores was the rise of a new business form in the 1930s: the supermarket. King Kullen in Queens, New York, is often regarded as the first supermarket, and like the supermarkets that followed its lead it prioritized high-volume self-service sales at blisteringly low margins. Most of the early supermarkets were independent stores or small regional chains, and consequently did not rely on nationwide centralized purchasing systems to keep costs low, instead focusing on accelerating stock turnover to maximize profit. Steep discounts offered in bare-bones warehouse-like settings earned the early supermarkets monikers such as "price wreckers" and "price crushers." What made supermarkets novel was not their low prices or self-service cash-and-carry approach, however, but the extraordinary array of goods and services they provided under one roof: fresh produce, dairy, meats, baked goods, and canned and packaged foods were to be had, but so were a stunning variety of other items and services. Before the advent of the supermarket, most shoppers would have visited multiple shops over several days for a week's food, perhaps stopping at a downtown public market for fresh produce, a chain or independent grocer for canned and dry goods, a butcher for meat, and a baker for bread. The Big Bear Market that opened in Somerville, Massachusetts, in spring 1933 in a 32,000-square-foot space on an abandoned factory floor included not only all those food products but also much more: a barber shop, cut flowers, dry cleaning services, a shoe repair, wallpaper, even a "chop suey" department. Major chains such as A&P maintained strict control over inventories, seeking to limit the range of goods on offer to minimize operating costs. Supermarkets, by contrast, maximized offerings, providing one-stop shopping in a carnivalesque atmosphere, attracting as many customers as possible into a store and bombarding them with steeply discounted items so they would leave with as many goods as their vehicle could carry.[7]

The supermarket model posed a substantial threat to established chain grocers such as A&P. A Big Bear in Elizabeth, New Jersey, reported weekly sales of a hundred thousand dollars in the early 1930s, equivalent to the entire weekly volume of sales at all one hundred A&P stores in the area surrounding that city. Despite competitors' impressive sales figures, A&P executives at first remained convinced that the price wreckers were a "passing fancy," a rowdy band of circus clowns roaring through town. As consumers continued to flock to supermarkets through the mid-1930s, however, A&P's directors saw the handwriting on the wall and quickly joined in the fray. By 1938 the firm was operating 1,100 self-service supermarkets (figure 1). Other chain grocery pioneers, including Kroger, Safeway, Piggly Wiggly, Grand Union, and National Tea, likewise converted small stores into larger supermarkets. Fusing the chain store's centralized buying practices with the supermarket's one-stop self-service approach was a necessary strategy for competing for consumers' tightly guarded food dollars during the Great Depression. Politically, however, the move of the chains into the supermarket field prompted a new round of attacks, including an effort by Congressman Wright Patman to institute a federal anti-chain tax in 1940, as well as a series of FTC and Justice Department antitrust investigations. But in contrast to the success of the anti-chain-store movement in earlier years, Patman's proposed tax bill went nowhere in Congress as consumer representatives made clear

Figure 1 A&P arrived somewhat late to the supermarket game, but in 1940, when this picture was taken by Jack Delano in Durham, North Carolina, the chain operated over a thousand supermarkets. (Library of Congress, Prints and Photographs Division, FSA/OWI Collection, LC-USF33-020523.)

their appreciation of the low prices available in the nation's ever-more-common supermarkets.[8]

Wartime conditions further allayed most remaining concerns about chain groceries and supermarkets. Independent grocers benefited from rationing and general consumer prosperity, making the chains temporarily less of a threat to the viability of Mom-and-Pop stores. Shoppers relied on small-scale local proprietors for access to rationed items such as meat and sugar as well as for personalized services—including sales on credit and home delivery—more readily available from independent stores than from chains. Chains furthermore generally complied more straightforwardly with rationing and price controls imposed by the Office of Price Administration, frequently making independent stores the only source of otherwise hard-to-find items such as sugar and steaks.[9]

Under such circumstances it might seem surprising that A&P was subject to a series of antitrust investigations during the war. Led by Thurman Arnold, the Department of Justice initiated several rounds of inquiry into the chain's business practices. A 1942 indictment of top-level A&P executives went nowhere and was ultimately withdrawn by federal prosecutors, only to be replaced in 1944 by a criminal suit that by any measure must be understood as one of the most significant antitrust cases in U.S. history. In *U.S. v. New York Great Atlantic & Pacific Tea Company,* Arnold's antitrust division charged the chain with abuse of monopsony power, declaring that the company used its buying practices to restrain trade and bully suppliers into submission. The criminal trial that began in April 1945 produced twenty-one-thousand transcript pages of testimony, with many more pages of analysis appearing in business, economic, and law journals for years afterward. Yet for all the documentation and disagreement, at heart the case was relatively straightforward. Both sides agreed that A&P sold food to consumers at lower prices than many of its competitors. Both sides also agreed that one important reason A&P was able to undersell competitors was its calculated efficiency in managing its supply network, using vertical integration and centralized purchasing to keep costs low and standardize quality. What they disagreed on, however, was the extent to which the firm's approach to cost-cutting either harmed or benefited consumers.

The defense maintained that A&P's low prices not only benefited consumers but provided indisputable evidence that the firm utilized resources better than its competitors did. The prosecutors, however, contended that any benefits consumers received in the short term were outweighed by A&P's overwhelming dominance of the grocery trade, which limited opportunities for other retailers to sell at similarly low prices. In September 1946 the federal judge hearing the case agreed with the prosecution and levied a ten thousand dollar fine on each of the named defendants. The battle nonetheless dragged on for years. A 1949 appeal was overturned, but even with that victory the Antitrust Division pressed forward with a civil suit, demanding that A&P break up its retail business into smaller units. Not until 1954 was the case fully resolved, when the Justice Department dropped its pursuit after A&P severed its produce brokerage subsidiary, the Atlantic Commission Company.[10]

The results of the antitrust case against A&P were mixed. On one hand, the firm's top executives were found guilty of restraint of trade in a criminal suit that generated headlines for nearly a decade. On the other, neither A&P nor other national chains suffered much in the way of loss of business. Indeed, by the mid-1950s the business practices perfected by A&P were being widely adopted by chains small and large as supermarkets came to anchor the American food retailing landscape. More broadly, the case represented one of the last sweeping efforts to use federal antitrust power to rein in perceived abuses of monopsony (as opposed to monopoly) power. Not until the mid-1960s would federal antitrust agents make a significant attempt to revive their pursuit of monopsonists, and even then they did so only fitfully and generally without much impact on business practices. The effects of monopsony on consumers were difficult to apprehend as a matter of antitrust policy at midcentury, and they remain so today.[11]

Yet for all the debates over how A&P's midcentury business practices impacted consumers, nearly everyone familiar with the antitrust case could agree that A&P's tight control over its supply network had significant, dramatic, long-term consequences for agricultural producers. As farmers came to be enrolled in the supermarket system that fed America's consumers, the industrialization of agriculture picked up pace substantially. American agriculture industrialized, fitfully at first in the late nineteenth century, then more consistently in the early twentieth century, as the Department of Agriculture funneled taxpayer funds into one of the most sustained scientific and technological research campaigns in world history. Innovations in chemical fertilizers and pesticides, hybrid seeds, grafting and cultivation of horticultural wonders, antibiotics and selective breeding for livestock, mechanized harvesters, and elaborate technological systems for moving milk, meat, vegetables, fruits, and grains to the marketplace—all relied to a great extent on direct or indirect government money and scientific research. The consolidated buying power of large-scale food businesses undoubtedly contributed to the rapid speed-up of U.S. agricultural industrialization that occurred from the mid-1930s through the rest of the twentieth century. In the hundred years leading up to 1935, annual productivity growth in U.S. agriculture proceeded at a pace of approximately 1 percent per year. By 1940, the annual growth rate in American agricultural productivity had at least doubled, and by some estimates tripled. This rate of growth, which continued on average until the end of the century, outpaced every other economic sector in the nation. Supermarkets were not the primary cause of agricultural industrialization, but their emergence and rapid rise in the 1930s was predicated on the state-supported transformation of the supply network that fed into their buying system. From the late 1930s on, chain supermarkets developed increasingly sophisticated systems for demanding more standardized, higher-volume agricultural production. In the process of supplying American consumers with abundance, supermarkets depended upon government actions hidden in plain sight. In the construction of the nation's supermarket supply chains, state power and market power were closely intertwined, with each abetting the other.[12]

The business practices for which A&P was both admired and reviled at midcentury were explicitly dependent upon a federally supported infrastructure of industrial agriculture. A 1944 A&P handbook for store managers made clear that this was well understood by top executives of the firm: "We believe that production and distribution of agricultural products are not separate activities." The handbook went on to explain that much of the firm's approach to supply-chain management mimicked core activities of the Department of Agriculture, as purchasing agents "have worked with [farmers] to improve the quality of the produce we offer consumers; to establish uniform standards for grade and pack; to find better, less costly, less wasteful means of moving food from farm to dinner table."[13]

The importance of standardization to A&P's business model is worth further consideration. The Cornell agricultural economist James E. Boyle noted the significance in a 1930 article published in the trade journal *Chain Store Progress,* explaining that "chains have most of their success in handling articles of higher standardization." Standards allowed for simplification, which in turn enabled chains to stock only items which consistently sold at high velocity. As Boyle further explained, if a store stocked several dozen kinds of a particular item, but half of those items accounted for a tiny percentage of sales, stock turnover was dragged into the region of unprofitability. Chain grocers—always keeping a close eye on the crucial metric of stock turnover—thus insisted that farmers produce only a limited range of goods. Boyle noted that in his home state of New York in 1930, farmers produced over "two hundred varieties of apples, but the chains who handle some of these apples are asking for only ten varieties. The chain store is becoming the main factor in teaching farmers to simplify their production." Standardized produce served to increase stock turnover ratios, but it also simplified the job of purchasing agents. As the Wharton professor John H. Frederick noted in 1931, "Chain store buyers can not go from farm to farm picking up enough to make a carload of some particular type of produce." Farmers who wanted to sell to the nation's biggest buyers needed to find ways to produce in the quantities and grades required by those buyers.[14]

For many top-selling items, a chain like A&P was able to capitalize on processes of standardization and industrialization that had been long under way at the behest of government agents. Take wheat. As the main ingredient in a range of packaged goods that consumers expected chain grocers to stock, including breakfast cereals and packaged bread, wheat was a crucial component of a supermarket's agricultural supply network. Since the 1870s, wheat had been thoroughly standardized, transformed into a commodity and carefully graded into forms amenable to processing into packaged cereals, breads, and biscuits. The farmers who produced wheat for commodity buyers at Chicago's grain exchanges, however, often struggled to produce the types and volumes of grain demanded by an industrializing nation. Doing so required intensive state backing, as federal government agents enabled American farmers to intensify and expand wheat production. Even before the Department of Agriculture became a permanent part of the executive branch of the federal government in 1862, government agents scoured the world looking for varieties of wheat suitable for planting on the expanding acreage of America's diverse climates and soils. In the early twentieth century, one of the most successful of these varieties was Marquis, introduced from Canada and tested by the Department of Agriculture in 1912–13. Within a few short years, Marquis had become the most planted wheat variety in northern U.S. grain regions. In 1900, the U.S. Department of Agriculture (USDA) wheat breeder Mark Alfred Carleton brought strains of Russian wheat to western Kansas, well-suited to the region's cool and dry climate; by 1914 the Russian strain Kharkof was accounting for about half the entire Kansas wheat crop. Integrating U.S. wheat farming into a system of international biological exchange allowed for dramatic geographical expansion of the cereal grain, but it also opened up farmers to imported biological threats, including insects, fungi, and other pests. Rust posed a particular risk to expanding wheat monocrops, and here again government-employed researchers served at the front lines, working incessantly to combat rust by breeding, importing, and encouraging the planting of rust-resistant wheat varieties. Without such government-led biological research, as the economic historians Alan Olmstead and Paul Rhode have demonstrated, the world-renowned productivity of American wheat lands could not have been maintained in the early twentieth century.[15]

Chain-store buying agents purchased wheat only in packaged, processed form, and so rarely needed to give much thought to how the grain supply network was actively industrialized and commoditized. But adopting the supermarket business model—in which chains sold not only packaged goods but also fresh meats, dairy products, and fresh produce—depended upon an even wider array of government actions. The meat and dairy economies of the early twentieth century were, like wheat, subject to intensive government-sponsored research aimed at boosting productivity. By the 1930s, beef cattle and hogs were being fed increasing volumes of corn to fatten them for slaughter at Chicago's great meatpacking houses. State-sponsored research into corn breeding produced dramatic results in the 1930s when farmers first began widely adopting hybrid seeds, locking themselves into a system in which commercial demands for high-yielding standardized seeds outweighed the farmers' long-maintained attempts to match self-selected corn varieties to local soil and market conditions. The extraordinary volumes of corn that flooded markets from the 1930s on in turn transformed the beef industry, as livestock raisers became ever more reliant upon cheap grains and confinement feeding operations to meet America's seemingly insatiable demand for red meat. In the dairy realm, government researchers in the early twentieth century deployed regulatory structures, inspection regimes, grading systems, and scientific research into animal breeding and disease prevention in a massive campaign to make milk and dairy products into central components of the American diet. Chain stores capitalized on such work, relying, for instance, on state inspection seals on butter packages to assure customers that a particular brand of butter could be trusted without the need for visual inspection that had characterized butter buying in a more localized economy.[16]

The agricultural productivity that enabled chains to sell the nation's consumers a wide range of standardized, affordable foods relied upon state intervention, but supermarket buyers also exercised significant power in managing their supply networks. This was perhaps especially the case for fresh fruits and vegetables, which were crucial to the supermarket business model by functioning as traffic builders in stores. It is worth returning to *Fortune* magazine's 1947 exploration of A&P's operations, and particularly the maps produced by Elmer Smith to accompany the article, to get a better sense of how A&P and other midcentury supermarkets exercised power over their produce supply chains. One of the central points that Smith was trying to visualize for *Fortune* was explained in the article text: namely, that A&P had to be understood as "one giant operation" devoted, first and foremost, to "an increasing centralization of buying." In other words,

A&P was aiming to act as a monopsonist, seeking to maximize its buying power in a market populated by many sellers (farmers, shipping agents, and food processors). And yet, as the *Fortune* article went on, the extraordinary centralization of buying practices at A&P was coupled with "paradoxically, many *decentralized* aspects."[17]

A map of A&P's produce network (figure 2) illustrates some octopus-like signs of economic centralization. Snaking through the nation is a 9,300-mile network of teletype cables connecting central purchasing agents in Chicago and New York to fifty-five far-flung terminal sales offices, each responsible for calculating at what price and from what regions to buy, say, potatoes in any given week. The teletype system enabled a rapid-response approach to produce purchasing, enabling A&P's central offices to keep a watchful eye on the price and quality of its fresh produce. Information conveyed along the teletype network included not only historical prices and divisional store sales data but also weather and pest reports. Thus, Detroit-based A&P buyers could discover in nearly real time that brown rot was appearing on Michigan peaches, enabling them to look to Colorado instead for purchases; and if Colorado's peaches were getting pricey for any reason, to move on to California or South Carolina. Furthermore, a handful of produce warehouses anchored the system. In those warehouses, raw produce was sorted, graded, and packaged into uniform commodities, compelled by the chain's marketing machinery to adapt to a sales system driven primarily by price, aesthetics, and convenience. Given the firm's strategy of pushing the largest possible volume of food through its retail stores at the fastest possible pace, such standardization was essential if customers were to be reliably and repeatedly drawn into A&P's stores.[18]

And yet, in the digitized map we also clearly see what *Fortune* labeled the "paradoxical" aspects of *decentralization*. Scattered

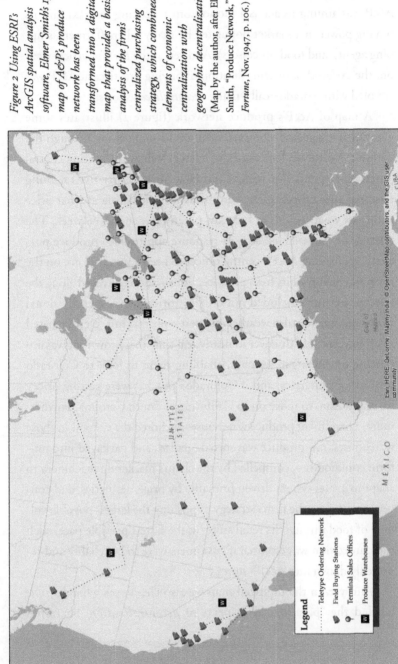

Figure 2 Using ESRI's ArcGIS spatial analysis software, Elmer Smith's 1947 map of A&P's produce network has been transformed into a digital map that provides a basis for analysis of the firm's centralized purchasing strategy, which combined elements of economic centralization with geographic decentralization. (Map by the author, after Elmer Smith, "Produce Network," Fortune, Nov. 1947, p. 106.)

Legend

- .... Teletype Ordering Network
- 🎒 Field Buying Stations
- ○ Terminal Sales Offices
- W Produce Warehouses

Esri, HERE, DeLorme, Mapmyindia, © OpenStreetMap contributors, and the GIS user community

UNITED STATES

MEXICO

Gulf of Mexico

CUBA

throughout the country are some hundred field buying stations: semi-temporary structures devoted to connecting, in space and time, knowledgeable humans—produce buyers—working for A&P's Atlantic Commission Company (ACCO) with other knowledgeable humans (farmers, shipping agents, members of cooperatives, wholesalers) who had produce to sell. These field buying stations operated within a shroud of secrecy, and they relocated regularly, both seasonally and annually. For the purposes of this analysis, it is important to note that while there are plenty of stations in the all-important fruit-and-vegetable-producing state of California (eleven), the other ninety or so sites are sprinkled in diverse places—South Carolina, Idaho, southern Illinois, and so forth. As A&P's manual for managers explained in 1944, "ACCO purchases fine produce from fields, groves, and orchards of forty-five of the nation's first-rank agricultural states." With its "vast facilities," ACCO enabled field buyers to "follow the harvest from the South to the North, and from the West to the East, purchasing fine crops direct from growers and shippers, and then dispatching them to your store by the most direct distribution routes yet developed."[19]

If we visualize the layout of A&P's combined centralization and decentralization systems, several points become apparent. For one, we can see that the industrial food-supply network constructed by the nation's leading supermarket chain at midcentury was anything but simple to construct and operate. In contrast with the fantasies of atomic-age futurists who envisioned a food-supply network composed solely of (California-based) factory farms delivering produce via pneumatic tubes to American kitchens, the supermarket supply networks of the mid-twentieth century were remarkably impermanent, flexible, and dynamically mapped and re-mapped onto a farm landscape characterized by diversity, regional specialization, and seasonality.

Take, for instance, a map (figure 3) illustrating the geographical proximity of A&P field buying stations and retail stores to the nation's top one hundred potato-producing counties. From these data certain patterns become clear. Perhaps surprisingly, we see that the most densely populated regions of the country, including the Eastern Seaboard, the upper Midwest, and coastal California—the areas most crucial to A&P's mission of pumping foodstuffs through its supply chain at high rates of stock turnover on razor-thin margins—were all quite close to major potato-farming centers. Furthermore, sixteen of the top hundred potato-producing counties had at least one A&P field buying station located either within or immediately adjacent to their borders; these sixteen counties together produced 122 million bushels of potatoes. Of the ninety-seven field buying stations represented on the map, fifty-four were located in close proximity to a major potato region. Drawing out the raw data in a different way, we can see that the median distance of an A&P store from a potato county was only forty-seven miles, and that 66 percent of A&P stores were located within a hundred miles of a major potato center. Stores in populous cities, including New York, Chicago, and Washington, D.C., were thus all quite close to potato sources.[20]

Field buyers of potatoes for A&P could thus meet the demands of a centralized, national provisioning system by locating themselves near regional potato-producing areas. But the productivity of those areas relied on much more than advantages of soil and climate. Commercial potato production, when practiced on the large scale that attracted A&P buyers to certain regions, required techniques and technologies for preventing pathogens from destroying an entire crop. One pathogen of great concern was the fungus *Synchytrium endobioticum*, the cause of potato wart, which had devastated European potato crops throughout the latter half of the nineteenth century. After the

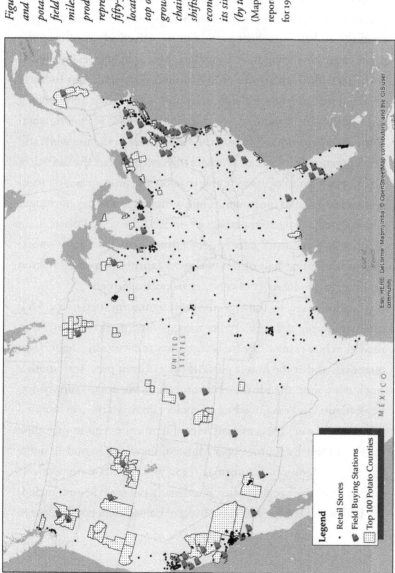

Figure 3 Field buying stations and major production areas for potatoes for A&P stores. Only field buying stations within 150 miles of a major potato-producing county are represented on this map. With fifty-four field buying stations located in close proximity to the top one hundred potato-growing counties, A&P's supply chain could rapidly respond to shifts in environmental or economic conditions affecting its single largest produce item (by tonnage) at midcentury. (Map by the author, using data reported in the agricultural census for 1950.)

S. endobioticum fungus was discovered on North American soil in 1909, the U.S. Federal Horticulture Board devised an embargo system, first deployed in 1912. Several million bushels of infested potatoes had, however, already made their way to the United States from Europe, and in 1918 an outbreak was discovered in Pennsylvania. Federal and state agents instituted strict local quarantines and strengthened the embargo on European imports, effectively confining the potato wart infestation to Pennsylvania. Meanwhile, federally funded scientists in the Department of Agriculture's Bureau of Plant Industry set about studying how infestations spread. This proved a challenging technical problem requiring decades-long analyses of experimental plots, as spores from the fungus can lie dormant in the soil while still being potentially infectious for more than twenty years. By the 1940s, USDA plant pathologists were able to select and propagate varieties of potatoes resistant to the fungus. Thus, although to this day the fungus is considered a dangerous pathogen—in 2002 the USDA placed it on a list of "bioterrorism" agents—the government-led assault on the fungus in the first half of the twentieth century prevented it from limiting the productivity of commercial potato farmers.[21]

Potatoes were, by tonnage, the most significant item in the A&P produce supply network. Yet as a major supermarket chain, A&P needed to buy many other fresh vegetables and fruits in reliably large quantities and at the lowest possible price. Green peas were another stock item, and provide a useful contrast to the potato supply network (figure 4). Peas grow best in cooler climes, so the top hundred pea counties were concentrated in cool temperate regions including the Pacific Northwest, the upper Midwest, the northern mid-Atlantic, and Maine. Stores in California, Texas, and Florida were relatively distant from their pea supplies, but densely populated cities, including Chicago, Detroit, and New York, remained remarkably close to their peas. Nonetheless, peas on average had to travel much farther through A&P's supply network than did potatoes. The median distance was 395 miles, with only 25 percent of stores located within a hundred miles of a major pea-producing county. Fresh peas at midcentury were seasonal products, available only for brief periods during the year, and consequently they posed a much greater challenge than potatoes as an item for nationwide distribution. This was one reason why A&P's produce field buying stations were so ephemeral; for a product like fresh peas, a field buyer needed to appear on the scene for only a matter of weeks. Yet when A&P buyers swooped into pea country, they were, as in the potato field, profiting from substantial state investments in scientific research that enabled supermarket-ready produce to be grown on a commercial scale. Especially important was the breeding of cultivars that produced the characteristics most aesthetically appealing to supermarket shoppers—particularly a dark-green pod holding large, perfectly spherical peas.[22]

Seasonality provided both an opportunity and a challenge to supermarket field buyers seeking large volumes of produce. In the case of peas, the ability to put unshelled peas on sale at key times of the year served as a crucial complement to the much larger volume of canned peas pulsing through the distribution chain. For certain other fruits and vegetables, however, consumers were both less willing to accept canned versions and more likely to demand items not locally available in certain seasons. Tomatoes provide an obvious example. A map of A&P's midcentury tomato network (figure 5) helps clarify why the company had so many field buying stations in Texas and the Southeast. Here we see clusters of field stations in close proximity to major tomato-producing counties in California, Texas, and Florida, as well as in the North Central and mid-Atlantic regions. The geography of A&P's field buying stations here clearly illustrates the firm's efforts to

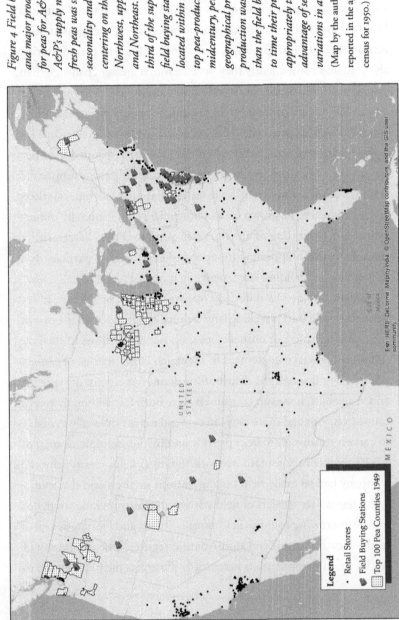

Figure 4 Field buying stations and major production areas for peas for A&P stores. A&P's supply network for fresh peas was shaped by seasonality and climate, centering on the Pacific Northwest, upper Midwest, and Northeast. Less than a third of the supermarket's field buying stations were located within 150 miles of a top pea-producing county at midcentury, perhaps because geographical proximity to production was less important than the field buyers' ability to time their purchases appropriately to take advantage of seasonal variations in availability. (Map by the author, using data reported in the agricultural census for 1950.)

Esri, HERE, DeLorme, Mapmyindia, © OpenStreetMap contributors, and the GIS user community

Legend
· Retail Stores
▲ Field Buying Stations
▦ Top 100 Pea Counties 1949

overcome seasonality of production, with locations shrewdly placed to collect first winter tomatoes from Sunbelt states and then summer tomatoes from the North. As of the late 1940s, the distance any given tomato traveled to an average A&P supermarket remained relatively short, if we do not take seasonality into account; the median distance of an A&P store from a top tomato county in 1949 was only thirty-two miles, and 72 percent of stores were within a hundred miles. Taking seasonality into account we see that winter tomatoes from Florida had to travel much farther than the overall median distance for most stores, while in summertime the availability of New Jersey tomatoes on the East Coast and California tomatoes on the West Coast would shrink certain regional arms of the national supply network. As of the late 1940s, most supermarket field buyers would have sought to minimize shipping distances, as fresh tomatoes at the time tended to suffer costly damage in railcars or truck trailers. Government-supported agricultural research would transform the tomato supply network in the 1950s and 1960s, however, as land-grant university and experiment station researchers bred and promoted the planting of varieties more amenable to both mechanized harvesting and long-distance transportation. As the centers of gravity for tomato production increasingly shifted to California, Texas, and Florida—and, later, to Mexico—supermarket field agents were also ready to move as needed.[23]

These data visualizations help reveal the otherwise invisible nature of the power embedded in a mass-buying system that combined centralization with decentralization. During A&P's long-drawn-out battle with the Antitrust Division of the Department of Justice, lawyers debated whether consumers were benefited or harmed by monopsonistic business practices, ultimately reaching uncertain conclusions about the impacts on competition in the retail grocery trade. Yet these maps show centralized buying power in action: a system that, by its very structure,

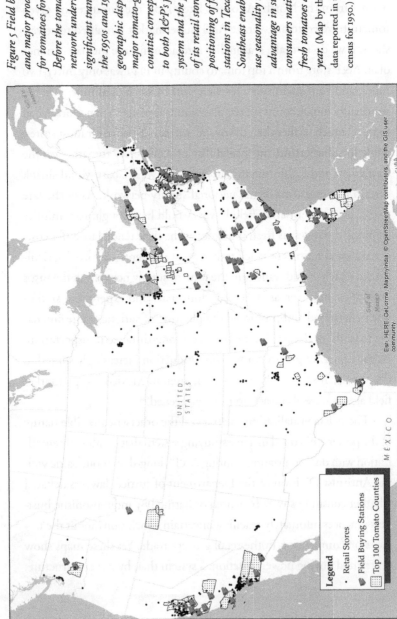

Figure 5 Field buying stations and major production areas for tomatoes for A&P stores. Before the tomato supply network underwent significant transformations in the 1950s and 1960s, the geographic dispersion of major tomato-growing counties corresponded closely to both A&P's field buying system and the preponderance of its retail stores. Strategic positioning of field buying stations in Texas and the Southeast enabled the firm to use seasonality to its advantage in supplying consumers nationwide with fresh tomatoes at any time of year. (Map by the author, using data reported in the agricultural census for 1950.)

Legend

- Retail Stores
- Field Buying Stations
- Top 100 Tomato Counties

Esri, HERE, DeLorme, MapmyIndia, © OpenStreetMap contributors, and the GIS user community constricted choice and produced asymmetries of knowledge. Shoppers at an A&P supermarket in the late 1940s regularly confronted what must have seemed a tremendous array of products from which to choose. But the economically centralized nature of the tightly coordinated supply network meant that, systemically, consumer choices were limited in the long run by the chains' need for standardization. That standardization, in turn, restricted the options available to farmers making decisions about what to plant in any given season. Importantly, the ways in which farmers were limited in their range of production choices came not by fiat—not by a system that was a simple hierarchical chain of command and control—but instead by their imbrication in a complex, dynamic network, with the highly informed, semi-autonomous tentacles of A&P's buying agents reaching out for supplies where and when they could be retrieved at lowest cost and highest (perceived) value.[24]

The supply network was not fully industrialized at midcentury, so even the world's largest supermarket chain did not exercise anything like complete control over agricultural production. Tomatoes ripened at different times of the year, fresh peas could not be efficiently grown in central Texas, and Irish potatoes thrived in Idaho and Maine but not Georgia. Furthermore, insects or blight or excess rain (or too little rain) could instantly transform a producing region into a blank spot on A&P's supply map. But because A&P had so many field buying offices, carefully distributed yet tightly tethered by teletype to A&P's Chicago and New York executives, only A&P had real power of choice—it could buy or not buy, it could haggle on price or set aesthetic specifications at will, and if those conditions were not met it would simply move its purchase, in something close to real time, to a site more amenable to its desires. Consequently, farmers hoping to sell to A&P's produce buyers were compelled through carefully controlled—not free—market forces to adapt or disappear. They might have to use more pesticides to keep their produce spot-free, install irrigation systems to ensure their peas were ready when A&P wanted them, ramp up production dramatically with fertilizers or mechanization, all in the hope (never guaranteed) that sales to the nation's biggest produce buyer would result and thus justify the expense and the effort.

This point was driven home by one of the most influential writings on the implications of the A&P antitrust case. The economists Joel Dirlam and Alfred E. Kahn, writing in 1952, noted that one of the troubling consequences of A&P's centralized buying system was its success in "*exploiting* (taking advantage of weak suppliers, lacking market information and an independent claim on the consumer's loyalty)." Without necessarily breaking the law or intentionally seeking to restrain trade, A&P's produce-buying agents could capitalize upon the structural imbalance of power and knowledge built into its supply network. As A&P explained in its 1944 manual for managers, "A man who buys nothing but fresh fruits and vegetables, and buys more of them than any other man in the world, is in a position to know more about them, and how to buy them properly, than the man who buys a little of everything." Left unstated here was the perhaps more crucial point: A&P's buying agents knew more about the nature of their agricultural supply chains than did any individual farmer. Field buyers were constantly surveying weather, soil, pests, quantities delivered (or not delivered), colors, smells, sizes of produce, and so forth. Because they shared this information along the central teletype network with other agents in the A&P system, their knowledge circulated on a national and not merely local scale. The supply network that A&P had erected to satisfy the needs of its retail stores by 1947 was thus capable of manipulating time and space to produce asymmetries of knowledge and market power. As a consequence, farmers who did not comply with the firm's demands for high-volume, standardized production were sure to be left outside the marketplace. In an effort to make sure they did not get left behind, farmers felt compelled to rely upon federally supported scientific research to avoid or eradicate pathogens, adopt commercially viable and mechanically harvestable cultivars, and otherwise industrialize operations to meet market demands.[25]

From the perspective of A&P executives in New York or Chicago, the structure of this supply network was not only necessary for its business model but also beneficial to the farmers who complied. To quote once more from the firm's managers' manual, A&P's executives "endeavored to build throughout the country a working relationship with farmers based on mutual confidence and helpfulness." Other major supermarket chains likewise sought to cultivate an aura of maintaining a "working relationship" with the nation's farmers. The most concrete example was a series of national "Producer-Consumer" campaigns orchestrated by the National Association of Food Chains in the 1930s, 1940s, and 1950s. The impetus for these campaigns was the perception that farmers supported anti-chain legislation at the state and federal levels in the 1930s. In the lead-up to a 1936 California referendum on anti-chain taxes, the National Association of Food Chains turned to the Lord & Thomas advertising agency to orchestrate a nationwide marketing campaign to transform a potentially devastating peach glut into a boon for the state's horticulturalists. The head of the National Association of Food Chains, John A. Logan, saw an opportunity to "improve relations with the farm community," and over five weeks in spring 1936 urged chain stores to promote California canned peaches as never before. Over 400 million separate advertisements drew nationwide attention to California peaches, along with elaborate floor displays topped with garish banners. Sales of peaches increased by 171 percent over the previous season, driving up prices for California's peach growers and eradicating the glut.[26]

Following the dramatic success of the 1936 peach campaign, the National Association of Food Chains held a meeting with major farm organization leaders at the New York Waldorf-Astoria Hotel in May. Chain-store representatives informed farm leaders that they intended to seek further opportunities for headline-grabbing surplus-reduction campaigns, and quickly followed through on the promise by promoting a June Nationwide Domestic Beef Campaign and a holiday-season turkey and chicken promotion. The following year the chains held a National Bumper Crop Grapefruit Sale as well as a massive campaign to introduce Americans to the largely unknown avocado. In following years more bumper-crop removals made their way into the public consciousness: apples, oranges, peas, apricots, raisins, eggs, lamb, cheese, pears, walnuts, potatoes, and tangerines were among the goods subjected to the Producer-Consumer propaganda machine. According to Douglas McPhee of the National Association of Food Chains, this "business approach to farm surpluses" provided clear benefits. Besides amassing a pile of statistical evidence on the increased farm prices produced by the campaigns, McPhee also claimed that "one farm mother in a Rocky Mountain agricultural area was able to have her baby at a hospital instead of at home, because of better returns from her husband's crop through chain outlets." The political message of the campaigns extended beyond a transparent attempt to combat anti-chain hostility at the state and federal level. As *Time* magazine explained in 1938, the Producer-Consumer campaign's "enthusiasts describe it as something to put AAA [the Agricultural Adjustment Administration] to shame, for it works on the positive principle of reducing surpluses." Chains, in other words, promoted their massive buying and selling power not as restraints on competition but as tools of free enterprise, seemingly capable of reducing the federal government's interventions in the American agricultural economy initiated at the start of the New Deal.[27]

Absent from the press releases touting the power of the Producer-Consumer campaigns, however, was discussion of the extent to which they relied on a form of state-sanctioned monopsony power in the farm economy. The "farm leaders" with whom chain representatives were meeting beginning in 1936 were by and large executives at marketing cooperatives, such as Charles C. Teague, longtime president of the California Fruit Growers Exchange. Teague's organization, best known as purveyors of Sunkist citrus fruits, had since its founding in 1893 pioneered the use of the cooperative form to bring farmers into line with the needs of an industrializing national economy. Calling Teague a "farmer," as the National Association of Food Chains propagandists were inclined to do, might have raised eyebrows for most Americans in the 1930s and 1940s. Besides heading the Exchange for thirty-four years (1926 to 1960), Teague was the president of two banks and owned several water-development companies in addition to more than three thousand acres of fruit and nut trees. Teague was among a select group of business leaders who promoted the agricultural marketing cooperative as a form of countervailing power, a means of uniting many atomized, individual producers into a coherent bargaining unit in an economic world that was increasingly dominated by vertically integrated corporations. In his 1944 memoir Teague bristled at the implication that cooperatives like the California Fruit Growers Exchange were "socialistic," insisting that they were "just as much a part of the business enterprise system as is manufacturing or any other form of industry." Indeed, marketing cooperatives did share much with the vertically integrated corporations they were designed to mimic and counterbalance; the Fruit Growers Exchange, for instance, successfully developed standards, grading, nationally advertised brands, and coordinated transportation systems to rationalize the production and marketing of citrus fruits. Yet there was one crucial difference between agricultural marketing cooperatives and corporations. When Congress passed the Capper-Volstead Act in 1922, it gave agricultural cooperatives a wide array of exemptions from antitrust laws. Marketing cooperatives were thus enabled to exert significant control over farm prices and to capture extraordinary market share without fear of legal reprisal. It is little wonder, then, that leaders of such cooperatives were among those most keen to participate in the National Association of Food Chains' Producer-Consumer campaigns from the 1930s into the 1950s.[28]

What made the American supermarket tick at midcentury was its ability to bring the abundance of industrializing agriculture into the baskets and shopping carts of the nation's consumers at consistently low prices. The success of a chain supermarket such as A&P was partly a product of a military-like strategic campaign to wring inefficiencies out of its supply network and boost stock turnover in stores, but those tactics in turn depended upon a state-supported campaign to industrialize and standardize American agriculture. Grains, meat and dairy products, potatoes and peas and tomatoes all illustrate the ways in which standardized, high-volume food production relied upon government-sponsored research. The Producer-Consumer campaigns demonstrated that chains could develop long-term partnerships with preexisting, state-sanctioned agricultural monopsonists who likewise urged farmers to standardize and boost their production. But what was a supermarket firm to do when executives sensed an opportunity for mass sales of a product that did not yet have an industrialized supply network?

The "Chicken of Tomorrow" contest provides the clearest example of an agricultural supply network willed into being by supermarket demands and constructed in tight collaboration with government agents. In November 1944, the national poultry research director for A&P informed a group of poultry researchers that chickens bred to produce large, meaty breasts would revolutionize the industry. As of the mid-1940s, chicken meat was for most Americans a relatively expensive item, essentially a byproduct of the much larger egg industry. Representatives of the A&P supermarket chain, however, were convinced that a meat-type chicken—a broiler, in the parlance of the industry—could transform the American diet if it could be successfully mass-produced and mass marketed. A meeting of the Committee for Improving Meat-Type in Poultry, composed of state cooperative extension agents, government-funded experiment-station scientists, and land-grant university researchers, was held in Lexington, Kentucky, in September 1945. Besides changing their name to the catchier Chicken of Tomorrow Committee, the group laid out plans for how to use fifteen thousand dollars provided by A&P. The cash, it was decided, would be divvied up as prizes to reward poultry breeders who could successfully raise a flock of birds with large breasts, white feathers (to minimize pluck-marks on the processed chicken's skin), disease resistance (to ensure volume of supply), and other qualities suitable for making chicken adaptable to supermarket distribution. The first Chicken of Tomorrow contests were held at the state level in 1946 and on the national level in 1948. Everyone involved understood that much more was at stake than a few thousand dollars in cash; winners of the contest were effectively guaranteed a mass market for what was in essence an entirely new product.[29]

The winners of the first national Chicken of Tomorrow contest vastly exceeded A&P's expectations. Vantress Hatcheries (originally a California firm, later based in Georgia) and Arbor Acres (of Connecticut) were among the top prizewinners, both effectively demonstrating the possibility of using genetic science to produce birds with white feathers and meaty breasts. Poultry growers in hard-hit agricultural regions of the United States—Delmarva Peninsula, the

Georgia upcountry, and northwestern Arkansas—were quickly enrolled in a new mass-production industry that depended on Chicken of Tomorrow–anointed chicks to provision the nation's supermarket chains. Within ten years, two-thirds of the nation's broilers could trace their genetic lineage to the Chicken of Tomorrow prizewinners. Along with new confinement methods, better disease control, and scientized feeding developed by government-supported scientists, the genetic transformation of the American chicken at the behest of the A&P supermarket chain had made Herbert Hoover's hyperbolic 1928 promise of a "chicken in every pot" a reality by the early 1950s.[30]

The Chicken of Tomorrow contest thus illustrates one of the ways in which a supermarket chain such as A&P could deploy its buying power to promote agricultural industrialization. Unlike California citrus fruits, chickens raised for meat production rather than egg laying had no preexisting cooperative organization that A&P could rely upon to push farmers into standardizing and ramping up their production. Unlike midwestern grains or Maine potatoes, broiler chickens in the early 1940s were not subject to an existing, well-funded scientific research program. For a mere fifteen thousand dollars in cash prizes, A&P was able to enroll USDA and land-grant university scientists in a coordinated campaign to develop an agro-industrial supply chain out of thin air. Entrepreneurs in poultry breeding and poultry feeding (including Don Tyson of Arkansas and Jesse Jewell of Georgia) rushed into the burgeoning field to meet supermarket demands. As explored further in Chapter 5, supermarkets continued to exercise significant power in the chicken supply network in the 1950s and later, though generally in ways that remained largely invisible to the consumers who frequented their stores.

"Do You Want Your A&P Put Out of Business?" bellowed full-page advertisements in some two thousand U.S. newspapers on September 20, 1949. If the American people wanted "to continue to enjoy low prices and better living," the advertisements threatened, they should reject the efforts of antitrust agents to break up A&P's integrated distribution system. They should also acknowledge their own role in abetting A&P's rise to the top of the retail food industry: "If A&P is big, it is because the American people, by their patronage, have made it big." This public relations gambit, typical of A&P's efforts to cultivate public favor during its long-drawn-out battle with the Department of Justice, echoed a point made nearly four decades earlier by Thomas Edison. "Selling and distribution," declared Edison, "are simply machines for getting products to consumers." Edison, speaking in 1910, was criticizing retailers for the inefficiency of their machinery in moving goods to customers; by contrast, A&P's 1949 PR campaign sought to convince the consuming public that its distributive machinery was as well-oiled a mechanism for improving the American standard of living as could possibly be desired. The supermarket stores operated by A&P and its competitors were indeed machines for selling, and A&P was correct in its claim that its distribution system was at the cutting edge of efficiency. But such advertising went a step farther, suggesting that supermarkets were machines not only for selling foods but for selling the concept that "free enterprise" was responsible for "low prices and better living." Such statements glossed over the significance of the state support for the industrial agriculture supply networks that had made supermarkets so successful.[31]

That omission did little, however, to stop an onslaught of declarations in the 1940s and 1950s that supermarkets were concrete embodiments of the economic promise of liberal democracy, not merely symbols of free enterprise but tangible enterprises for enabling

consumer freedom. U.S. food corporations had long upheld themselves as promoters of democracy; before World War II, advertisers
commonly proclaimed that a purchase of a product such as Campbell's soup or Kellogg's breakfast cereal was not simply an economic
transaction but a form of "election" akin to casting a ballot for a political candidate. During the Cold War era, however, U.S. food corporations, including supermarkets, increasingly promoted a definition
of democracy centered on consumer abundance rather than on individual autonomy. A&P's supermarkets packed enormous spaces floor
to ceiling with tens of thousands of food products, as did the stores of
competing firms (who by the end of the 1950s beat A&P at its own
game by driving ever more products through even larger stores in suburban settings). Foods that had previously been available only in specific seasons were increasingly to be found year-round on supermarket
shelves. Americans ate more, and more cheaply, than ever before.
Food buyers were supposedly freed from seasonality as well as every
other constraint on their choice. Supermarkets, in *Fortune*'s words,
could "show socialism how to work"—they could even be conceived
of as weapons in the Cold War battle between the capitalist West and
the communist East.[32]

2

The Farms Race Begins

In May 1942, Vice President and former Secretary of Agriculture Henry A. Wallace spoke of a "century of the common man" before a gathering of liberal internationalists in New York City. World War II, Wallace told the Free World Association, was a "fight between a slave world and a free world," part of a "long-drawn-out people's revolution" aimed at making freedom reign around the globe. Wallace was explicit about his definition of freedom: it was not a product of anti-statist individualism or untrammeled "free enterprise" but instead a result of liberal governance and collective approaches to the fair distribution of the fruits of industrial capitalism. American science and technology provided the means and the model for expanding freedom around the world, particularly in undergirding agricultural abundance. As "an essential part of the people's revolution," science had "made it technologically possible to see that all of the people of the world get enough to eat." Emphasizing the third freedom (freedom from want) laid out in President Franklin Roosevelt's "Four Freedoms" speech of January 1941, Wallace declared that "men and women cannot be really free until they have plenty to eat." Implicitly inverting the propaganda line "Food Will Win the War," Wallace suggested that an Allied victory over the Axis powers would win food for the hungry peoples of the freedom-yearning world. Wallace envisioned a future in which abundant food supplies produced by government-supported, technologically sophisticated capitalist agriculture would not only enable real freedom; they would justify and in fact require American leadership on the global stage.[1]

"I am not fighting for a quart of milk for every Hottentot," retorted James Witherow, the conservative president of the National Association of Manufacturers, in response to Wallace's speech. Witherow may have been more comfortable with the more aggressive framing of an "American Century" proffered in *Life* magazine by its publisher Henry Luce in February 1941. Outlining a vision for the United States to formally join the Allies in World War II and thereafter exercise its power on the world stage, Luce declared it was the "destiny" of the United States to share "with all people . . . our Bill of Rights [and] our magnificent industrial products." Luce, a vocal critic of Franklin Roosevelt's New Deal economic policies, argued for an expansion of U.S. military and economic power as a necessary means for spreading free enterprise around the world, "lifting the life of mankind from the level of the beasts to what the Psalmist called a little lower than the angels." Luce's American Century, in other words, outlined not a New Deal for the world but a world of "free enterprise" in which American corporate capital took primary responsibility for raising global living standards. Luce's famous essay has been carefully examined by generations of scholars, but it is striking how few have recognized that Luce, much like Wallace, understood food security to be a crucial determinant of victory in the fight for freedom. "It is the manifest duty of this country," Luce wrote, "to undertake to feed all the people of the world." But whereas Wallace's vision could be ridiculed by conservatives for its idealism, Luce's understanding of American food power came with an important disclaimer: the United States should only undertake to feed those "whom we can from time to time reach consistently with a very tough attitude toward all hostile governments."

Access to abundant food, suggested Luce, should be provided only to nations that rejected communism. Food in the American Century could in fact be understood, ominously, as analogous to military weaponry: "For every dollar we spend on armaments, we should spend at least a dime in a gigantic effort to feed the world—and all the world should know that we have dedicated ourselves to this task."[2]

Luce's essay and Wallace's speech prefigured in important ways the rhetoric and policies of the Cold War Farms Race. Both individuals, like many other public figures at the time, understood America's food abundance as a crucial component of U.S. foreign policy, a tool for building political and military alliances as well as a metric of America's mission to raise global living standards in the postwar world. In the aftermath of World War II, such thinking about the place of the U.S. food economy in global geopolitics would harden into a Farms Race with the Soviet Union, one that had material and political consequences for the course of the Cold War. One aspect of this Farms Race was a rhetoric of consumer abundance, which, as a number of Cold War historians have noted, played a key role in America's attempts to propagandize the "American Way." A second facet of the Farms Race was the notion, expressed especially in Luce's "American Century" essay, that U.S.-style food abundance could serve a counterrevolutionary purpose in Cold War foreign policy, a diplomatic carrot and stick that by the 1970s would come to be known as "food power." In addition, both Wallace and Luce suggested that industrial agriculture provided a concrete and morally justifiable model for exercising American power on the global stage, whether the United States was seen as engaged in a "long-drawn-out people's revolution" (Wallace) or spreading "free enterprise" (Luce).[3]

During Harry Truman's presidency, Wallace's idealism would be most clearly reflected in the Point Four Program providing technical assistance for developing countries that was announced in January 1949. Under Point Four, the United States sought to deploy American technology to feed the hungry world, thereby establishing a beach-head in the emerging economic contest with the Soviet Union. When Dwight Eisenhower entered the White House, the harder edge of economic militancy expressed by Henry Luce came to the fore in such policies as "trade not aid" and PL 480, both of which explicitly identified American agricultural abundance as a capitalist weapon against communism. Truman and Eisenhower thus contributed in key ways to the onset of the Cold War Farms Race, enlisting American farmers and agribusiness corporations in a series of rhetorical, diplomatic, and economic proxy wars with the Soviet Union. In this chapter I shall emphasize the rhetoric and policies of government officials in establishing the outlines of the Farms Race in the late 1940s and early 1950s; later I shall return the focus to the role of private enterprises, particularly supermarkets, as businessmen seized opportunities to engage in, and profit from, the economic battles of the Cold War.[4]

The roots of the Farms Race were planted well before the onset of World War II. The idea that American food could be understood as a weapon was explicitly declared by Herbert Hoover, head of the U.S. Food Administration during World War I. Under Hoover's direction, the Food Administration parceled out American food aid during the war as a strategic mode of supporting the Allies. Hoover considered wartime grain and meat shipments as effectively equivalent to munitions and other military supplies. At war's end, furthermore, Hoover used food relief to combat widespread starvation in central Europe in an explicit attempt to forestall the influence of Bolshevism. As one of Hoover's aides announced: "Bread is mightier than the sword." Such rhetoric resurfaced during World War II. The introduction to the 1945 annual report of the secretary of agriculture carried the title "Our Food as a Weapon of War," asserting that "food ranked with ships, planes, tanks, and guns" in the fight against the Axis powers.[5]

America's agricultural productivity was not always framed in militaristic terms, however. The emergence of an agenda for rural development during the interwar years was a more important precursor to the Cold War Farms Race than wartime "food as a weapon" rhetoric. Although development projects would come to fit squarely into the U.S. Cold War economic agenda—particularly after Truman's Point Four Program was announced in 1949—the origins of development ideology were strongly rooted in New Deal approaches to modernizing the American countryside. As the historian Sarah Phillips has demonstrated, New Deal agricultural reformers "instituted novel ways of assisting, financing, even compelling cooperation with a nationwide vision of resource use and general rural development." In the 1930s, liberals who developed such programs as the Soil Conservation Service and the Tennessee Valley Authority sought to modernize the countryside as part of a broader goal of nation-building, in terms of both securing the livelihoods of rural Americans and building state capacity to manage natural and social resources on (for the first time) a national scale. The Tennessee Valley Authority (TVA) in particular served as a model for grand-scale rural development. Intended to shatter the vestiges of plantation agriculture in the South by simultaneously deploying technocratic regional planning and participatory governance, the TVA brought in its wake electricity, fertilizer, flood control, transportation infrastructure, and farm credit. According to the historian David Ekbladh, the TVA was, in short, "a living example of how to undertake modernization on a large scale," and in later years it would provide a model for those who sought to extend the development agenda beyond the borders of the United States.[6]

It was by no means inevitable that the ideology of development forged in the context of modernizing the rural American South would be extended beyond U.S. borders. Yet even the most internally oriented agricultural development policies of the New Deal era emerged in an international context. A group of influential agrarian reformers—including the U.S. ambassador to Mexico Josephus Daniels, the historian Frank Tannenbaum, and the New Deal economic adviser Rexford Tugwell—explicitly understood the problems of the Cotton Belt to be analogous to the challenges faced by Mexican peasants. From that premise emerged a key New Deal agricultural program, the Farm Security Administration. The framers of the administration drew on American interpretations of Mexican farm problems to shape a program to provide U.S. dirt farmers with access to land and credit in an attempt to break the pernicious plantation mentality of the rural South. Such transnational analogical thinking was furthermore crucial to the establishment of the Rockefeller Foundation's first effort to engage in agricultural modernization schemes outside the United States: the Mexican Agricultural Program, launched in 1943. Many historians see the Rockefeller Foundation's efforts in Mexico as the onset of the "Green Revolution," particularly because substantial Rockefeller funding was provided to the plant breeder Norman Borlaug to develop high-yield varieties of wheat. As the historian Tore Olsson has demonstrated, however, the early efforts of the Mexican Agricultural Program were at first modeled on the Rockefeller Foundation's rural development campaigns in the impoverished American South. Directly encouraged by Henry A. Wallace (who became vice president in 1940), the Rockefeller Foundation's foray into Mexico combined scientific research on "peasant-friendly" plant breeding with efforts to extend credit to small farmers and build an infrastructure for a more productive, if not necessarily an industrialized, agriculture. Throughout the

New Deal and World War II era, agents of rural modernization were guided not by a quasi-militaristic ideological campaign but by a vision much like that expressed in Wallace's "century of the common man" speech. When the Cold War set in, however, rural development schemes, including the Rockefeller Foundation's work on breeding high-yield grains, would quickly be transformed into much more aggressive components of U.S. foreign policy.[7]

One consequence of the Cold War's impact on U.S.-led rural development programs was the increasing acceptance of technology as an inherent and universal good. Agricultural productivity could be measured by the universal metric of yield per acre, and in the idealized rural landscapes envisioned by modernization theorists, that yield could be produced in any place, regardless of local ecological, historical, or cultural conditions. Such a universalizing vision for agricultural development, particularly when pursued as an ostensibly philanthropic project guided by purportedly apolitical scientific elites, meshed well with broader U.S. Cold War foreign policies that sought to extend American power and influence in South and Southeast Asia and Central and South America. Thus the Rockefeller Foundation took the Mexican Agricultural Program model to Colombia and elsewhere in Latin America beginning in 1950, and then began similar projects in India from 1955 on. The Ford Foundation, urged on by the CIA and the State Department, offered substantial support for explicitly anticommunist rice research in the Philippines beginning in 1960. That same rice research would soon be militarized as part of the U.S. Cold War campaign in Vietnam.[8]

Although it may seem inevitable in hindsight, it took significant time, money, and work to transform agricultural development into a component of America's Cold War arsenal. Nelson A. Rockefeller, of the petroleum dynasty, emerged as a crucial network-builder who witnessed and aided the transition from the sympathetic agricultural development schemes of the 1930s and early 1940s to the more aggressive modernization campaigns that characterized the Cold War Farms Race. Like Wallace—with whom he liked to play tennis when in Washington, D.C.—Rockefeller developed an intense interest in the economic problems of the Latin American countryside in the 1930s. A business trip to check on his family's petroleum investments in Venezuela in 1935 "changed his life," convincing him to return home to New York and take a crash course in Spanish. He returned to Venezuela in 1937 as director of the Creole Petroleum Corporation, a division of Standard Oil of New Jersey (founded by his grandfather John D. Rockefeller). Harboring ambitions to move from the business world into politics, Nelson Rockefeller began formulating plans for developing Latin American commercial relations with the United States.[9]

Rockefeller's plans took a more urgent turn after 1938, when Mexico nationalized its petroleum production, setting a precedent for the potential disruption of U.S. investments in Latin American oil refining. Soon thereafter he wrote to President Franklin D. Roosevelt, insisting that sustained U.S. investment in Latin American economies would ensure the success of Roosevelt's "Good Neighbor Policy." In response, Roosevelt appointed Rockefeller coordinator of the Office of Inter-American Affairs (OIAA), charging him with overseeing a range of economic and cultural programs intended to ensure "stability" in Latin America. Fears of growing Nazi influence in Latin America persuaded Congress and a host of private investors to provide Rockefeller's office with a budget of $38 million by 1942, money that was pumped into cultural propaganda campaigns, food provisioning, and health services to keep Latin American countries in the Allies' corner. The package of technical assistance, agricultural modernization schemes, and cultural propaganda pioneered by the OIAA not only served as a concrete model for later Cold War campaigns; it also laid out, according to David Ekbladh, "the clear outlines of how development should operate as part of an ideological confrontation."[10]

As head of the OIAA during World War II, Nelson Rockefeller built networks, found funding, and secured political support from a range of private and public actors for what he hoped would be a self-perpetuating development program. From the beginning Rockefeller feared that Congress would have little stomach for funding a long-term economic development program in Latin America, so he worked assiduously to build political support in host countries while also drumming up funds from corporate investors. Key to the OIAA's approach was the *servicio,* a bureau located in the appropriate department (say, the Ministry of Agriculture) in the host country, actively managed by a U.S. representative of OIAA but formally responsible to the host government. Much like the early-twentieth-century efforts of the Rockefeller philanthropies in the American South, the OIAA worked to build institutional capacity both inside and outside the state for erecting infrastructure, improving public health, and demonstrating the productivity of scientific agriculture to rural citizens. Rather than a strictly "high modernist" vision of technocratic development, then, Rockefeller's wartime OIAA agenda aligned at least in part with emerging ideas about "community development," in that a cooperative mentality and respect for local expertise and political authority were promoted alongside the American-led push for scientific and technological modernization.[11]

Food was high on the Office of Inter-American Affairs' agenda. In Venezuela during World War II, for instance, the OIAA sent a staff of American agricultural scientists into Venezuelan fields to coax farmers into producing more milk, potatoes, wheat, and vegetables—products that were primarily imported rather than domestically produced and thus especially prone to escalating prices under wartime conditions of scarcity. By 1944, however, the Venezuelan staff of the Office of Inter-American Affairs had decided that boosting agricultural production alone would not bring food prices down for urban consumers. Venezuela had little transportation or distribution infrastructure to connect even its most productive farms with consumers. Oranges produced in the valley of Montalbán in 1944, for instance, were left to rot in orchards. The cost of transporting them to urban markets far outweighed the price ($3 per thousand) offered by wholesalers—this, at a time when oranges sold in Caracas for $33.33 per thousand. Rockefeller, aware of such circumstances, took from his experience in the OIAA a lesson: if lasting economic development were to take root in Latin America after the war, modern techniques of food distribution would have to be closely coupled with efforts to step up farm production. Such thinking would form the foundation for Rockefeller's creation of the International Basic Economy Corporation in 1947, a private development agency that, unlike many development programs in the Cold War, understood food abundance to require effective technologies of distribution, not simply capital-intensive agriculture.[12]

The OIAA offered a model for development, but that model was not inherently hardwired to become a weapon in the Cold War. Yet as World War II came to a close, a rising sense of fear in foreign policy circles brought new urgency to considerations of agriculture's place in the postwar world. By the autumn of 1945, with the Red Army advancing through Eastern Europe, U.S. military planners were openly worrying that Soviet leaders intended to assert territorial control in agriculturally productive Eastern European countries, in part to deny crucial foodstuffs to Western Europe. After the war's end, widespread hunger set in across Europe and much of Asia; harvests failed as wartorn farmlands were hit by droughts and exceptionally hard winters.

Assistant Secretary of State Dean Acheson informed President Truman in spring 1946 that Eurasia was in the throes of a "most critical period of the world food crisis" that threatened "general disorder and political upheaval." Eurasian hunger, it seemed, was a direct threat to postwar democracy, capitalism, and American foreign policy goals.[13]

One important response to the perceived threat was the establishment of the United Nations Food and Agriculture Organization (FAO). Emerging from a 1943 conference held at Hot Springs, Virginia, FAO embodied the vision outlined by Henry Wallace in his "century of the common man" speech. The declaration adopted by the Hot Springs attendees announced that when the war ended the signatory nations had to "concert our efforts to win and maintain freedom from fear and freedom from want." Confident in the power of science and technology to win the battle against hunger, the Hot Springs Declaration continued: "Production of food must be greatly expanded; we now have knowledge of the means by which this can be done." Formally founded as a division of the United Nations in 1945, FAO joined a host of other multilateral postwar institutions such as the World Bank and the World Health Organization geared toward raising living standards around the globe.[14]

The agricultural economist Mordecai Ezekiel was one of the most prominent promoters of the Food and Agriculture Organization's approach to the problem of world hunger. An influential figure who played a key role in nearly every farm policy deliberation of the New Deal era, Ezekiel was one of a host of liberals who moved into the international realm during and after World War II. In 1945 Ezekiel penned an essay for the antifascist magazine *Free World* extolling both the Tennessee Valley Authority's and the Soviet Union's five-year plans as admirable models for economic development capable of staving off hunger. In Ezekiel's formulation, the fight to "win" the war against global hunger did not necessarily entail a contest between the United States and the Soviet Union, nor did it necessarily require a capitalist economic system. What the fight against hunger required was science, technology, and central planning—and, according to Ezekiel, the two superpowers were equally well equipped to engage in the battle.[15]

As tensions with the Soviet Union escalated after 1945, however, the idealism embodied in FAO's Hot Springs Declaration and in Ezekiel's essay was replaced by a more aggressive understanding of what a "win" in the battle against global hunger would entail for the United States. A consensus developed that hunger was a cause of communism. As Congressman John Flannagan (D-VA) declared in 1946 on the House floor: "The dictator nations exist upon hungry bodies and befuddled minds. If you want to dispel the gloom of Nazism and communism from the face of the earth, the thing to do is to feed and educate the peoples of those nations." Such thinking emerged most prominently in Secretary of State George C. Marshall's June 1947 speech at Harvard University outlining what would become the multibillion-dollar Marshall Plan for rebuilding Western Europe's postwar economy. Marshall did not directly mention either the Soviet Union or communism in his speech, declaring that U.S. foreign policy was "directed not against any country or doctrine but against hunger, poverty, desperation and chaos." Marshall's Harvard audience could read between the lines, however, and applauded most enthusiastically when the secretary made veiled threats against the Soviets. Soviet leaders, for their part, perceived the aggressive implications of the Marshall Plan and refused to allow Eastern European nations to partake of American largesse. Truman, meanwhile, understood the economic aid to Western Europe as a necessary complement to the policy of containment formalized in the 1947 Truman Doctrine; as he once put it, the Truman Doctrine and the Marshall Plan were "two halves of the same walnut." Premised on the belief that hunger could breed "chaos" (meaning communism) among European citizens—many of whom had become increasingly skeptical of capitalism and liberal democracy—the Marshall Plan included $10 million in agricultural aid in its first three years of operation.[16]

The Marshall Plan specifically targeted Western Europe, and the majority of its $12 billion in expenditures between 1948 and 1952 prioritized industrial rather than agricultural recovery. The result was by most accounts a successful rejuvenation of Western Europe's mass-production industries, enabling a revival of trade between the United States and Western European countries unparalleled since before the Great Depression. As a project in economic development, however, the Marshall Plan was unlike most later U.S. schemes targeting the less-developed world. Although it was originally sold to Congress and the American people as a way to stave off hunger, it rested on the assumption that Western Europe was inherently more "advanced" than the postcolonial nations of what would come to be known as the Third World. In those regions, U.S.-led development during the Cold War emerged from anxiety, mainly produced by fears of rural Eurasian peasants engaging in revolutions against the capitalist underpinnings of the old colonial order. References to a "long-drawn-out people's revolution" had seemed only positive to Henry Wallace in his "century of the common man" speech, but as the Cold War escalated after 1947 such language inflamed rising anticommunist anxieties in the United States. (Wallace's political career collapsed in the face of such fears during the presidential campaign of 1948, when, running on the Progressive ticket, he was repeatedly and viciously painted as a Soviet sympathizer by a range of more centrist liberals, including Truman.)[17]

Even if the Marshall Plan was an outlier in the emerging Cold War ideology of development, the idea that food abundance could simultaneously bolster capitalist democracies while undermining communist advances in Europe and Asia persisted. The same year that President Truman signed the legislation initiating the Marshall Plan, Chester Bowles delivered a speech titled "America's Food in a Hungry World" to a group of supermarket executives. Bowles was a successful businessman who had retired a multimillionaire in 1941 at the age of forty and thereafter devoted himself to public service. He became intimately aware of the political significance of food and agriculture during his stint as head of the Office of Price Administration from 1943 to 1946. In that office Bowles oversaw one of the most dramatic expansions of U.S. government economic intervention in the name of protecting domestic consumer access to affordable goods, particularly foodstuffs. In his 1948 speech to supermarketers—many of whom remained viscerally appalled by memories of the Office of Price Administration's profit-dampening price controls during the war—Bowles suggested that a global fight to make food affordable for all was an essential component of the emerging contest with the Soviet Union. Much as Secretary Marshall had implied at Harvard, Bowles pinned the rise of revolutionary leftist movements on "the hunger and hopelessness of the masses." Bowles further declared that the survival of liberalism required dramatic action on the food front: "We will need nothing less than a revolution in world agriculture." But unlike Marshall, Bowles explicitly named the enemy to be defeated: "Let me remind you that, much as we dislike it, Communism is an *idea,* and ideas cannot be destroyed by atomic bombs and B-36s. . . . We will have to provide a more dynamic and more convincing answer to world poverty than that provided by the Soviet Union." Mindful of his audience of supermarket executives, Bowles concluded his call to arms by suggesting that engaging in this worldwide battle of food systems was simply "good business." In a single speech, Bowles outlined the three key elements of the Cold War Farms Race that was about to begin in earnest: food abundance as effective propaganda (a "convincing answer" to the Soviets), the counterrevolutionary potential of keeping the "hungry masses" in nonaligned countries from turning to communism, and, crucially, a morally justifiable yet also profitable role for U.S. businesses in waging an economic assault on communism.[18]

Bowles's speech might warrant little historical attention had it not so neatly prefigured crucial elements of Point Four of Truman's 1949 inaugural address. In Point Four, sometimes seen by historians as the first declaration of development as an official component of U.S. foreign policy, Truman explained to the American public that hunger overseas was a clear and present danger to U.S. national security. "More than half the people of the world are living in conditions approaching misery," Truman intoned. "Their food is inadequate." Attacking that misery, Truman announced, was not just morally right but a crucial defensive strategy in the fight against world communism: "Their poverty is a handicap and a threat both to them and to more prosperous areas." The inspiration for Truman's Point Four announcement came from a memo prepared by Benjamin Hardy, a former small-town newspaperman from Georgia. Working on public relations for Nelson Rockefeller in the OIAA in Brazil during World War II, Hardy helped promote the agency's technical assistance programs. After the war, Hardy worked as a speechwriter in Truman's State Department, and remained in contact with Rockefeller, who was mulling over ideas for a "bigger program" to attack poverty in the postwar world. When Truman's aide Clark Clifford asked State Department officials for ideas to include in Truman's inaugural address, Hardy sent a memo to Francis Russell, director of the public affairs office at State, titled "Use of U.S. Technological Resources as a Weapon in the Struggle with International Communism." Hardy's memo differed in one crucial respect from Bowles's 1948 speech in that it prioritized government programs rather than the activities of private enterprises. Like Bowles's speech, however, Hardy's memo outlined the propaganda power and counterrevolutionary potential of waging war on hunger, and in doing so offered a succinct strategy for initiating a Cold War Farms Race.[19]

The United States, insisted Hardy, held a "potent weapon" that was ready to launch: its "immense technological resources." Technologies for "increased production of food, clothing, and other consumer goods" could be deployed around the world as part of a "dramatic, large-scale program that would capture the imagination of the peoples of other countries." Modeled on the rural development campaigns of the New Deal era and of the OIAA in Latin America, technical assistance programs including "soil conservation, flood control, the TVA concept, sanitation, and many others" would enable the United States to "repulse Communism and create a decent life [for] the earth's millions." What made the American "weapon" especially powerful, Hardy suggested, was that it "would bear almost immediate fruit," demonstrating to the world's rural poor in a concrete manner the superiority of capitalism to communism. It would "appeal to the masses in a direct and understandable way—more food to eat, more clothes to wear, better housing, improved living conditions and a definite promise of better life and greater opportunities for their children." Hardy furthermore suggested that such a program of technical assistance would be much less expensive than the Marshall Plan.[20]

Despite Hardy's optimism and Truman's stirring rhetoric, Point Four's grand vision proved challenging to implement from the outset. Congressional hearings immediately opened up a rupture that would ultimately lead to the program's demise, as Republican representatives and business lobbyists pushed to minimize government funding while maximizing opportunities for private capital to undertake economic development. Backers of the Truman administration, however, insisted on the importance of government funds; Point Four was, after all, meant to demonstrate the government's commitment to winning the economic contest of the Cold War. Nelson Rockefeller played a prominent role in reconciling the two sides, arguing strongly before Congress that it was possible to spend significant government moneys on technical assistance without precluding opportunities for private investment. As he put it, "How can we get more buying power in the hands of the other peoples of the world? How can we help them get more dollars without just giving it to them?" The answer lay, according to Rockefeller, in "increasing the availability of capital, technical and scientific knowledge, and managerial experience," and cooperation between public and private organizations would be necessary to achieve that goal. After lengthy debates, multiple cuts to the proposed budget, and various amendments ensuring private capital's access to developing markets, Congress relented. On June 5, 1950, Truman signed into law the Foreign Economic Assistance Act, which provided the Department of State with a first-year budget of $25 million to put Point Four into action. In October of that year, Congress approved the creation of a new agency within the Department of State to administer the program, the Technical Cooperation Administration (TCA), first headed by Henry G. Bennett, a former president of Oklahoma Agricultural & Mechanical College.[21]

Specific plans for how Point Four would work in practice remained uncertain. Stanley Andrews became the second head of the TCA after Henry Bennett died in a plane crash in 1951. Andrews recalled in a 1970 oral history that "nobody seemed to know just what was involved in the final hammering out of what we were to do." Representatives from State, Agriculture, Commerce, and several other agencies met with President Truman in the Cabinet Room seeking feedback on various proposed approaches. Bennett, Andrews later remembered, gave the final presentation. He pointed to the globe Truman kept handy and "sketched out what he thought were the greatest needs of the new nations at that time emerging in the world as the outcome of World War II." Bennett singled out Ethiopia, which he had visited the previous summer, as an example of a nation with "marvelous natural resources" that was nonetheless "steeped in poverty, disease, and hunger," and declared: "These people must have a chance to at least glance into the door of the Twentieth Century." Truman, according to Andrews, turned to the group and announced, "That's the kind of a program I was talking about." Bennett's vision for Point Four, approved by Truman, marked the postcolonial nations of what would soon be termed the Third World as distinctly different from the recipient nations of the Marshall Plan. While Western Europe received an influx of cash for reviving industrial economies and reengaging with the United States as an equal trading partner, the Technical Cooperation Administration was meant to spend its money teaching host nations how to build their own TVA-like dams, using irrigated agriculture and flood control to secure their food supplies and prevent mass instability in the countryside. When Andrews—who before his involvement with Point Four was director of the Office of Foreign Agricultural Relations in the Department of Agriculture—took over the helm of the TCA from 1952 to 1953, he continued to push for what he understood as Bennett's vision of "slow educational patient work" in helping host nations build infrastructures for agricultural productivity. It was, according to Andrews, "a white knight business . . . an antidote to war." Others in the State Department, however, chafed at the TCA's limited funding as well its operating assumption that host countries, rather than the State Department, should take the lead in setting priorities for how to use aid money. There were thus significant tensions built into the Point Four Program from the outset, yet there was also consensus that the United States had a morally justifiable role to play in boosting agricultural production outside its own borders.[22]

Meanwhile, outside the State Department alternative visions for Point Four's implementation returned to the question of whether private enterprises might more effectively achieve Truman's vision than government agencies. In November 1950 Truman appointed Nelson Rockefeller chairman of the Advisory Board on International Development. Rockefeller took the opportunity to canvas major U.S. business interests to draw up a blueprint for implementing Point Four on a more massive scale than Congress had been willing to support. Compiling the results in a report, "Partners in Progress," delivered to Truman in March 1951, Rockefeller's committee announced that America's business leaders were prepared to support the government in waging economic warfare against "Soviet imperialism" by joining forces in "an economic offensive to root out hunger, poverty, illiteracy, and disease." "Freedom," concluded the report, "has little meaning to a man who is starving." Truman wrote a warm thank-you note to Rockefeller, agreeing that "economic development is the spearhead of the forces of freedom," but chose to ignore Rockefeller's suggestion of enrolling private businesses more directly in the Point Four agenda. As David Ekbladh notes, the report met with "a cool reception" and "thousands of copies simply sat in storage."[23]

Rockefeller may have forgotten one of the key phrases used by Truman in his 1949 inaugural, when the president claimed that "the old imperialism—exploitation for foreign profit—has no place in our plans." Rockefeller and his corporate colleagues seemed convinced that, even if the United States was not rebuilding an "old" empire, perhaps foreign aid programs could nonetheless open up a "new" empire of U.S. economic dominance outside of North America and Western Europe, conveniently freed from the bothersome trappings and trade restrictions of colonial rule. Historians continue to debate the extent to which Point Four illustrates the emergence of a "new" American imperialism. Some suggest that the ulterior motive was to enroll resource-rich nations as peripheral subjects in a European-American-centered world economic system. Others give more credence to the humanitarian sentiments behind Point Four but nonetheless acknowledge that the push for foreign development initiated by the Truman administration "shifted the Cold War onto entirely new ground," marking the territories of less-developed nations as crucial battlegrounds in an emerging Cold War "grand strategy" that "privileged economic power [as a means] to contain the USSR." Whether or not Point Four should be understood as the onset of a new era of empire or hegemony, it is clear that its formalization of economic aid as a component of U.S. foreign policy marked a turning point. Before the war, it would have seemed strange to equate economic modernization with military weaponry. By 1950, the analogy had crystallized, such that American-style food abundance and agricultural productivity seemed an obvious fit alongside nuclear armaments in the U.S. Cold War arsenal.[24]

The Farms Race had thus begun, but the question of whether it would be waged primarily by public or private organizations remained unsettled. When Dwight Eisenhower stepped into the White House in 1953 promising to cut federal expenditures, corporate interests and Republican politicians redoubled their efforts to tip the balance toward private enterprise. High on the agenda was dismantling the Point Four Program. Immediately after winning the 1952 election, Eisenhower called on Nelson Rockefeller to chair the Advisory Committee on Government Organization. By April 1953 the Rockefeller

Committee had sent the president twenty reports with 140 recommendations for streamlining government agencies. Among those recommendations was a reiteration of the central points of the "Partners in Progress" report so coolly ignored by Truman, including a call for the Technical Cooperation Administration to be merged with the Mutual Security Agency, an organization created by Congress in 1951 to funnel increased military assistance to allied nations.[25]

This was not simply bureaucratic reshuffling. John Foster Dulles, Eisenhower's choice for secretary of state, informed Congress during his confirmation hearings that Point Four activities could be done "largely by private enterprise." Once in office, Dulles expressed further concerns about Point Four, declaring, "We are trying to get away from" foreign aid programs, which he viewed as "abnormal." He suggested that liberalized trade relations would be "perhaps of greater advantage," for they could be "set up as one of the attractions which may eventually tend to disintegrate the attractiveness of the captive world, the Communist world." Here Dulles echoed a core theme of Eisenhower's presidential campaign, summed up by the pithy phrase "trade not aid," which was supported by business interests, including the National Association of Manufacturers. But perhaps most problematic, according to Dulles, was Point Four's bureaucratic autonomy and unclear connection to defense goals; economic development projects proceeded in response to host country requests, regardless of whether the host country provided quid pro quo access to military bases. For Dulles, Point Four was all carrot and no stick.[26]

In June 1953 Congress responded to the pressure from the Eisenhower administration and merged the Point Four agency, along with the Mutual Security Agency, into a new Foreign Operations Administration. Harold Stassen—former governor of Minnesota and three-time Republican presidential candidate—took charge of the merged agency. By September, Stassen had dismissed Point Four administrator Stanley Andrews without appointing a successor and given the ax to most of the Technical Cooperation Administration's high-level employees. Under Stassen's directorship, foreign aid delivery would have to depend upon promises from the host country to participate in "mutual security" arrangements—that is, allowing U.S. military bases on their territory. Furthermore, as Stassen had informed the Senate Committee on Foreign Relations earlier in the spring, the new mutual security apparatus would be characterized by "increased reliance upon private capital for all phases of economic accomplishment." It was not the end of foreign aid as a component of U.S. foreign policy. Indeed, Eisenhower would, over the course of his presidency, come to distance himself from the simplistic call for "trade not aid" and reiterate the significance of economic development as an important anticommunist strategy. Nonetheless, the dismantling of the Point Four Program in 1953 was a bitter disappointment to those, including Stanley Andrews, who had committed themselves to the humanitarian vision outlined by Truman in his inaugural address.[27]

In the first years of Eisenhower's presidency, domestic farm politics also pressed upon foreign policy, encouraging the rising chorus of calls for "trade not aid." The president, conscious of the precarious nature of the farm vote in key midwestern states, struggled to lay out a farm policy agenda that would satisfy his party's call for reining in New Deal–era farm price supports without alienating farmers who had come to depend on those programs. Eisenhower was not helped on the domestic political scene by appointing as his secretary of agriculture the hard-right conservative Ezra Taft Benson, who entered office with blistering calls to dismantle agricultural price supports and throw farmers on the mercy of the markets. Foreign trade of American agricultural products offered a much less controversial approach to solving the "surplus problem" faced by highly productive U.S. farmers operating in an environment of escalating costs and declining farm prices. As Eisenhower noted in 1954 to a group of grocers: "We must quit piling up storage [of farm products] that alarms everybody, and upsets the business and farming community, and get things to be used—to find, establish, and sustain markets everywhere." Eisenhower's suggestion that expanded foreign trade, spearheaded by private enterprises actively seeking new markets, could take the lead in solving the U.S. farm problem was not entirely new. During the 1920s farm crisis, proponents of surplus-dumping schemes, especially Senator Charles L. McNary (R-OR) and Representative Gilbert N. Haugen (R-IA), believed that world markets could be forced to accept excess American farm products without endangering trade relations. Various iterations of McNary-Haugen export-dumping bills were repeatedly blocked in Congress, however, and the collapse of international trade during the Great Depression made such approaches even less palatable. But by the 1940s, some prominent farm figures, particularly in Republican circles, became convinced that a modified approach to surplus dumping might do the trick.[28]

One such figure was John H. Davis. As executive secretary of the National Council of Farmer Cooperatives in the mid-to-late 1940s, Davis actively promoted Hooverian associationalist approaches to American farm policy. The farm cooperatives that Davis represented were exempt from antitrust laws under the 1922 Capper-Volstead Act, which enabled some cooperatives—including the purveyors of Sunkist-branded citrus fruits, Land O'Lakes butter, and Diamond walnuts—to develop mass-marketing programs to stabilize farmer-member incomes. Upholding the success of cooperatives in addressing the "farm problem" by developing (and controlling) markets for farm goods, Davis repeatedly pushed Congress in the 1940s to think as much about food markets as about farm prices when formulating agricultural policy. A logical consequence of Davis's vision was for the government to reconsider foreign development programs in terms of their potential benefits for American farmers. As Davis testified before Congress in 1949, "In the long run, the demand for American farm products can be greatly stimulated through the industrialization of the more underdeveloped countries." Rather than promote agricultural development in the hungry world, Davis suggested, U.S.-supported industrialization of developing economies would "make possible the building up of balanced purchasing power [to] develop a demand for more farm products than these countries can produce." This was not a statement of "trade not aid" but a call for industrial aid, more akin to the Marshall Plan than to Point Four, to enable expanded trade of American-produced agricultural products to the hungry nations of the world.[29]

Secretary of Agriculture Ezra Taft Benson agreed with Davis's position on the need for expanded trade of American agricultural products. One of Benson's first actions as secretary of agriculture was a thorough reorganization of the structure of the USDA, in part to reduce the power of agencies such as the Bureau of Agricultural Economics, which were viewed by conservatives as too closely tied to New Deal farm programs. One component of this reorganization was a boost of the Foreign Agricultural Service to the highest levels of the USDA bureaucracy, headed by a new assistant secretary of agriculture. In September 1953, Benson appointed John H. Davis to head the newly empowered service. Testifying before the Senate Appropriations Committee in spring 1954, Davis laid out the mission of this "new, revitalized arm" of the Department of Agriculture. "Its job," announced Davis, "is to help American agriculture and American agricultural industry hold the foreign markets that they now have, regain some of the markets that have recently slipped away, and build new expanded markets in the future." Importantly, as Davis saw it, this was not "a Government program as we usually think of Government programs, but . . . an essential service to American farmers and to private trade." Private enterprise, supported by USDA research and funding, would be called upon to engage in "aggressive merchandising" to reduce U.S. stockpiles of agricultural commodities. Feeding a hungry world, in Davis's vision, was undoubtedly good business.[30]

In 1953 Congress, at the request of Benson and Davis, began considering legislation to fund a permanent and substantial program for disposing of agricultural surpluses "among friendly peoples abroad" to "further the foreign policy of the United States." Signed into law by President Eisenhower in July 1954 as Public Law 480, the legislation's language made clear that sales of farm commodities to "friendly peoples" could serve militaristic purposes. Though redubbed by President Eisenhower the "Food for Peace" program in 1959, PL 480, as crafted by Congress, was designed as a weapon for the Farms Race. Representative Fred Marshall (D-MN) declared on the House floor in June 1954 that "we have never made the use of food as a weapon as effectively as we should in this fight against the insidious effects of communism." Arkansas Democratic congressman Lawrence Hays agreed, denouncing the country's agricultural surpluses as a "disgrace . . . rotting on our hands as a hungry world looks on." Hays suggested that "with proper use these surpluses can be made a far more poten[t] means of combating the spread of communism than the hydrogen bomb."[31]

Tensions over how to use PL 480 to attack communism developed early in the program's administration. Secretary Benson and members of the congressional farm bloc pushed for dramatic and immediate expansion of exports, thinking of the law primarily as a means of boosting U.S. farm prices. Davis, however, worried that overly aggressive surplus dumping would disturb world markets and strain trade relations with allies. Officials in the State Department agreed with Davis, and further insisted that exports had to be limited and carefully calibrated to the foreign policy goal of drawing "friendly countries" into the U.S. orbit—military as well as economic. The compromise that resulted from these debates was that private enterprise was pushed to the front lines of the battle to expand world markets for American agricultural products. In 1954 Davis left the Department of Agriculture to accept a professorship at Harvard Business School, where he would coin the term *agribusiness* to describe the specific corporate form he believed should engage in the "aggressive merchandising" of farm products at home and abroad. Speaking to a group of Iowa farmers in 1955, Davis explained that vertically integrated modern corporations—agribusinesses—held the power to coordinate and launch an economic assault on the global agricultural marketplace, "very much the same way we established theaters of military operations during World War II."[32]

By the mid-1950s, the Cold War Farms Race was fully under way. Though some aspects of the Farms Race had been prefigured by wartime "food as a weapon" rhetoric and interwar rural modernization schemes, it was only during the Truman and Eisenhower administrations that three distinct lines of thinking about American agricultural abundance were fused into a relatively coherent component of U.S. Cold War foreign policy. First, the propaganda power of promoting American-style food abundance gained a sharper edge as hopes for a century of the common man were replaced by the bifurcated Cold War world, defined in no small part by an economic contest between capitalism and socialism. Second, the notion that American agricultural surpluses could be strategically deployed to build global alliances likewise became intertwined with American military and defense goals in ways that few could have imagined before World War II. Finally, the concept that America's food system could and should serve as a concrete model for exercising U.S. leadership in the world, while hotly debated before the war, came to be accepted as a given across the political spectrum by the late 1940s. Discussions of the extent to which that food system should be rooted in public action versus private enterprise certainly continued, but even so a consensus developed in which few could legitimately question the idea that America's food abundance was a powerful, just, and deployable weapon.

When Harry Truman effectively launched the first weapon of the Farms Race with Point Four, he called for agricultural development without "the old imperialism" of "exploitation for foreign profit." Two years into Dwight Eisenhower's presidency such thinking had been replaced by an explicitly pro-corporate agenda for using U.S. agricultural abundance as a weapon against the communist world. Among the American business leaders who responded most enthusiastically to the call to arms was none other than Nelson Rockefeller, who aimed to launch an arsenal of supermarkets against the threat of world communism.

3

Supermercado USA

The arrival of American supermarkets in Venezuela in 1949 was supposed to spark an instantaneous passage into modern consumer capitalism. "It was hard," according to Bernardo Jofre, a consultant for the International Basic Economy Corporation (IBEC), "for Venezuelans to realize the importance of modernizing the retail food stores and operating them on the basis of greater sales volume and less profit margin." Long accustomed to the "classical 'casa de abastos' or 'bodega,'" Venezuelans were, according to Jofre, ill-prepared to foresee the revolutionary benefits to be gained by shopping at American-style supermarkets. Those benefits were envisioned by Nelson Rockefeller when he founded IBEC shortly after World War II. Supermarkets would, Rockefeller imagined, transform Venezuela from a petroleum-dependent autarky with a restive peasantry into a reliable U.S. ally with a diversified economy, openness to foreign trade and investment, and a solidly middle-class electorate. By 1956, Venezuela was home to eight American-operated *supermercados,* and according to Jofre's report to IBEC headquarters, it could "truthfully be said that the modern supermarkets are displacing the old fashioned 'bodegas.'" The decline of the bodega, for Jofre, heralded the beginning of the end for the Venezuelan political economy, marked by divisive radicalism, rampant inequality, and antagonistic relations with the United States. The rise of the supermarket portended a new future, of broadly shared prosperity, stable democracy, and cooperative relations with North American capitalists.[1]

Nelson Rockefeller was an internationalist, a moderate Republican, and a scion of the most recognized business family in the United States. In 1947 he pooled $2 million in personal and family capital to create the International Basic Economy Corporation. Founded on the optimistic notion that a corporation could pursue philanthropic developmental goals while turning handsome profits, IBEC would score its greatest successes from the late 1940s through the 1960s with a chain of Venezuelan supermarkets. These stores were deeply politicized entities, appearing on the world stage as the first exemplars of U.S.-driven efforts to use American-style food retailing as a weapon in the Farms Race. Supermarkets, Rockefeller and his IBEC colleagues imagined, would reach back into the small-scale localized agriculture of countries such as Venezuela, forcing rapid adoption of technological systems for lowering the price of food for urban populations. The power of American capital, brought to bear on high food prices, would silence political leftists who demanded the ouster of "Yanqui imperialistas." As Rockefeller would declare in the mid-1950s, "It's hard to be a Communist with a full belly." In contrast to the oft-touted "supermarket revolution" that swept the United States after the 1930s, in other words, IBEC introduced American-style food stores as forces of anticommunist counterrevolution in Cold War Latin America.[2]

Rockefeller's supermarket project was both similar to and markedly different from other, better-known development institutions that emerged after World War II. The United Nations Food and Agriculture Organization, for instance, worked to fight global hunger at least in part to quell political radicalism. Yet according to the historian Amy Staples, such development agencies were staffed by well-intentioned technical experts who "derived no monetary profit from

their work." Rockefeller's IBEC was similarly staffed by internationalists harboring a mix of humanitarian and anticommunist intentions,
but profit was the company's raison d'être. Development without
profit, for Rockefeller, was no development at all. In this respect
Rockefeller's thinking aligned well with shifting ideas about American
development projects in the 1950s, when nonstate actors, including
U.S. corporations, rapidly expanded their global activities as explicit
components of the country's mission to prove capitalism's superiority
to communism.[3]

Rockefeller's understanding of the role of corporate capital in the
postwar world was not solely a product of a Cold War calculus. For
Rockefeller—whose enormous personal fortune was hardly kept under
wraps—the post–World War II moment offered an unprecedented
opportunity to reconceptualize the relationship between profit and
philanthropy. In the nineteenth-century Anglo-American economic
vision, profit was inseparable from social welfare. In Andrew Carnegie's influential 1889 essay "Wealth," for instance, the windfall profits
accrued by industrial capitalists were the necessary and logical result of
managerial success in bringing basic comforts to average workers. Industrialization brought enormous inequality of wealth, admitted
Carnegie, but when "the poor enjoy what the rich could not before
afford," profit and social welfare are one and the same. Thus, only the
most successful capitalists, who had proved themselves worthy in the
industrial marketplace, could be trusted to employ their accumulated
wealth toward charitable purposes. According to Rockefeller, however,
this nineteenth-century vision no longer applied in a world racked by
the devastation of two world wars and a global depression. "The record
of the last century," Rockefeller explained to a Brazilian business group
in 1948, "shows that capital then went almost invariably to the area
promising greatest profit. Today this is not enough. Today capital must

go where it can produce the most goods; render the greatest services; meet the most pressing needs of the people." Like Carnegie, Rockefeller believed firmly in the power of both capital and philanthropy. In contrast with Carnegie, however, Rockefeller sought to merge philanthropy with profitability, rather than pursue them in separate life stages, and to do so on a global scale. This optimistic understanding of corporate capitalism's potential for social uplift was not Rockefeller's alone at midcentury. The management guru Peter Drucker was among the many influential thinkers who argued that American corporations were spearheading a massive transformation in the world economy. The modern corporation, declared Drucker, was replacing the anarchic free-for-all of nineteenth-century markets with a rationalized, socialized, and planned political economy in which multiple stakeholders—workers, consumers, communities, nations—benefited from the spoils that had once gone primarily to shareholders.[4]

Charged with the multipronged mission of satisfying hunger, staving off communism, and churning out profits, IBEC's managerial team descended on Venezuela in the late 1940s and set to work establishing supermarkets. Their bold attempts to transform the entire nation's food economy led to mixed results. By the mid-1960s, the company had established more than two dozen thriving, profitable supermarkets in a Latin American country that had operated no supermarkets before IBEC's arrival. But simultaneous efforts to establish industrialized agriculture to supply the country's basic food needs never produced the desired results. By the end of the 1960s, IBEC was shedding all semblance of altruism as it transformed into a multinational agribusiness firm seeking profit for profit's sake.

The notion that supermarkets could function as agents of capitalist development emerged in the context of the burgeoning Farms Race. In post–World War II Venezuela, that context was deeply colored by petroleum. Since his earliest days as a director of Creole Petroleum in Venezuela, Rockefeller had fretted about the possible impacts of communist agitation on U.S. diplomatic and business relations in Latin America. After World War II, the apparent threat of communism took on added force. As the *New York Times* reporter W. H. Lawrence noted in an article that Rockefeller's staff clipped for his personal files, the "economic ills of Latin America, basic and temporary, have made that area a fertile field for Communist agitation." Repulsed by communism but also concerned about Creole's bottom line, Rockefeller was spurred into action when Venezuela's postwar reformist party, Acción Democrática, responded to leftist pressures by imposing steep taxes on foreign oil companies. To stave off further impositions on the oil companies, Rockefeller convinced the petroleum firms to pony up $15 million to help Acción Democrática and President Rómulo Betancourt confront a worsening food crisis in Venezuela.[5]

The result, in May 1947, was the formation of a subsidiary of IBEC, the Venezuelan Basic Economy Corporation (VBEC). Half of VBEC's capitalization came from the oil companies and half from the Venezuelan government, thus making it into something like a for-profit version of the wartime OIAA's servicio. Like its parent company, VBEC was a profit-oriented corporation with an explicit social mission. Its certificate of incorporation declared that VBEC would "promote the economic development of Venezuela, and particularly its agricultural economy, to increase the production and availability of goods, things and services useful to the lives or livelihood of its people, and thus to better their standards of living." Supermarkets, VBEC's organizers quickly decided, would play a crucial role in achieving these goals. A February 1947 press release touting the proposed company declared: "It is the general impression of the mission that food supplies at more reasonable prices can be made available by improving methods of food distribution." The lessons learned in Venezuela under the Office of Inter-American Affairs were applied to VBEC's formation, as Rockefeller and his aides were determined to introduce "improvements in warehousing, transportation, and marketing facilities," not simply boost agricultural production at the farm level.[6]

Supermarkets became the centerpiece of the VBEC counterrevolutionary campaign because of the problem of spiraling food costs in postwar Venezuela. Kenneth J. Kadow, IBEC development consultant and a former plant pathologist at the University of Delaware, informed Rockefeller in March 1947 that one of the core problems of the "backward countries of the world" was reliance on "generally antiquated methods and equipment in nearly all phases of agriculture." Kadow suggested a three-pronged attack on Venezuela's "antiquated" agriculture: introduce service industries such as warehousing and agronomical research; push "the industrialization of agriculture for the conversion of bulky inexpensive raw materials into finished or semifinished high priced consumer goods"; and develop model farms to demonstrate the benefits of "modernization, mechanization and industrialization of agricultural production." Once exposed to the miracles of American-style agriculture, Venezuelan peasants could play key roles in bringing down the cost of food in the nation.[7]

The next month, Rockefeller received another scouting report emphasizing the need for supermarkets to spur industrialization of Venezuelan agriculture. The analyst, Dwight H. Mahan, informed VBEC executives that most Venezuelan consumers purchased their food from small merchants located in large open markets. Operating bodegas no larger than four hundred square feet, retailers generally carried less than a thousand dollars' worth of stock. Because of the "small stocks and very moderate sales," these food-store proprietors had to "take high markups to earn a living." With little capital and no consolidated buying power, merchants could exercise no leverage over their supply chains. Venezuela had neither commission houses for buying fresh produce nor American-style marketing cooperatives for farmers. In short, Mahan declared, the marketing end of the country's food economy was "primitive" and in dire need of modernization. Without consolidated retail and wholesale facilities farmers would have little incentive to intensify production and expand food supply; consequently, food prices would remain high.[8]

Stacy May of IBEC took the lead in formulating plans for using the American supermarket model as a tool for profitable agricultural development. May was an economist who had headed the U.S. Bureau of Research and Statistics of the War Production Board during World War II. His work centered on the theoretical implications of increasing raw-material production, especially agricultural production, for economies in crisis. During the war, for instance, May informed the Academy of Political Science that the industrial demands of military mobilization could not be met without simultaneous attention to the food needs of civilian populations. Along with his theoretical interest in the relationship between agricultural and industrial sectors of national economies, May hewed close to Rockefeller's vision of agricultural development as an anticommunist weapon. May was just the kind of big-picture thinker favored by Rockefeller at IBEC's New York headquarters, but unlike many of Rockefeller's associates he had little sense of the day-to-day operations of actual businesses. So May turned for advice to Clarence Francis, who had overseen the rise of General Foods since its incorporation in 1922 into one of the world's largest marketers of branded, packaged convenience foods. Francis informed May that an American-style food distribution system in Venezuela could be "an extraordinarily profitable venture" and suggested that May contact other leaders in the food industry to gain insight into how U.S. businesses, including Seeman Brothers (a major food wholesale outfit) and the National Tea and First National supermarket chains, had successfully lowered food prices.[9]

May took Francis's advice, but continued to stamp his own theoretical gloss and wartime experience on VBEC's plans for centralized food distribution facilities. In April 1947, he wrote a lengthy letter to John Camp, a forester and veteran of the Rockefeller-funded Institute of Inter-American Affairs who served as the initial head of operations for VBEC. May explained to Camp the importance of radically transforming Venezuela's food-supply chains. Venezuela's economy, he insisted, "paralleled, in many ways, the war-time economy of the United States," with full employment, high wages, and high demand for limited consumer goods. Petroleum refineries pumped money into the economy, much as U.S. wartime spending boosted industrial production and workers' wages. Production of basic goods from food to shelter failed to keep pace, however, causing rampant inflation. The key to enabling food abundance was "vigorous competition" in the food distribution field. To initiate this competition, May proposed that VBEC start by providing centralized food procurement for oil companies— firms employing many North Americans already accustomed to supermarket-style food products. Food costs for oil employees would decrease, something that from May's viewpoint would have the added benefit of relieving labor union demands for higher wages. Supplying food for the oil companies' commissaries would furthermore provide "sufficient volume [of sales] to allow us to set up a really efficient wholesale procurement and distribution system" that would form the basis of a supermarket retailing system for Venezuela's domestic market. "Above all," May proclaimed, the food-procurement approach would give VBEC "definite goals and specific location-factors for our entire program for increasing agricultural production."[10]

In one stroke, it seemed, an American-style food distribution system would stabilize Venezuela's overheated economy, quell union militancy, and introduce Venezuelan shoppers to the economies and conveniences of modern-day living provided by self-serve supermarkets. Furthermore, May and other IBEC executives hoped that focusing on food distribution and lowering food costs would defuse protests from Venezuelans who sensed that Rockefeller had a hidden agenda. One editorialist declared in a Caracas newspaper, for instance, that Rockefeller's secret goal was to buy up local farmlands and "convert agricultural production into another political weapon . . . of British-American imperialism." Or as Bernardo Jofre suggested in 1947, the upcoming Venezuelan election might turn in part on claims that "Betancourt has sold the basic economy of the country to Yankee imperialism." Supermarket-style food distribution, IBEC's planners believed, offered a politically savvy method of fending off such attacks on U.S. oil interests or the reformist Betancourt administration.[11]

These plans went into action in the summer of 1947, as VBEC formed a subsidiary dedicated to building an American-style food distribution network in Venezuela. Compañia Anónima Distribuidora de Alimentos (CADA) was headed by the Puerto Rican–born Anthony B. Toro, who had established the Tom Thumb chain of supermarkets in Dallas, Texas, in 1945. The original plans for CADA called for new food distribution centers in the Venezuelan capital of Caracas as well as the oil refining city of Maracaibo. In the oil regions, CADA would at first focus solely on wholesaling endeavors, providing the petroleum firms' commissaries with local and imported foodstuffs. In Caracas, however, CADA would establish retail food stores, intending "to obtain more direct leverage on the price of food to the consumer, with a view to keeping prices as low as possible." CADA's original plan acknowledged that much of the early business volume would depend on imports from the United States, but it was hoped that contracts with local farmers would stimulate the agricultural production of farmlands surrounding the major urban centers.[12]

Enormous challenges immediately confronted CADA. Most important, CADA's planners were overly optimistic about the "revolutionary" potential of supermarkets in a non-U.S. context. They failed to acknowledge the dense network of technological infrastructure, scientific research, and government policy making that had sowed the seeds of agricultural industrialization in the United States. Supermarkets alone had not been responsible for the dramatic changes in U.S. agriculture after 1930. This is not to say that VBEC's planners were unaware of the importance of mechanized agriculture, genetically modified hybrid seeds, scientifically selected animal breeds, or chemical fertilizers and pesticides as the bases of America's vast agricultural productivity. In fact, VBEC also formed a subsidiary to foment a productivity revolution in Venezuelan agriculture—Productora Agropecuaria Compañia Anónima (PACA). Three model farms were set up—the 7,800-acre (3,150-hectare) Central Bolívar southwest of Lake Maracaibo; the 20,000-acre (8,000-hectare) Agua Blanca between Maracaibo and Caracas; and 6,000 acres (2,450 hectares) in the Chirgua Valley that included an abandoned coffee estate once owned by Simón Bolívar himself. Along with Granja Avícola, a model poultry plot near Caracas, the PACA farms were designed as demonstration sites that would "undertake production of farm staples with modern equipment and farming methods."[13]

The barriers to industrialization of agriculture in Venezuela, however, were legion for both CADA and PACA. Dwight Mahan's spring 1947 report on the farm and food economy of Venezuela highlighted some of the major challenges CADA and PACA would face. Geography was one. The two largest cities, Caracas and Maracaibo, were located far from the best farmlands (figure 6). Warehouses established in the inland commercial centers of Valera and Barquisimeto, nearer important agricultural regions, had had to be shut down by the end of 1949 when operating costs proved prohibitive. Transportation of goods was extraordinarily expensive, particularly for the largest cities. As Mahan put it, "There are no railroads worth mention," and truckers charged shockingly high rates for overland transport. The oil companies in Maracaibo relied heavily on expensive air freight for butter and meat from the livestock-producing regions of southeastern Venezuela, more than four hundred miles away. Many foodstuffs traveled even farther. Mahan estimated that the country produced "probably less than one half" of its own basic food commodities. Absentee landowners lived in cities while their diseased cattle produced minuscule quantities of milk. Small-scale farmers produced coffee, sugarcane, and pineapples without machinery or access to credit. A group of consultants from Cargill—one of the world's largest transnational grain-trading firms, based in the U.S. Midwest—echoed Mahan's observations in a July report to IBEC's directors. Farming in Venezuela, the writers declared, was "incredibly backward, almost biblical," and relied on ancient technologies: "fire, stick, and hoe." To the horror of the Cargill representatives, Venezuelan farmers did not even practice systematic seed selection of open-pollinated corn—let alone use the scientifically pollinated hybrid strains responsible for enormous yield boosts in the United States.[14]

Neither Mahan nor the Cargill consultants could fathom that there might be legitimate ecological, economic, or sociohistorical reasons for Venezuela's farmers to rely on nonchemical, nonmechanized approaches to agriculture. Everyone involved in the project tended to

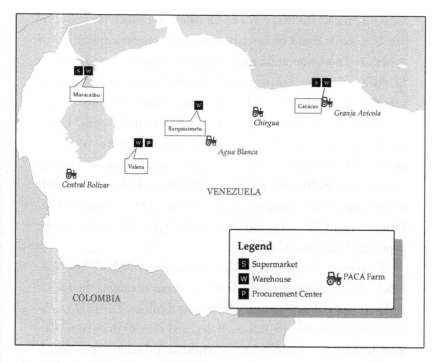

Figure 6 Locations of PACA farms, warehouses, procurement centers, and supermarkets in northwestern Venezuela as of early 1949. Retail stores and warehouses were initially located in relatively affluent urban areas, such as Maracaibo and Caracas. Procurement stations and warehouses located near agriculturally productive regions of the country, such as those at Valera and Barquisimeto, had closed by the end of 1949 due to lack of profitability. Transportation expenses plagued three of the four PACA farms, although the poultry demonstration plot at Granja Avícola was within easy reach of Caracas.

(Map by the author, based on Morrison G. Tucker, "Report of the Activities of PACA, Year 1949," March 11, 1950, Microfilm Reel R-94, International Basic Economy Corporation Records, Series R, Rockefeller Archive Center, Sleepy Hollow, N.Y.)

view Venezuela's landscape as a blank slate upon which the midwestern U.S. farm could be inscribed with the proper application of American know-how and capital. The PACA farms were, according to VBEC operational manager John Camp, "set up on the basis of a mixed farming enterprise with field crops, livestock, etc., worked out on a diversified basis such as we have in the United States." Camp considered this approach clearly superior both to the small-scale agriculture of local peasants and to the hyper-extractive monocropping promoted by multinational food corporations in Latin America such as the United Fruit Company. A diversified midwestern-style farm, Camp assured IBEC executives, was the "type that could best be copied by Venezuelans."[15]

Optimistic about airlifting Iowan agricultural methods into Venezuela, PACA's managers immediately set about saturating their fields and pastures with several tons of synthetic fertilizer. The IBEC technical consultant Robert P. Russell declared that all the Venezuelan acreage should be doused with the synthetic herbicide 2, 4-D, which American farmers had used to achieve "major yield increases." Russell held a master's degree in chemical engineering from the Massachusetts Institute of Technology. Before becoming the chief of development for Standard Oil, he had worked during the war to develop improved flamethrowers and incendiary bombs. Given his abiding interest in the chemical cutting edge, he was especially gratified to learn in spring 1948 that "PACA plans large scale field trials of DDT, Toxaphene, and benzene hexachloride." Petrochemicals were assumed to be responsible for America's dramatic increase in farm productivity at midcentury, and so were seen as essential to success in Venezuela.[16]

Experience repeatedly showed, however, that American-style chemical warfare did not guarantee American-style productivity. Despite initial optimism, PACA's monthly reports to IBEC headquarters began to read like Old Testament catalogues of plagues. In the summer of 1948, armyworms attacked PACA's 2,500 acres of corn. Five power dusters and two chemical sprayers roved the fields for "a quick application of poison." After the third spraying of DDT, the armyworms retreated—but in the meantime, the "necessity for concentrating all manpower and equipment to fight worms" prevented the application of the desired amount of fertilizer. Heavy rains drowned plants. Virulent weed growth prevented effective harvesting by machine. Yields were abysmal, and PACA reported massive monetary losses. "To say that we were upset," VBEC manager Morrison Tucker informed IBEC executives, "is to put it mildly." Tucker was particularly annoyed to notice, in January 1949, that "one of our neighbors (Sr. Camacho) was doing what looked like a better job" than PACA in developing healthy pastures—and Camacho was not applying any chemical fertilizers or pesticides. Other evidence of "Venezuelan know-how" further impressed Tucker. Local farm operations, for instance, employed individuals who understood that the climate and soils of tropical agriculture were different from those of Iowa—and who could speak Spanish. PACA's original management, Tucker noted, "had never been in the tropics, . . . apparently paid no attention to the local technical advice offered it, and could not speak the language."[17]

Executives at IBEC's New York headquarters turned to outside consultants for help in understanding PACA's miseries. In 1949, the Venezuelan farms received a visit from Charles F. Seabrook. Seabrook, known by some as the "Henry Ford of Agriculture," owned an industrial vegetable farm in southern New Jersey that produced most of the frozen vegetables for General Foods' Birds Eye brand in the late 1940s. After touring PACA's farm operations, Seabrook wrote a blistering report to Nelson Rockefeller, noting that managers had spent ridiculous sums of money to assemble a "weird assortment" of tractors, harvesters, and other farm machines. The lack of standardization meant that "more than 50% of your equipment is frequently out of operations." Without a radical change in management, Seabrook suggested, the farms were doomed to failure.[18]

The on-the-ground reality of PACA's operations contrasted starkly with IBEC's public pronouncements. Robert Russell published a glowing report on PACA's work in the September 1949 issue of *American Magazine,* announcing that the Venezuelan farm project was engendering an "economic revolution." Venezuelan peasants were "tossing out ox-old methods of producing, storing, and distributing food, substituting in their stead the latest scientific and marketing techniques imported from the United States." Employing the rhetoric of the Farms Race, Russell declared without irony that PACA was engaged in a "Revolution, the American Way," a successful campaign of "selling industrial democracy" to Venezuelan peasants.[19]

Such hubris made for impressive copy but bad farming. PACA's farm managers relied on techniques developed in an American industrial agriculture context, rather than looking to local producers for insights. Through 1951 and 1952, PACA continued to face the reality that farming in Venezuela was entirely unlike farming in Iowa. Heavy rains in early 1951 drowned pastures and washed away workers' mud houses. In tropical conditions, weeds thrived even when repeatedly doused with the DuPont chemical company's latest offerings. IBEC's directors, exasperated with appalling losses, decided to liquidate PACA in 1953. Although VBEC would continue to invest in efforts to boost dairy production and industrialize chicken production in Venezuela, the attempt to ramp up grain, beef, and vegetable production was an unmitigated failure.[20]

There was a deep, generally unacknowledged problem at the heart of PACA's efforts to summarily industrialize Venezuelan agriculture.

Blinded by a deep-seated faith in the power of "free enterprise" and goaded by the sweeping anticommunist rhetoric of the Farms Race, PACA's managers fundamentally misread the history of the U.S. industrial agriculture model upon which they based their approach. As I explored in Chapter 1, the twentieth-century transformation of American farms was due in no small part to the interventions of government agencies and technical experts. Capital and technology were essential to the industrialization of American agriculture, but their application was guided at every stage by the actions of bureaucrats and scientists in the Department of Agriculture, farm bloc congressmen, and technical experts in the land-grant university and federal extension complex.

In Venezuela, despite friendly relations with the Betancourt regime, IBEC confronted a state ill-prepared to implement either a "high modernist" or a "low modernist" agenda on the nation's farm fields. The country's Ministry of Agriculture became an independent federal agency only in 1936, while the U.S. Department of Agriculture had been actively building its institutional capacity since 1862. Venezuela's oil wealth allowed the ministry to fund impressive laboratories and experimental farms staffed by research scientists, but little effort was made by ministers of agriculture to translate such research into practical applications in the field. As an American member of the Office of Inter-American Affairs noted in a wartime survey, the "so-called experiment stations" in Venezuela did "not have a coordinated program of work," kept no systematic records on their scientific research, and made little effort to introduce their book-farming methods to actual farmers. The Rockefeller Foundation (with which Nelson Rockefeller had only limited connections) briefly funded a single obscure geneticist and four fellowships for promising young Venezuelan agronomists in the 1940s, hoping to introduce the U.S. experiment-station model of research. Even that limited program was canceled in 1949 due to lack of results. Without a strong state apparatus for promulgating methods of industrial agriculture to the countryside, PACA imported its own technical experts from the United States, but the expense of a robust technical staff serving just four farms clearly outweighed the benefits.[21]

Farming the "American Way" in the twentieth-century United States was built upon an elaborate state infrastructure dedicated to making farms into factories. State-supported scientific and technological research made American farms the most productive in the world. The "free enterprise" vision of American agriculture that inspired PACA could not easily be replicated in Venezuela. Indeed, it had never existed in the first place.

Supermarkets and not the state, then, were to serve as CADA's primary tool for agro-industrialization in Venezuela. Although CADA supermarkets would prove to be the single most profitable component of the International Basic Economy Corporation's diverse portfolio in the 1950s, in the late 1940s they repeatedly fell short of expectations. In March 1949 Anthony Toro, manager of supermarket operations for CADA, wrote to Nelson Rockefeller with a sober report. Early plans for CADA had assumed that its wholesale operations would, through mass buying from local food producers, spur expanded farm production while streamlining distribution to local retailers. Instead, Toro noted, "the greater part of the food" purchased by CADA was coming from Seeman Brothers and other giant U.S. grocery wholesalers. Rather than eliminating intermediaries from the Venezuelan food-supply chain, CADA was functioning merely as "another local wholesaler and importer of foods with no greater volume than several of the local wholesalers." Up to 80 percent of CADA's goods were U.S. imports.[22]

Dependence on imports was a sticky political problem. For one, it required Nelson Rockefeller to cash in many of his chits in Washington to convince the Departments of State and Agriculture to permit massive exports of U.S. foodstuffs to a single corporation in Venezuela. VBEC's demands for a special export license in 1948 would have instantly doubled U.S. food exports to Venezuela, threatening U.S. trade relations with other Latin American countries and thus infuriating the State Department. The Department of Agriculture, meanwhile, refused to let VBEC export as much meat as it wanted at a time of tight meat supplies back home. High domestic meat prices produced constant headaches for the Truman administration's agricultural policy makers; a dramatic transformation of beef export policies would not go over well with citizens clamoring for steaks and roasts after the rationing of World War II.[23]

Venezuelan politics made CADA's reliance on imports doubly damning. As Rockefeller well knew, the mere mention of the name Rockefeller in Venezuela evoked images of ruthless Yanqui capitalist imperialists bent on profiting from the country's oil reserves. The continuing power of anti-Rockefeller sentiment was confirmed by a letter delivered in late 1948 to Rockefeller by Armando Capriles, the head of Venezuelan operations of the Chicago meatpacking firm Armour and Company. According to Capriles, a "bad atmosphere" had infected local wholesalers and retailers, who sensed that CADA intended to drive both them and their Venezuelan suppliers out of business by importing U.S. food products. This bad atmosphere posed particular problems for the Rockefeller enterprises in November 1948, the month in which Marcos Pérez Jiménez orchestrated a coup that replaced Rómulo Betancourt's reformist government with a military junta for the next ten years. An editorial program on Maracaibo's Radio Mara that month declared that the Rockefeller enterprises were seeking to make Venezuela into "an immense farm of economic slaves," while Venezuela's central bank labeled Rockefeller "public enemy no. 1" for allowing CADA to purchase most of its goods from the United States in dollars rather than from Venezuelan merchants in local currency. In 1947, VBEC's planners had believed that wholesaling would provide a soft landing on Venezuelan soil for American food distribution practices. By the end of 1948 it was clear that wholesaling alone was not going to achieve the expected results.[24]

In the summer of 1949, a new head of VBEC, William Coles, shifted CADA's focus from wholesaling to retailing. Rather than attempt to build a food distribution network piecemeal, CADA would henceforth plunge into the world of American-style supermarketing. Facing political attacks as well as "increasing losses, rising costs, and static sales," CADA would need "drastic revisions" in its planning. Retailing expert Anthony Toro would be given power to "do everything possible" to build supermarkets in Caracas. Coles also called on another American supermarket manager to help implement the plans—Richard Provost. The son of a Kansas supermarket owner, Provost had spent three years working with his flamboyant uncle, the Kansas entrepreneur Dick Boogaart, setting up nine grocery stores in Mexico. Fluent in Spanish yet all-American in his approach to supermarket management, Provost oversaw the opening of the first VBEC supermarket in Maracaibo in December 1949, adding to the supermarkets already in operation in Caracas under Toro's management. The Maracaibo supermarket immediately enjoyed flourishing sales.[25]

Sales were helped by the fact that the supermarket was opened on the avenida Bella Vista in a ritzy section of Maracaibo. As IBEC executives would discover over the next decade, their supermarkets—whether in Venezuela, Brazil, Argentina, Peru, or Italy—tended to perform best in affluent areas, especially areas with significant populations of North

Americans already accustomed to self-service shopping. One of the Caracas supermarkets, located in the upscale Las Mercedes district, provided 208 parking spots for automobiles, a commodity only well-heeled residents of Caracas could afford. The supermarket was prominently featured in the magazine *Progressive Architecture* for its luxurious modernist aesthetic. For North American managerial employees of the oil companies of Maracaibo and Caracas, as well as for affluent urban Venezuelans, Toro's and Provost's supermarkets offered the amenities and the gendered norms that U.S. consumers had come to expect in their suburban shopping experiences: air conditioning, a "phalanx of meat counters" carrying prewrapped meats, "even frozen-whipped potatoes for the woman who has not the time . . . to whip up a dish herself." The fact that average Venezuelans were not the main shoppers at VBEC's supermarkets was underscored in 1951 when one store raffled off a new Ford. The automobile was won by a woman from Denmark who had spent only three months in Venezuela—enough time, apparently, to purchase thirteen raffle tickets.[26]

Even with affluent customers forming their core market, the supermarkets gained widespread attention. VBEC's Maracaibo supermarkets—operating under the name TODOS (Spanish for "everything" or "everyone")—gained "public acceptance . . . beyond all expectations," with prices running about 10 percent lower than their competitors'. Most promising from the standpoint of VBEC's broader political objectives, the TODOS supermarkets were forcing local grocers to operate on thinner margins. Although CADA took a net loss for the 1950 fiscal year, its sales of nearly $5 million heartened IBEC executives in New York, as did TODOS's net profit of $282,000 on sales of $3.2 million. Particularly impressive were TODOS's low operating expenses, which rang in at almost half those of comparable U.S. supermarkets, thus allowing the stores to make a profit even though gross margins compared unfavorably to those of U.S. super-markets on most items.[27]

For the supermarkets to achieve long-term success, however, they would have to develop centralized buying power to drive down pur-chasing costs and gross margins. As U.S. food retailers had been learn-ing from the 1920s on, mass sales and rapid turnover of stock depended on a reliable, high-volume supply chain, which in turn relied on sub-stantial warehouse capacity. A large warehouse, whether owned by an independent wholesaler or by the retailer itself, required a minimum of five retail stores—and ideally ten to twelve stores—in order to keep goods flowing steadily out the warehouse door and thus minimizing costly "dead time" as products sat idle. The imperative to expand retail operations was thus built into the business model, and VBEC quickly poured capital into building new stores in Caracas and Maracaibo. By 1956, VBEC was operating eight supermarkets in Venezuela. All were turning steady profits on remarkably high sales volumes.[28]

Those profits accrued in part because by 1956 the supermarkets had successfully tapped local sources for a majority of their purchases. In 1953, only half of TODOS's sales involved locally produced items, mainly "canned goods, paper products, dairy foods, fresh fruits and vegetables, staples, fish, and meats." But in 1956, IBEC's treasurer J. W. Hisle noted that he was "surprised that there are so many items which we are now purchasing locally because of their availability." Fewer than 6 percent of TODOS goods, in fact, were at that time imported from the United States. IBEC's 1957 annual report to investors declared that nearly all the Venezuelan supermarkets' most popular items—rice, meat, poultry, and lard—were being procured from Venezuelan pro-ducers. Meanwhile, "substantial amounts of fruits, vegetables, eggs, and other items" also came from within Venezuela. Supermarkets, rather than model farms, seemed to be effectively providing incentives to "agriculture, the livestock industry, and food processing plants in Venezuela" to boost production.[29]

As weapons in the Cold War Farms Race, however, VBEC's supermarkets were expected to be more than profitable operations. They were also meant to dramatically demonstrate the superiority of U.S.-style consumer capitalism. To be sure, the TODOS and CADA supermarkets were popular with consumers, who liked the clean, well-lit stores and their low prices. Julio Ramos, a popular columnist for *El Universal* (a relatively conservative middle-class newspaper), announced in 1956 that VBEC's efforts to "produce meat, milk, potatoes, corn, and rice so as to bring to the people the basic foods at low prices . . . could not be more generous [or] more plausible." Ramos was clearly responding to widespread grumbling about the American supermarkets, however. Bernardo Jofre, IBEC's itinerant ear-to-the-ground consultant on political conditions in Latin American countries, reported in 1957 that he had heard members of the Caracas Chamber of Commerce plotting a "campaign against growth of the IBEC [supermarket] chain." The Chamber of Commerce members were convinced that Rockefeller's enterprise intended to create a "monopoly" in Venezuelan food distribution. Jofre assured IBEC's executives in New York that such claims were baseless. Altogether IBEC accounted for "a drop in the bucket" of food sales, with public markets in the city of Caracas alone making five times the volume of sales of all of IBEC's supermarkets in Venezuela combined.[30]

Venezuelan opponents of the supermarkets had legitimate reasons to worry. IBEC was quickly expanding its operations, and the more stores the company built, the greater its sales volumes and hence the greater its profits. By 1960, IBEC subsidiaries had built seventeen supermarkets in Venezuela. Steadily increasing Venezuelan sales provided IBEC headquarters with its most reliable cash cow. By 1960, the company was the largest retailer in the country, outperforming second-place Sears, Roebuck by $1.2 million in annual sales. In 1961, IBEC's Venezuelan supermarkets made sales of $34.6 million, reaping "greater than expected" profits.[31]

That same year witnessed the first of a series of violent attacks on IBEC supermarkets in Venezuela. A bomb exploded in Las Mercedes shopping center in Caracas in February 1961, causing significant physical damage but no bodily harm. In November 1962, guerrilla fighters hijacked one of CADA's trucks, took it up to a hillside hideout, and distributed the food Robin Hood–style to locals. According to Dick Provost, "there must have been one helluva banquet in the barrio that evening," as the truck was filled with a "sufficient supply of wines" and imported foods. In September 1963, a year in which CADA reported record profits, six members of the leftist group Armed Forces of National Liberation held up seventeen supermarket employees, forced them to disrobe, and set fire to a storage room. A month later, another bomb exploded at Las Mercedes shopping center. This "campaign of terror," IBEC executives believed, was aimed at "discrediting the government of Rómulo Betancourt," who had returned to power in 1959 after wresting control from the conservative dictator Pérez Jiménez. Although Betancourt pursued populist reforms, including redistributing lands to small farmers and joining OPEC to boost Venezuela's petroleum revenues, Betancourt's administration also actively persecuted leftist organizations, whose members responded with violent protests.[32]

Betancourt's alienation of union members and leftist students, however, was only one factor contributing to widespread dissatisfaction in a country racked by extreme inequality, persistent hunger, and limited access to medical care. Even after Betancourt vacated the presidency in 1964, attacks on IBEC's supermarkets continued. In April 1965, protestors armed with machine guns and stones attacked several of CADA's twenty-four locations to protest the U.S. Marines landing troops in the Dominican Republic. Several teenagers hijacked a CADA truck in Caracas, and after opening it up outside the city limits and finding it empty, riddled it with machine-gun fire out of frustration. At least for some Venezuelans by the mid-1960s, IBEC's supermarkets represented something more sinister than mere collusion between domestic politicians and North American capitalists. The supermarkets, it seemed, were symbols of unwanted economic imperialism, and if they were weapons in a broader political-economic contest, then violent protests against their machinery seemed warranted.[33]

The most persistent hostility came not from armed young revolutionaries, however, but from Venezuelan business elites. A group of influential Venezuelan businessmen, including many grocery wholesalers, formed the Pro-Venezuela Association in 1962 to denounce foreign capitalist intervention. The group specifically targeted IBEC's supermarkets for using "discriminatory maneuvers" to prioritize sales of processed foods produced by non-Venezuelan-owned companies. The Pro-Venezuela Association persuaded the national legislature in April 1965 to consider outlawing foreign capitalists from operating food businesses. In response, Provost met with Alejandro Hernandez, president of the group. Hernandez declared that foreign firms were taking over the economy, intending to leave Venezuelans with "only the flag and the national anthem." Provost noted the irony, however, that the wives of Pro-Venezuela's members "all shop in our stores and enjoy both the conveniences and the economies."[34]

Not everyone enjoyed the economies of IBEC's supermarkets, however. In November 1966, four CADA supermarkets were attacked—two in drive-by shootings, two with bombs. IBEC's managers began considering sloughing off the CADA supermarkets, which seemed to be "at or near the peak of efficiency and effectiveness" and thus ripe for sale. Despite the ongoing protests, IBEC had increased its sales in 1966 by 20 percent over the previous year, with profits up by 10 percent, and was now operating twenty-nine stores in Venezuela.[35]

By 1966, with Nelson's son Rodman Rockefeller now at the helm of IBEC, the legacy of the experiment in revolutionizing Venezuela's food economy seemed mixed. The supermarkets begun in Venezuela had proven remarkably profitable. Those profits had spurred similar projects in Brazil, Peru, Argentina, Puerto Rico, and Italy. At the same time, the company's efforts to introduce American-style agricultural practices in tandem with American-style retailing had proven largely unsatisfactory. PACA's attempts to re-create midwestern chemical-dependent farms in the Venezuelan countryside had failed miserably. Whereas the supermarkets, by contrast, had established a strong market presence as buyers of locally produced foods, they had not developed anything like the centralized buying power deployed by American supermarkets such as A&P and Kroger in their efforts to transform agricultural production. Yet the buying power the Venezuelan supermarkets had been able to consolidate had fomented violent protests against "Yanqui imperialistas," undermining the central political goal of promoting a pro-U.S. consumer culture in the Latin American republic. Rodman Rockefeller, faced with these results, reiterated his determination to expand IBEC's supermarket endeavors—but rejected his father's broader vision of doing so as part of a comprehensive plan for agricultural development. As an IBEC Food Group planning report announced in 1966, "We are very conscious of the need for growing profit," and the profitable operations of the supermarkets indicated that "clearly the growth potential is relatively greater at the processing and distribution end" of the food chain—not on the production side. An agricultural development project born of the Cold War Farms Race was, by the late 1960s, being converted into a transnational agribusiness corporation—a theme to which I shall return in Chapter 6.[36]

The failings of Nelson Rockefeller's counterrevolutionary project seem most apparent in the context of his 1969 tour of Latin America. Rockefeller, at the time serving his third term as governor of New York, was sent as a proxy by President Richard Nixon to visit countries in the Southern Hemisphere where he had worked for decades to build goodwill. He was greeted with anything but. Repeatedly burned in effigy by protesters, Rockefeller was denounced as a capitalist imperialist in the streets and in the press. On June 26, 1969, thirteen incendiary bombs, concealed in bags of flour and tubes of toothpaste, exploded simultaneously inside various IBEC supermarkets in Argentina. The purpose, according to protesters, was to draw attention to the "looting of our continent" by U.S. investors and their allied "government captives" in the Southern Hemisphere. Whether such violence emerged from a broader rejection of Rockefeller, IBEC supermarkets, or American capitalism more generally remains open to interpretation. The historian Ernesto Capello, having analyzed letters written to Rockefeller's office after the tour, suggests that a vast "pliable center" of Latin American citizens was more interested in economic opportunity and cooperative relations between the United States and its southern neighbors than in violent protest.[37]

Indeed, the profitability and rapid expansion of IBEC's supermarkets in the 1960s suggest that many Latin American citizens enjoyed the abundance of goods associated with twentieth-century U.S. capitalism generally and supermarkets specifically. But without industrialized agricultural supply chains, such abundance proved difficult to establish and maintain. Unable to industrialize Venezuela's agricultural production through mechanization or chemical spraying alone, the would-be Americanizers retrenched, falling back upon a more limited goal—rapidly turning over stocks of frozen foods, pre-packaged meat, fresh produce, and brand-name canned goods in well-lit, air-conditioned stores. IBEC's supermarkets were ultimately sold off in 1975–76 to Latin American investors in order to stanch rapid capital losses at the parent company.[38]

By all of Nelson Rockefeller's measures for successfully introducing a "private Point Four" in Latin America, then, IBEC's Venezuelan project would seem a failure. Even so, IBEC's efforts to deploy supermarkets as counterrevolutionary weapons may have established an important pattern for later imitators. As I shall explore below, IBEC's focus on capturing profits at the consumer end of the developing world's food chain would, by the 1990s, become a widely adopted practice. In the wake of late-century global economic restructuring, less-developed nations around the globe would witness the rapid penetration of their food economies by multinational supermarket firms, including Carrefour and Walmart.

Understanding how the IBEC Venezuelan experiment served as a bridge from Cold War development thinking to post–Cold War globalization, however, requires deeper exploration of the ways in which American supermarkets were positioned in the 1950s, both rhetorically and figuratively, as weapons in the Cold War Farms Race—as will be seen in the divergent responses to the 1957 Supermarket USA exhibit in communist Yugoslavia and to the 1959 American National Exhibition in Moscow—site of the landmark Kitchen Debate between Richard Nixon and Nikita Khrushchev.

4

Socialist Supermarkets and "Peaceful Competition"

If Latin America was the first region to be targeted for the deployment of American supermarkets as Cold War propaganda weapons, communist Europe loomed as the primary focus in the 1950s. One salvo hit Yugoslavia in September 1957 when a group of American officials and businessmen opened the Supermarket USA exhibition at the Zagreb International Trade Fair, the first fully operational American-style supermarket in a communist country. Waving the abundance of American consumer capitalism under the nose of Yugoslavia's leader Josip Broz Tito, the organizers of Supermarket USA celebrated when communist officials envied, admired, and ultimately tried adopting the American system of mass food distribution. Two years later, Americans once again declared victory when Vice President Richard Nixon, standing amid an intentionally embarrassing display of American consumer goods, taunted Premier Nikita Khrushchev at the so-called Kitchen Debate in Sokolniki Park, Moscow. Automatic dishwashers, self-service food stores, ranch-style homes, sips of Pepsi-Cola—how could communism possibly continue in the face of such an onslaught of unattainable American consumer goods?

From an American point of view, the 1957 Supermarket USA exhibit and the 1959 American National Exhibition both served a clear purpose. When confronted with towering displays of capitalist abundance, socialist consumers were expected to lose all faith in the communist officials who had failed repeatedly to deliver the goods. When citizens in Zagreb or Moscow saw how easily Americans could procure prepackaged beefsteaks and frozen apple pies, their socialist utopias were bound to founder. Although the U.S. Air Force never carpet-bombed the Soviet Union with nylon pantyhose, wristwatches, and plastic yo-yos as the sociologist David Riesman suggested in his 1951 farce "The Nylon War," the exhibitions in Yugoslavia and the Soviet Union in the late 1950s came close. In anything but farcical terms, though, their organizers celebrated the events as indisputable symbolic victories for capitalism.[1]

These two installments of 1950s U.S. Cold War psychological warfare were about much more than consumer politics, and their impacts resonated in Eastern Europe in ways never imagined by American propagandists. If we consider both the Zagreb and the Moscow exhibitions as pivotal events in the Farms Race, we can see that, for communist leaders on the receiving end of these campaigns, the key question was not how embarrassing were the American riches on display. Rather, it was how best to achieve socialist abundance to match—or even surpass—that so arrogantly paraded by the Americans. Farms, farmers, and farm policy, it turned out, were at the top of the communist list of concerns when it came to addressing socialist citizens' demands for better living standards. In the United States, supermarket promoters touted midcentury food distribution as a product of free enterprise instead of state-supported industrial agriculture. In socialist Eastern Europe, however, the question of urban food provisioning was always intertwined with the state's attempts to squeeze more farm production out of the countryside. In Marshal Tito's Yugoslavia, supermarkets had become commonplace in urban areas by the late 1960s, as Communist Party leaders sought to harness their centralized buying power to transform Yugoslavian agriculture. In the Soviet Union, by contrast, supermarkets were less attractive to communist officials who sought state-centric means for revolutionizing agricultural production in the Khrushchev years.

Despite important differences between Yugoslavian and Soviet approaches to food politics, however, communist leaders in both countries put little stock in America's claims that free enterprise was itself capable of producing consumer abundance. The rules of the Farms Race were quite different, it turned out, in Yugoslavia and the Soviet Union, as the leaders made no efforts to mask the hand of the state in constructing socialist food systems in the 1950s and 1960s. When farm production and food availability improved significantly in socialist Europe in the late 1950s, leaders such as Tito and Khrushchev had reason for optimism. Khrushchev in particular announced in no uncertain terms that the Soviet Union would ultimately out-farm the United States, bringing specificity to his often misunderstood claim that state socialism would "bury" the capitalist West. Yet such explicit efforts to link political legitimacy to agricultural productivity and food availability also meant that communist leaders bore the brunt of consumer dissatisfaction when farms faltered or shelves went unstocked. Although U.S. propagandists of the 1950s imagined the American supermarket as a powerful weapon that would undermine socialism from the bottom up, the reality by the 1970s was that socialist regimes were undermining their own legitimacy from the top down by promising that socialist industrial agriculture would meet the consumer desires of urban citizens. Just what sort of weapon a supermarket was at the height of the Cold War Farms Race, then, depended on who was wielding it.

A gathering of American reporters learned in July 1957 that a supermarket was about to invade communist Yugoslavia. John A.

Logan, the head of the National Association of Food Chains, announced that Supermarket USA, part of an "industry-Government program of technical assistance," would thrust ten thousand square feet of consumer capitalism behind enemy lines. Logan noted that his organization's demonstration of a supermarket in Rome the previous year had been "very successful," hardly a necessary reminder for those among the assembled reporters who had penned sensational accounts of Italian women who "shrieked with surprise and envy" upon sight of the range of foods in the American Way *supermercato*. But Rome had been just the opening act. Supermarket USA would involve airlifting four thousand consumer items to avowedly communist soil. John A. Logan had reason to view the Yugoslavian project in militaristic terms.[2]

When Logan spoke in Zagreb on September 6 to mark the opening of the exhibit, he toned down the talk of invasion. He focused instead on how the low food prices available in supermarkets could create "peace and harmony among nations." A placard at the entrance, visible to the more than one million Yugoslavian citizens who passed through the supermarket that fall, presented President Dwight Eisenhower's similarly banal emphasis: "the knowledge of science and technology available to this age" promised a "more widely shared prosperity."[3]

Such claims about producing peace and prosperity were duplicitous. Relations between the United States and communist Yugoslavia were undoubtedly friendlier than those between the United States and Soviet Bloc countries formally under the Kremlin's sway. Yet Logan and Eisenhower knew full well that the purpose of Supermarket USA was to shatter the Yugoslavian citizens' faith in their communist leadership. By 1957, "selling" American consumerism to citizens of the world had become a central component of the Eisenhower administration's Cold War strategy. The representatives of the Department of Commerce and the National Association of Food Chains who cooperatively staged Supermarket USA intended nothing less than to stun visitors with their array of America's prepackaged abundance. Piles of fresh fruit, appealing cuts of plastic-wrapped meat, and towering aisles of sugary breakfast cereals awaited the gawks, gapes, and gasps of socialist consumers, who had experienced serious privation in the wake of World War II. One university student, examining Birds Eye frozen foods arrayed in more than a dozen refrigerated display cases, noted that he had seen "lots of pictures in magazines" of American supermarkets, but actually seeing this plethora of convenience foods firsthand was bewildering: "You can even touch these things. They are real" (figure 7).[4]

Figure 7 Yugoslavian visitors to the 1957 Supermarket USA exhibit gaze at stacks of American breakfast cereals and refrigerated cases stocked with Birds Eye frozen foods. (Box 2, Record Group 489-TF, National Archives and Records Administration II, College Park, Md.)

Such astonishment made for compelling propaganda. Canned press releases from the Department of Commerce's Office of International Trade Fairs, for instance, led U.S. reporters to declare that Yugoslavian Communist Party leaders were "visibly embarrassed" by the supermarket's "enormous appeal to visiting crowds." None too subtly, the Americans provided every hundredth Yugoslavian visitor with a ticket redeemable for a bag of free food—obtainable at a location conveniently situated for waiting photographers to snap a picture (figure 8). In order to make a spectacle out of the quotidian act of self-service shopping, female students from a local university were hired to push wheeled carts—a novelty to shoppers used to carrying baskets

Figure 8 Throngs of lucky ticketholders await free bags of groceries at Supermarket USA, providing U.S. propagandists with a staged photo opportunity. (Box 1, Folder 1, Record Group 489-OF, National Archives and Records Administration II, College Park, Md.)

on their arms—through the aisles. The young women occasionally borrowed a baby to place into the carts, while explaining to the rapt audience the efficiencies and conveniences of American-style food distribution. In short, John Logan had reason to tout Supermarket USA as "effective propaganda for the democratic way in Eastern Europe."[5]

For the dozens of U.S. corporations that donated the infrastructure and goods on display at Supermarket USA, however, the potential for accessing untapped socialist markets appealed at least as much as the chance to embarrass communist officials. Since 1954, when the Eisenhower administration had significantly stepped up its propaganda efforts, corporate executives had been largely expected to foot the bill when it came to selling the American Way overseas. Partly this was because American exhibits at international trade fairs like the one in Zagreb were supposed to promote "free enterprise," not the U.S. government itself; partly it was a result of an attempt to disguise the propagandistic motivations behind, say, demonstrating a station wagon in a European city devoid of driveways or private garages. But by 1957, some corporate observers were convinced that business-government cooperation could produce tangible and immediate returns. As *Time* magazine editorialized, international trade fairs provided not only "one of the best ways to spread the gospel of free enterprise" but also opportunities for U.S. exporters to rack up "millions in sales."[6]

Corporate sponsorship made Supermarket USA possible. At the 1957 Zagreb fair, corporate sponsors included all the major U.S. meat-packers, Coca-Cola and Minute Maid, General Foods and General Mills, Nabisco and Quaker Oats, the food-packaging producers Dow Chemical and DuPont, and dozens of other firms eager to strike deals with Yugoslavian importers. At Supermarket USA, as at other trade fair exhibits of the late 1950s staged by U.S. propagandists, the goal was to sell "goods as well as ideas." Still, American businesses often had to be cajoled into participating. In May 1957, for instance, Department of Commerce representatives attempted (unsuccessfully) to persuade executives at Nelson Rockefeller's International Basic Economy Corporation to help construct Supermarket USA. The IBEC executives declined, apparently too occupied at the time with building their own anticommunist supermarkets in Latin America and Italy.[7]

But it was Yugoslavians, who were decidedly not interested in undermining their communist state, who first proposed the Zagreb trade fair exhibit on food distribution. Yugoslavian officials and business leaders had their own agendas and ambitions, which could be served by creative adaptation of American models, much as Western Europeans had demonstrated during the Marshall Plan when they selectively resisted or adopted American business practices to suit their own local problems and strategies. Risto Bajalski, secretary-general of the Federal Commercial Chamber of Yugoslavia, had earlier traveled to the United States, where he became "enthusiastic" about American supermarketing techniques. Bajalski shared his enthusiasm with various elites at home, including the Belgrade city official Jovan Janković and businessman Milorad Jovanović, who in turn pushed American planners of the 1957 exhibit at Zagreb to consider demonstrating a full-scale supermarket. The efficiency of American supermarkets, with their streamlined machinery for moving goods from farm to table, undoubtedly appealed to Bajalski, and indeed to his many like-minded compatriots in East Germany and Hungary who also sought to build socialist supermarkets in the 1950s. But at a broader level, Supermarket USA tantalized Yugoslavian officials with its potential for radically transforming the politics of wresting food out of the Yugoslavian countryside.[8]

Supermarket USA landed in Zagreb nine years after Marshal Tito openly defied Soviet leader Joseph Stalin. Multiple long-standing tensions lay behind Yugoslavia's ejection from Cominform in 1948, although key among them was Tito's desire to forge a path to socialist economic planning independent of the Kremlin's dictates. Stalin responded to Tito's perceived insolence by imposing a blockade that cut off much-needed shipments of farm machinery, seeds, and fertilizer. With famine threatening Tito's grip on power, desperate Yugoslavian officials turned to the United States for food aid in 1950. Truman's secretary of state, Dean Acheson, saw an opportunity to "promote fissures within the communist world" by propping up Tito's regime as a model of how a communist state—even a dictatorial one—could defy Moscow. In October 1950 Truman demanded Congress send "emergency" food aid to "assist Yugoslavia to maintain its independence," and Congress complied with remarkably little debate. During congressional hearings held that November to determine whether to authorize an additional $38 million in U.S. food aid on top of an already approved $30 million package, Representative Jacob Javits of New York inquired whether the aid should be considered "economic warfare." Assistant Secretary of State George Perkins openly acknowledged that the goal was to attack "the Stalin breed of communism." Foreign policy makers would spend much of the rest of the decade finding ways to funnel American farm surpluses and taxpayer dollars to Yugoslavian officials. But as a January 1951 document signed by the Yugoslavian foreign minister Edvard Kardelj declared, the Yugoslavian government had no intention of remaining dependent on the United States. Belgrade would instead "take all appropriate economic measures . . . to encourage increased production and distribution of foodstuffs within Yugoslavia, and to lessen the danger of future conditions of food shortage similar to the present emergency."[9]

Yugoslavia's ability to produce food on its own terms was thus an essential component of Tito's resolve to remain independent of Soviet control. Where U.S. foreign policy makers saw Yugoslavia's near-famines in the early 1950s as a chance to wage economic warfare against the Soviet Union, Yugoslavian policy makers perceived a pressing need for agricultural self-sufficiency. After Tito fell out with Stalin, Yugoslavian leaders redoubled their efforts to build their own variant of state socialism in the early 1950s. Kardelj and his successors explored opportunities for trade with Western European nations and the United States. Domestically, Yugoslavian leaders instituted various economic reforms, including "workers' self-management," a decentralized form of industrial policy making that set the socialist state apart from Soviet-style centralized planning. Food remained a high priority in both domestic and foreign economic policy for Yugoslavia, even after relations with the Soviet Union improved when Khrushchev came to power. In 1956 Khrushchev visited Belgrade, offering to send shipments of grain to ease an ongoing bread shortage in Yugoslavia in exchange for closer ties between the two countries. Despite the reconciliation, however, Tito repeatedly rebuffed Khrushchev's pressure to hew closer to the Moscow line. Both American and Soviet officials sought Yugoslavia as an ally in the broader Farms Race, even as Titoists struggled to find an independent third way to food self-sufficiency.[10]

When Yugoslavian officials tasked the U.S. Department of Commerce with putting on a "particularly impressive show" with the theme "Farm to City Table" for the 1957 trade fair in Zagreb, then, the request was understood by all involved as one of utmost significance. In May 1957, U.S. trade exhibition planners drew up a rough draft of the Zagreb exhibit's script: "In view of Yugoslavia's predominately agricultural interests the accent will be on food production and distribution."

The exhibitors hired Professor A. B. Hamilton of the University of Maryland as an "agricultural consultant" for the project, seeking his "specialized knowledge of Yugoslavia's agricultural problems." As Branko Novaković of the Yugoslav Information Center explained at a July 1957 press conference, Yugoslavian leaders expected Supermarket USA to "show our [agricultural] cooperatives and enterprises the importance of packaging, presenting, preserving of foods," while John Logan touted the chance to demonstrate to Yugoslavian farmers how to "broaden their markets." With expectations running high, American scouts scoured Yugoslavian food markets for produce to stock the soon-to-open supermarket, only to discover that local fruits and vegetables were small, ugly, and entirely lacking in uniformity. The Penn Fruit Company, an American supermarket chain, stepped in with a solution: it would provide, via airlifts on KLM commercial flights every five days, apples from Oregon, tomatoes from New Jersey, lettuce from California. Shipping costs for the exhibit would ultimately tally more than $26,000, but the cornucopia of giant, uniform, aesthetically pleasing American produce provided an "impressive show" indeed (figure 9).[11]

The lesson was clear for many of the socialist citizens who visited Supermarket USA. "Here," noted a visitor impressed by the fruits of California's industrial farm fields, "one can see the strength of the American soil, the influence of men over nature." Another visitor admired an ear of "beautiful corn" as she calculated how much the enormous cob would cost at her local outdoor market. Marshal Tito visited the exhibit. Although he expressed appreciation for the "beautiful building" (designed by Walter Dorwin Teague Associates), he nonetheless seemed most impressed by the American farm equipment and descriptions of hybrid corn that visitors saw when they exited via the supermarket's rear doors (figure 10).[12]

*Figure 9 Large, uniform, and plentiful American fruits and vegetables, provided
courtesy of an airlift campaign orchestrated by the Penn Fruit supermarket chain,
were prominently displayed at Supermarket USA in Zagreb.* (Box 1, Folder 1,
Record Group 489-OF, National Archives and Records Administration II, College Park, Md.)

The possibility that American-style supermarkets could serve as
tools for agricultural transformation could not but appeal to Yugosla-
via's communist leadership. Farm politics had played an outsize role in
Yugoslavian politics for decades. Before the devastation of World War
II, Yugoslavia was one of the world's most important grain exporters.
During the war peasants were among the most crucial supporters of
Tito's communist Partisans in their ultimately successful resistance to
Nazi occupiers. Once in power, Tito's communists set about imposing

Figure 10 Visitors leaving Supermarket USA passed by images and artifacts that presented American industrial agriculture as the source of the abundance contained within the exhibition walls. (Box 1, Folder 1, Record Group 489-OF, National Archives and Records Administration II, College Park, Md.)

Soviet-style collectivized agriculture in the Yugoslavian countryside. By 1951, 17 percent of the country's peasant households had been forced or persuaded into state-run collective farms. Collectivization was immensely unpopular, however. Following the farm crises of the early 1950s and resulting American emergency food relief, the Yugoslavian government abandoned the most heavy-handed attempts at collectivization. Compulsory deliveries of produce to the state, for instance, were largely abolished as of 1952, and further retreats followed soon after. Peasants in the federated republic of Yugoslavia, for whom land was one of the only reliable forms of security in a world repeatedly tossed into upheaval by war, refused to cooperate with the government's plans to eradicate private ownership. Yugoslavian officials consequently spent much of the next decade seeking tools and policies for building socialist agriculture, premised on collective land ownership and centralized farm management, without using the brute force of Soviet-style collectivization. Supermarkets, with their centralized purchasing power and insistence upon industrialized agricultural supply chains, potentially offered exactly such a technological fix to the government's peasant problem.[13]

The official American position on the matter of private farm ownership could not have been more different. From an American perspective, the Eastern European peasants' stubborn attachment to private land seemed a crucial crack in the foundation of communist rule. As Stanley Andrews, director of the USDA's Office of Foreign Agricultural Relations, informed Congress in 1950, Yugoslavia's "little farmers . . . are a tough bunch of cookies," which for Andrews was a compliment of the highest order. American foreign policy makers in the 1950s and 1960s expected Eastern European peasants to resist state-directed agricultural modernization by holding on to their small-scale farms. In no small irony, at the same time U.S. agronomists such as Norman Borlaug were pursuing agricultural modernization projects—which, after 1968, would be referred to as the Green Revolution—in Latin America and Asia with the explicitly anticommunist goal of shattering small-scale farming in those regions. American modernization theorists and development agencies saw peasants in the Third World as threats, and peasant-based agriculture as a precursor to communism. In the "Second World" of communist Europe, by contrast, the peasantry seemed to be potential allies on the American side of the Farms Race.[14]

One consequence was that Radio Free Europe, one of the longest-lasting propaganda weapons in the U.S. Cold War arsenal, devoted significant resources through the 1950s and 1960s to undermining the tenets of socialized agriculture. A 1963 summary of Radio Free Europe's position on agricultural collectivization put it bluntly: "There is ample evidence that the peasantry is profoundly dissatisfied." Rural dissatisfaction offered Radio Free Europe staff an opportunity "(by carefully planned and timed [propaganda] campaigns) to hasten the erosion of collectivization." Reports from Radio Free Europe, the policy statement elaborated, should provide Eastern European citizens with detailed accounts of the unproductivity of collective farms and the injustice of a system that did not allow a farmer "to make his own decisions about such matters as whether the land he tills should be communal property or his own." A certain violence undergirded these propaganda campaigns; as one Radio Free Europe memorandum suggested, the "long-run objective" of such efforts was "total destruction of the soviet-collectivized system." With this goal in mind, Radio Free Europe staff carefully documented the persistence of small-scale agriculture in Yugoslavia in the 1950s and 1960s, recording and broadcasting in impressive detail just how recalcitrant that "tough bunch of cookies" was proving to the communists in power.[15]

From the perspective of Yugoslavia's leadership, something had to be done. Small-scale, labor-intensive peasant farming in fact dominated Yugoslavian agriculture in the years leading up to the Supermarket USA exhibit. Despite backing away from the most coercive attempts at collectivization in 1952 and 1953, the Yugoslavian government remained dedicated to socializing agriculture in the country. A major reform of early 1953 allowed farmers to voluntarily withdraw from collectives.

According to Edvard Kardelj, however, this move was not "an aban-
donment of the line of socialist transformation of agriculture" but instead a recognition that the state needed to pursue "different means
than heretofore" in order to socialize Yugoslavian agriculture. Between
1953 and 1957, the central government experimented with a variety of
techniques but generally saw little change in the countryside. Peasants
could legally own land, but only 25 acres maximum. At a time when
the average U.S. farm spread over 272 acres, the average Yugoslavian
plot comprised just 11 acres. Those tiny farms, however, accounted for
the overwhelming majority of the populace engaged in agriculture,
and also produced a majority of the country's meat, produce, and dairy
products in the 1950s. Peasant production was thus crucial to yet
politically problematic for Tito's regime. As he declared in November
1955, "There cannot be two production systems, socialist and capitalist," in a country attempting to "realize socialism in full." This was
publicly illustrated in spring 1956 in a purge of Communist Party
apparatchiks who had allowed private farmers to rent land and lease
tractors, apparently forgetting that "reorganization" of collectives did
not entail "renunciation" of the principles of socialist transformation of
the Yugoslavian countryside.[16]

In early 1957, the Yugoslavian government redoubled its efforts. In
April the National Assembly openly denounced collectivization as a
"negative influence" that had discouraged Yugoslavia's farmers from
producing food for the socialist cause. In place of collectivization, the
state would now pursue a policy of "socialist cooperation"—farmers
could continue to own small plots of land privately, but state-run collectives would be made "as attractive as possible to the private farmers." Private farmers could work cooperatively and voluntarily with the
state farms to gain access to technical advice, machinery, and seeds, but
they would also be expected to market the resulting produce through

the state system. The Assembly laid out its reasoning thus: small-scale peasant farms were "old-fashioned" and produced "low yields," whereas a socialist nation—especially one working to maintain its independence from the Kremlin—required "a fast development of agriculture," which in turn required "the application of modern technology and organization of work." This would not be American-style farm policy. The Assembly noted that government crop subsidies would be "a State-capitalistic way of development" that would ultimately "preserve the backward agricultural structure." Henceforth, Yugoslavia would strike its own path toward agricultural modernization. The heavy-handed methods of the Soviet Union were out. But so was the duplicitous approach of the United States, where policy makers lauded American family farmers and European peasants while subsidizing the industrial agriculture that uprooted both from their land. In the new Yugoslavian agricultural policy, by contrast, "gradual socialization of agricultural production" would be the abiding goal, but the state would present no "forcible danger to the individual ownership of property."[17]

Yugoslavia was in the midst of a remarkable experiment in agricultural policy making, then, when Supermarket USA opened. The strategy was in keeping with the idiosyncrasies of Titoist economic policy that the American scholar Dennison Rusinow once labeled "laissez-faire socialism." With "socialist cooperation," the regime sought to use market incentives to gain Western-style agricultural productivity from its farms. Simultaneously, however, the Communist Party kept a firm grip on the central levers of power in the farm economy. As the physician Stevo Julius remarked in a memoir of his life in 1950s Yugoslavia, Titoist market-based economic reforms allowed the Party "to congratulate itself" on its innovations while maintaining "a stranglehold on all aspects of life." In effect, the Communist Party was engaged in constant—albeit nonmilitary—conflict with the peasantry. Any policy tool, economic reform, or technological system that could benefit the nation's state farms at the expense of private producers without provoking a rural uprising was thus of paramount interest. Socialist supermarkets, in this vision, might provide a powerful weapon for pursuing a third way to industrialized agriculture, relying neither on the brute force of collectivization nor on the utter disregard for rural livelihoods that accompanied capitalist agricultural transformations.[18]

Perhaps this is why Milorad Jovanović, immediately upon the closing of the 1957 Zagreb trade fair, procured funds to buy up the entire Supermarket USA exhibit. Every refrigerator, stock shelf, shopping cart, magazine rack, and cash register now belonged to Jovanović's Belgrade-based state-owned enterprise Vračar. To help set up the socialist supermarket in Belgrade, Jovanović hired as a consultant J. Rollin Moon, a supermarket manager from Atlanta, Georgia. Writing to John A. Logan of the National Association of Food Chains on April 30, 1958, Jovanović expressed his satisfaction at having opened his nation's first permanent self-service supermarket. It was "very difficult to [i]ntroduce such a novaute [novelty] at our market," especially when the new supermarket at Belgrade's Cvetni trg (Flower Square) took the place of twenty-one butchers, twenty-three produce stalls, and an open-air *pijaca* (farmers' market). It was nothing short of a "revolution in our commerce," crowed Jovanović. He would soon learn the same lesson that IBEC's would-be supermarketers had learned a decade earlier in Venezuela: building one supermarket effectively required building several more if any efficiency was to be gained. So in 1959 Vračar built eight more supermarkets. Within a decade, Vračar operated twenty-five supermarkets, most in Belgrade, while other state-owned firms constructed similar stores in other regions of the country.[19]

Yugoslavia consequently joined the dozens of European countries that adopted American-style supermarkets in the 1950s and 1960s. The earliest adopters were not communist countries; the United Kingdom, Switzerland, and Sweden developed self-service supermarkets earlier and more pervasively. Italy introduced supermarkets beginning in 1957 under American guidance, when executives at Nelson Rockefeller's International Basic Economy Corporation selected Florence and Milan as the firm's first non–Latin American sites for extracting profits while undermining leftist politics. West Germany had thoroughly integrated self-service and branded packaged goods into its food retail system by the 1960s. And yet even in these capitalist European countries, American-style supermarkets did not inherently entail a "revolution in commerce." Differences in local customs, gender norms, regulatory structures, technological infrastructures, and business practices ensured that even in the most prosperous capitalist nations of Western Europe a supermarket was not necessarily a tool of "Americanization." This would have been obvious to the communist officials who actively promoted and constructed supermarkets in Hungary and East Germany in the 1960s. There, as in Yugoslavia, supermarkets were never intended to "revolutionize" consumer culture; they were expected to bring the machinery of centralized distribution to bear on a key problem in socialist economic planning: how to satisfy citizens' incessant demands for affordable, desirable food.[20]

The adoption of American-style supermarketing thus proceeded relatively quickly in Yugoslavia, Hungary, and East Germany in the 1960s. Yet supermarkets did not appear in the Soviet Union until the 1970s. In stark contrast to the positive Yugoslavian response to the American model of supermarket-driven industrial agriculture, Soviet leaders of the 1950s and 1960s remained deeply skeptical of the power of Western food distribution practices to achieve the desired revolution in socialist farm production. Nikita Khrushchev, who rose to power after Joseph Stalin's death in 1953, made a point of declaring Yugoslavian economic policies heretical to Marxist-Leninist ideology. As he put it to Marshal Tito in 1956 with an apt metaphor, "It is impossible to look at socialism as a commodity at a grocery store where one could come in and say 'give me a kilogram of Yugoslav socialism' and another person '[give] me [a kilogram] of Soviet.'" In 1959, *Pravda*—the Communist Party's official mouthpiece—denounced Yugoslavian farm policies for enriching landholding peasants (derogatorily referred to as kulaks) while undermining the long-term socialist cause. The timing of *Pravda*'s attack on Titoist farm policy was significant. In 1959, communist leaders in Moscow were participating in a wide-ranging discussion of a bold seven-year economic plan aimed at boosting Soviet consumer abundance, particularly the availability of highly desired foodstuffs. It was also the same year that Richard Nixon flew to Moscow to debate with Khrushchev the relative merits of capitalism and socialism in a canary-yellow kitchen at the American National Exhibition. Soviet leaders, much like Yugoslavian leaders, felt the immense burden of providing food to their urban citizens in order to legitimate the socialist strategy. Unlike the Yugoslavians' response to Supermarket USA, however, Soviet leaders in the Khrushchev years placed their Farms Race bets on the machinery of socialist industrial agriculture, not on the machinery of supermarket-style centralized food distribution.[21]

It is difficult to overstate the importance of farm and food policy in the Khrushchev era. It certainly figured with extraordinary prominence in Khrushchev's rhetoric. In his first major speech as leader of the Communist Party in September 1953, Khrushchev declared, "Communist society cannot be built without an abundance of grain, meat, milk, butter, vegetables, and other agricultural products." The early years of Khrushchev's reign were dominated by earnest efforts to produce plentiful food, even at the cost of ideological revisionism. As he informed an audience in Leningrad in April 1955, "The people put it to us this way: Will there be meat to eat, or not? Will there be milk, or not? Will there be decent pairs of pants? This isn't ideology, of course, but what good does it do if everyone is ideologically correct but goes around without trousers?" Khrushchev may have addressed the issue of unsatisfactory standards of living for Soviet consumers with his notorious humor, but the matter was of grave concern to the Soviet state in the 1950s. As the historian Susan Reid has demonstrated, Khrushchev prioritized efforts to deliver better and more affordable foodstuffs and other consumer goods to Soviet consumers, marking the pursuit of consumer satisfaction as a defining feature of his never-ending bid for political legitimacy and respect. As the portly leader once declared, "It is not bad if in improving the theory of Marxism one throws in also a piece of bacon and a piece of butter."[22]

Never at a loss for words, Khrushchev made the matter of Soviet farm productivity a topic of constant high-level policy discourse. In 1956, Khrushchev startlingly declared to a group of Western diplomats: "We will bury you!" Although Americans would for years remember the line as a threat of nuclear Armageddon, Khrushchev had meant only to summarize his take on the Marxist-Leninist conviction that socialism was destined to outlast capitalism. Among the features of Soviet socialism most likely to demonstrate the inferiority of capitalism in the long run, Khrushchev was convinced, was a collective approach to agricultural production that prioritized the needs of workers and consumers over those of profit-seeking corporations and absentee landowners. Within a year of the "bury you" pronouncement, Khrushchev began repeating a much more concrete threat, one that would characterize his rhetoric leading up to the Kitchen Debate. Within just "a few years," Khrushchev announced, the Soviet Union would surpass the United States in meat and milk production. This threat was not veiled. As Khrushchev elaborated in May 1957, the Soviet Union's inevitable overtaking of the United States in farm production would be the equivalent of hitting "the pillars of capitalism with the most powerful torpedo yet seen."[23]

One reason for Khrushchev's bellicose rhetoric on farm productivity was that Americans so consistently touted the superiority of capitalist food systems in the 1950s. Eisenhower-era propaganda campaigns seized on the disparity between American and Soviet food costs as a key strategy for trying to convince communist citizens of the illegitimacy of socialist economics. A U.S. Information Agency propaganda brochure from 1953, for instance, noted that Moscow workers had to work twice as long for a pound of bread as did New York City workers, while Soviet beef required five times the purchasing power of American beef, and milk six times. Lauren Soth, in a 1955 Pulitzer Prize–winning editorial in the *Des Moines Register*, suggested that if it was "more meat" Khrushchev wanted, he should send a delegation to Iowa ("the heart of the greatest feed-livestock area of the world") to see how capitalist farmers got the job done. Even when acknowledging that Soviet farms could produce a remarkable quantity of food, American anticommunists called into question the diversity of Soviet diets, suggesting that lack of choice in the food marketplace was a frightening symptom of the lack of political freedom under communist rule. The U.S. Chamber of Commerce president Arch Booth, for instance, once informed a group of American businessmen that while Khrushchev might have been able to produce "more goulash," communist enterprises were not capable of "better goulash—not frozen, or dehydrated, or irradiated goulash—not '57 varieties' or '20 delicious flavors.' Just 'more goulash.'" Americans apparently thought, or liked to think, that Soviets ate nothing but borscht in between stints of waiting in line at state-run food shops.[24]

A wish to counter such perceptions undoubtedly contributed to the combativeness of Khrushchev's Farms Race rhetoric, but so did his desire to stake out his nation's leadership role as an economic—not just military—superpower. In the May 1957 speech in which he announced his plan to overtake the United States in meat and milk production, Khrushchev made clear to the assembled farm workers that their harvests were of global significance: "Today the United States is impressing the entire Western world with the account of its [agricultural] production." With "colonial countries . . . agog," Khrushchev intoned, it was incumbent upon Soviet farm workers to prove to the entire world that socialist agriculture was the only model worth imitating. Two years before that speech, a Soviet delegation had toured several South Asian countries, primarily with the aim of frightening the Eisenhower administration into thinking the Soviets were capable of launching a major development campaign there. For both superpowers the possibility that development projects, including agricultural "modernization" campaigns, could win the allegiance of emerging leaders in the postcolonial Third World became a structuring feature of foreign policy in the 1960s. Symbolism mattered for Khrushchev on the world stage, but so did numbers. The Soviet leader knew that racking up impressive production statistics, whether in agriculture or industry, served to bolster Soviet influence among less-developed countries looking for models for economic growth. And when American observers believed the Soviet statistics, as they often did in the mid-to-late 1950s, the fear produced was priceless. In an important sense, statistical measures—including the per-capita consumption of milk and meat products—were crucial weapons in the Soviet Cold War arsenal.[25]

One problem with Khrushchev's rhetorical contributions to the Farms Race, however, was that quantitative measures could not entirely account for either the successes or failures of socialist agriculture. Even as Khrushchev repeatedly declared his intent to out-farm the United States, the reality was that postwar Soviet agricultural reformers always sought to do much more than simply produce more food. A desire for power animated agricultural reformers in Moscow who hoped, as the historian Jenny Leigh Smith has argued, to "get a better handle on the vast and poorly governed Soviet countryside." Yet those same power-hungry communists also expected that boosted farm productivity would "relieve millions of rural workers from the tedium of manual labor, and create a model, sustainable system of socialist agriculture." From a Soviet perspective, the 1950s Farms Race was as much about how best to create political legitimacy out of available natural and human resources as it was about out-producing the United States.[26]

Khrushchev was in fact entranced by American agricultural productivity, particularly the vast cornfields of Iowa. Four years before the Kitchen Debate, the Soviet leadership received an unexpected invitation from the Iowa seed dealer and corn-hog farmer Roswell Garst to visit his spread near Coon Rapids and "find out how the Iowa corn belt worked." The Soviets responded with enthusiasm, sending a delegation of agricultural experts in 1955 to Garst's farm to learn about chemical herbicides, hybrid seeds, and the entire panoply of science and technology that made Iowa's fields so productive. The Soviets were impressed enough to invite Garst in turn to visit the Soviet Union, where he toasted his hosts with the phrase "peace through corn" and promised that if they purchased his hybrid seeds they would see a 30 percent boost in yields and plants more easily harvested by machine. He managed to sell the Soviets $3 million worth of American corn seed and farm machinery.[27]

Two factors drove the Soviets' attraction to Iowan corn. First, Soviet agriculture minister Vladimir Matskevich was convinced that Iowa's agricultural productivity was due not to a capitalist approach to farming per se, but rather to the scale of the enterprise—and of course agricultural projects of industrial scale had long appealed to Marxist farm theorists. Second, and perhaps more important, the Iowa model held up by Roswell Garst concerned corn-hog farming. All those acres of corn were not being grown in Iowa for direct human consumption, but for feeding livestock. For Soviet leaders bent upon providing more meat and milk to their citizens, any method of boosting livestock production was attractive. Especially after 1955, the Soviet Union's food abundance was to be built on corn. This marked a departure from the effort begun in 1954 to plow up the steppes of the "Virgin Lands" of the Kazakh Republic for wheat cultivation (wheat being intended primarily for human consumption). Vice chair of the Council of Ministers P. P. Lobanov informed a group of farmers in the northwestern Soviet Union in 1955 that "corn can be cultivated everywhere," even in northern climes that had proven unsuitable for wheat. Khrushchev followed up on Lobanov's report by rattling off statistics meant to convince cooperative and state farm managers that growing corn would lead to much fatter pigs per unit of land. Just as important Khrushchev suggested that growing corn—even in northern latitudes—would "produce the greatest quantity [of grain] per man-day worked." Overall quantity of agricultural production mattered tremendously in the international Farms Race, but on the Soviet domestic front what mattered even more was how efficiently state-run and collective farms could deliver the products that urban consumers desired most—meat and milk.[28]

Corn seemed key to these goals, so much so that Khrushchev gained the nickname *kukuruznik* (corn fanatic) for his public obsession with the crop. Where to plant this communist corn? Khrushchev was convinced that maize would adapt particularly well to Soviet lands that were then producing oats and rye as well as perennial grasses for grazing sheep. The fact that the Soviet climate and soils were not remotely comparable to Iowa's did not deter Khrushchev from embarking on a vigorous personal campaign to promote corn as the "queen of the fields," nor was he fazed by the relative paucity of chemical fertilizer available to Soviet farmers, who would now be required to plant the extremely nitrogen-hungry crop. In the long run, the encroachment of corn on fields previously planted to less nitrogen-dependent crops led to devastated soils and disastrously low yields. But in the short run, from 1954 to 1958, favorable weather conditions helped boost Soviet grain production to impressive heights, with increases of as much as 50 percent in yields (even when measured by outside observers). Not only was Iowa-style corn adopted without the environmental conditions that made it so productive in the American Midwest, its cultivation was pursued in strictly socialist fashion. Despite some agricultural reforms under Khrushchev that provided farmers with incentives to boost production, the Soviet model of agriculture in the late 1950s remained fully dependent on collective and state-run farms, in contrast to the "decollectivization" being pursued at the time in Yugoslavia, Hungary, and Poland.[29]

By 1957 Khrushchev thus felt confident that the communist, collectivized adaptation of the American corn-livestock complex was a success. This was the context for his public pronouncements that year that by the turn of the decade the Soviet Union would surpass the United States in per-capita production of meat and milk. A few days after his provocation, Khrushchev informed the CBS reporter Daniel Schorr in a televised interview that he liked "the very idea of our country now being able to compete with the United States, which is a very rich country indeed." Insisting that his plans for agricultural dominance were entirely compatible with his vision for "peaceful co-existence," Khrushchev nonetheless rephrased his "we will bury you" statement from the previous year. "Your grandsons," he informed Schorr, "will live under socialism in America, too. I can foretell this." Soviet cornfields were producing bumper crops, and the overall Soviet economy was expanding at a record-breaking clip. Khrushchev had reason to be confident, even bombastic, in challenging the United States to an economic competition he earnestly intended to win.[30]

Khrushchev's calls for peaceful coexistence served multiple pur-poses. For one, he knew the high costs of the Soviet Union's participa-tion in the nuclear arms race. When Khrushchev told Schorr on CBS television, "Let us live in peace, let us develop our economy, let us compete," he was imploring U.S. leaders to allow him to redirect lim-ited Soviet resources to build up his nation's agriculture and industry rather than its weapons stockpile. Soviet citizens expected better food and better housing. While Khrushchev had no intention of ending the arms race he nonetheless hoped a reduction in nuclear tensions with the United States could help his domestic agenda for economic growth. On another level, the call for peaceful coexistence emerged from a desire to shift international attention away from the taint of the brutal Soviet repression of the Hungarian popular uprising of October–November 1956. As was often the case with Khrushchev's proposals, the plan for peaceful existence was simultaneously genuine and disingenuous.[31]

With so much on the line, the gears of communist bureaucracy quickly went into motion to provide evidence of the Soviets' agricul-tural might. Managers at state and collective farms systematically in-flated their production figures to please their political superiors. Some farm managers, for instance, bought meat and dairy products in state-run cooperative stores then redelivered them to other state procurement stations, so the same pound of meat or butter might be counted as many as five or six times as a fresh delivery by state accountants. Soviet food buyers, meanwhile, continued to wait in long lines at cooperative stores for meager offerings unless they chose to pay black-market prices at peasant markets. Although Khrushchev would later acknowledge the perversity of the "distorting mirror" of Soviet farm statistics—noting in a 1970 memoir that "the stores and our people's stomachs give better testimony than the statistical agency about the real state of affairs [in Soviet agriculture]"—as of the late 1950s he remained convinced of the potential of communist agriculture to meet the demands of Soviet consumers for more meat and dairy products.[32]

The Soviets' entry into the Farms Race was thus at full stride when the United States Information Agency began plans to erect the American National Exhibition in Sokolniki Park. The exhibit figures often in historical accounts of Eisenhower-era propaganda campaigns. Rarely have historians paid much attention, however, to the actual food that was on display in the American kitchens there. Yet the competition between the United States and the Soviet Union in agricultural production was paramount in the minds of both the Soviet leadership and the American planners of the exhibit. In the early planning stages, U.S. organizers had considered developing a show more like the 1957 Zagreb display, focused on farm and food abundance rather than on housing. Harold "Chad" McClellan, a California paint manufacturing titan and former assistant secretary of commerce, was appointed by President Eisenhower to head the project. McClellan began a White House press conference in January 1959 devoted to the exhibition by worrying aloud that a nearby Soviet agriculture–dominated pavilion—the Exhibition of Achievements of the National Economy

(VDNKh)—would be "tough competition." McClellan mused that it might be worthwhile to display farm equipment used by American family farmers—"things [Soviet farmers] don't know about, that the average guy will be tickled to have, like trailers, farm machinery for a small unit farm"—to counter the Soviet displays of gigantic machinery permanently on exhibit at VDNKh.[33]

More pointedly, Daniel Schorr of CBS asked McClellan why the plans did not include a supermarket, "which was so successful in Zagreb." The architect and industrial designer George Nelson, the mastermind behind the pavilion layout, maintained that there was no room, although it seems likely that Nelson had aesthetic objections to a warehouse-like building dominating the pavilion, which was to be anchored by a futuristic geodesic dome. Yet Schorr pushed the point further, declaring that "the one great crying need in Russia is for better [consumer] service. Their distribution system plods along. People are irritated by not being able to buy things that are theoretically available without queuing up." As Schorr implied, a supermarket display would impress upon visitors that the Farms Race could not be won by the Soviets. In a fully stocked supermarket, socialist citizens would see that America not only out-produced the Soviet Union agriculturally; it also made its abundance available to ordinary consumers through its retail distribution system. A supermarket, Schorr seemed to suggest, would expose the distance between the inflated statistics of Soviet agricultural production and the ground truth faced by consumers anxious to buy the meat and milk repeatedly promised by the Khrushchev regime.[34]

Schorr's critique might have been even sharper had he been aware of the "secret" objectives of the American mission in Sokolniki Park. Publicly, U.S. Information Agency officials maintained that the exhibit was benign in intent, meant to "increase understanding by the peoples of the Soviet Union of the American people, the land in which they live, and the broad scope of American life." Secretly, according to an internal memo from January 1959, the pavilion's planners intended the exhibit to fundamentally undermine Soviet citizens' faith in the socialist system and their communist leadership by overwhelming visitors with the *"freedom of choice and expression,* and the unimpeded flow of diverse goods and ideas [which] are the sources of American cultural and economic achievements." Supermarkets, with their self-service shopping, low prices, and cornucopias of meats, produce, and packaged goods, might have fit this bill particularly well, especially given the consensus within the U.S. Information Agency that the 1957 Zagreb supermarket had been a smash propaganda hit. Furthermore, the National Association of Food Chains, which had orchestrated the Zagreb exhibit, protested volubly to the Eisenhower administration about being left out of the planning for the Moscow event. And in January 1959, Soviet Deputy Premier Anastas I. Mikoyan had visited a Giant Food supermarket in White Oak, Maryland, where he bought $9.29 worth of food and ruefully acknowledged, "We don't have stores like this in Russia."[35]

Ultimately, though, the U.S. propaganda team chose to focus on "typical" American housing at Sokolniki Park. The expectation was that a display of a split-level ranch house with a modern kitchen would deeply impress apartment-dwelling Soviets still smarting from a postwar housing shortage and the admitted failures of Stalinist attempts to communalize kitchens. Near the model house, the pavilion would also include a demonstration of a small apartment-style kitchen and a futuristic "Miracle Kitchen" designed by General Electric/Whirlpool. Reading over the early plans for the exhibit, Llewellyn E. Thompson of the American Embassy in Moscow chided organizers for not including a supermarket in the design, fearing that the housing approach would be seen as too blatantly propagandistic and would not in fact "make the Soviet people dissatisfied with the share of the Russian pie which they now receive." Other Americans familiar with Russian culture and privy to the plans for the exhibit voiced similar concerns, and repeatedly urged the U.S. Information Agency to consider airlifting in American meats and fruits, and particularly items available out of season, as in U.S. supermarkets. Exhibitors ignored this advice. Instead, the demonstration kitchens at the exhibit were stocked primarily with frozen foods—shipped to Moscow free of charge by the General Foods Corporation, marketer of Birds Eye frozen foods—including 416 pounds of frozen asparagus and 148 pounds of "fish bites."[36]

"There is keen interest in convenience foods in communist lands," insisted General Foods executives. Propagandists at the U.S. Information Agency were particularly open to suggestions from the world's largest producer of frozen foods. The corporation was contributing food and money to the exhibit, along with a professional home economist who would demonstrate how Americans prepared their convenience foods. Furthermore, the corporation's longtime chairman and president, Clarence Francis, had served in the Eisenhower administration since leaving General Foods in 1954. Yet State Department officials and others who had lived in the Soviet Union knew that Soviet citizens had little hope of owning a home freezer and were primarily interested in having reliable access to affordable staples, not convenience foods.[37]

After its opening in July, the American Exhibition immediately secured its place within America's popular consciousness as an undeniable display of the inevitable triumph of capitalism over communism. Vice President Nixon's aggressive sparring with Khrushchev, staged before rolling color television cameras, undoubtedly made the event resonate on the American side of the Atlantic. In the estimation of many observers, Nixon's performance secured his previously uncertain place on the Republican presidential ticket in the 1960 election.[38]

From a Soviet perspective things looked quite different. The event was certainly popular, drawing close to three million visitors. Yet for a populace long accustomed to propagandistic claims of economic prowess, it was all too easy to call the Americans' bluff. *Pravda* ran numerous articles dismissing the claim that typical American workers could afford to own a well-appointed ranch-style home. Khrushchev declared the model home flimsy and likely to be in need of razing within twenty years. Such claims might have surprised Soviet citizens living in newly constructed single-family apartments derided for their shabbiness as *khrushchoby*—a derisive portmanteau of "Khrushchev" and the Russian word for "slums." But for all his bluster, Khrushchev could legitimately puncture American expectations that Soviets would be "amazed" or "dumbfounded" by opulent displays of "mere gadgets." Although it was certainly not true that ordinary Soviets had "all these things in our new apartments," as Khrushchev insisted, it was nonetheless the case that since the 1930s the Soviet state had taken pains to cultivate and satisfy consumer desires as a crucial aspect of building real socialism. For Soviet economic planners, mass consumption was intended to serve a social purpose and bolster the legitimacy of the Communist Party, not cultivate selfishness or crass materialism, or—as the Americans so clearly desired—to equate economic choice with political freedom.[39]

Khrushchev's critique of the gender norms on display in the model kitchens offers an important example. Nixon claimed that the household technologies in the exhibit—automatic dishwashers, push-button stoves, a robotic floor cleaner—were intended to "make easier the life of our housewives." Khrushchev countered that such a view smacked of "a capitalist attitude toward women." In the years following the Kitchen Debate, Soviet functionaries would in fact make a concerted effort to trumpet the superiority of the rationally designed communist kitchen as a tool allowing women to work for wages outside the home, rather than simply making their homebound lives "easier." Men's expectations that women would do the double duty of building socialism for pay outside the home while also continuing to shoulder most unpaid household duties never dissipated in communist Europe. In contrast to the Americans' gender assumptions, however, socialist state planners consistently sought technological fixes for easing women's burdens as a way of shoring up the legitimacy of one-party rule among a crucial segment of the populace.[40]

Soviet citizens were, furthermore, well equipped to dismiss shiny consumer goods as fetishistic commodities. "What is this," demanded a young patriot in the pages of *Izvestia,* "the national exhibition of an immense country or the branch of a department store?" Comments collected by the U.S. Information Agency suggest that this attitude was relatively widespread among visitors, although the prevalence of remarkably similar phrases suggests that many visitors were formally coached in their dissatisfaction. One anonymous reviewer chided "you Americans" for attempting to "surprise us with the glitter of your kitchen pans" rather than "show something grandiose, something similar to Soviet sputniks." One official response to the exhibition indicates that state functionaries, at least, believed grandiose agricultural displays were more in tune with the mood of the Soviet people: when it was learned that the United States would be exhibiting a "Circorama" panoramic film produced by the designers Charles and Ray Eames, Soviet crews rushed to build their own, larger panorama, which projected "great fields of grain being reaped by tractors" with "wheat growing as far as the eye could see." Even the head of the U.S. Information Agency, George V. Allen, later remembered these images as "quite a spectacular sight."[41]

If the model home and gleaming kitchens were less effective propaganda weapons than the U.S. Information Agency had hoped, would a fully stocked American supermarket have better served the "secret" intentions of the exhibition? We can only speculate, as the American National Exhibition included only a tiny demonstration of supermarketing methods—a "Food-O-Mat" self-service food counter, sponsored by the Grand Union food chain (figure 11). The Soviet novelist Arkady Perventsev, writing in the widely circulated newspaper *Trud* a month after Nixon's arrival in Moscow, noted that it would be "worth our while to learn from the Americans how to organize self-service markets." Perventsev lambasted the Food-O-Mat display, however, as a boring exercise in pedantry, built with little regard for the central importance of efficient food distribution for a socialist society. Soviet citizens wanted more grain, meat, milk, and fruit, Perventsev acknowledged, and it was going to take "new forms of realization, storage and delivery" to satisfy that demand. But where American propagandists had intended to embarrass communist leaders with American riches, Perventsev had seen only "tin cans with the bright labels." As Perventsev certainly knew, Soviet planners since the late 1940s had been forging their own noncapitalist approaches to mass food distribution, seeking ways to be less reliant on the omnipresent refrigeration and petroleum-fueled transportation networks that undergirded the American food system. Fast-food carts and ice-cream pushcarts, for instance, had brought small luxuries to the Soviet masses by the 1950s, and even understocked state-run stores reliably carried the shelf-stable tinned pork product *tushonka*. Operating an American-style supermarket would require regularized, just-in-time deliveries of massive quantities of perishable goods—a very tall order in a nation all too familiar with periodic famines and systematic food shortages.[42]

Figure 11 Grand Union's small "Food-O-Mat" display at the 1959 American National Exhibition ("self-service food store" reads the Russian sign), underwhelming in comparison to Supermarket USA. (Box 1, Folder 1, Record Group 306-HVM, National Archives and Records Administration II, College Park, Md.)

The American National Exhibition was, in short, no Supermarket USA. Yugoslavian officials had embraced Supermarket USA—indeed, literally purchased it wholesale—as a tool for transforming the path of socialist food from farm to table. Soviet officials in the Khrushchev era instead pinned their hopes on the productive promise of collectivized agriculture, particularly the new cornfields sprouting throughout the Soviet Union at Khrushchev's urging. Yet the aftermath of both Supermarket USA and the American National Exhibition suggests one important shared experience between Tito's Yugoslavia and Khrushchev's Soviet Union. In both cases American propagandists attempted to torpedo the pillars of communism with symbols of capitalist plenty, yet when the Americans headed home, the onus remained on communist officials to provision citizens with socialist abundance. Farms and foodstuffs continued to figure prominently in both countries' efforts.

A month and a half after the Kitchen Debate, Nikita Khrushchev traveled to the United States. On September 21, he toured a San Francisco supermarket, where he expressed delight over a package of plastic-wrapped apples. Later that evening he spoke to a reception of local city and business leaders, and declared his "admiration" of the supermarket. "It was, I believe, excellently organized," Khrushchev noted, and it made him "just a little bit envious." Nonetheless, the always-combative Khrushchev tweaked his audience, announcing that "we will certainly produce as much as you are producing now." The next day the Soviet premier traveled to Iowa, where he enjoyed his first taste of an American hot dog and effused over the state's "highly mechanized" agriculture and "fine achievements in livestock breeding." Yet even amid Iowa's towering corn, Khrushchev declared Soviet agriculture to be inherently superior. Capitalist farming was premised on ruthless competition that drove small farmers off the land, whereas Soviet *kolkhozy* and *sovkhozy* (collective farms and state farms) provided work for all who were fit. "We challenge you to a competition," Khrushchev proclaimed, "in the output of meat, milk, butter. . . . This is far more beneficial competition than competition in stockpiling hydrogen bombs. . . . May there be more corn and meat, and no hydrogen bombs at all!"[43]

In the last days of his U.S. visit, Khrushchev doubled down on the Farms Race rhetoric. He complimented a herd of dairy cattle at a USDA research center in Beltsville, Maryland, as "very good cows" but then declared that "in the course of three years the average milk yield per cow in our country has risen by 600 liters." And on a nationally broadcast televised speech just before his departure, Khrushchev once again announced that the Soviets would best the United States in per-capita farm production within a few short years. Returning to Moscow, Khrushchev reveled in adulatory speeches on his overseas performance. One Communist Party official told a Moscow gathering that Khrushchev had convinced American capitalists that "the Soviet Union is no longer that ragged Russia where the only fare of the poverty-ridden *muzhik* [peasant] was thin cabbage soup." Increased milk and meat production, the speaker went on, was the "most striking proof . . . that the Soviet system is bringing the working people greater benefits than the capitalist system. (Applause.)"[44]

There were two essential problems with Khrushchev's constant repetition of promises of agricultural plenty. First, if the Farms Race were solely about quantity of production, the odds were clearly rigged against the Soviets. A group of Iowa farmers touring the Russian countryside in late 1959, for instance, took one look at Khrushchev's highly vaunted cornfields and instantly dismissed them as "30 years behind" the United States. Or, as Richard Nixon put it in a 1960 campaign speech before a group of South Dakota farmers, "If it is a food torpedo that is to be fired, it is going to be shot by American farmers and ranchers at the foundations of communism." In both relative and aggregate terms, there was little question that the United States was well ahead of the Soviets in quantifiable measures of farm productivity. The central challenge for American farmers and policy makers in the 1950s and 1960s was overproduction, not shortages, a problem that Soviet economic planners no doubt wished they could have as their own.[45]

The second problem for Khrushchev was that by promising plentiful food so often, with equal measures of self-assurance and self-congratulation, he had set himself up for a fall. In attempting to satisfy consumers' desires for abundance through state-dictated agricultural reforms, Khrushchev would find his economic policies discredited by the Soviet people in the mid-1960s. The year after the Kitchen Debate and his visit to the United States, Khrushchev learned that his country was experiencing the worst farm yields since Stalin's death. Meat and dairy products, the centerpiece of his campaigns to boost living standards through agricultural productivity, were in dire shortage. Although the state embarked on a crash campaign to boost yields, the harvest of 1961 was bitterly disappointing, and meat production fell to levels below those seen in 1959. Discontentment spread widely, as citizens began directly questioning the ability of Khrushchev's regime to deliver on the repeated promises of meat and milk. In December, workers in Siberia hung posters declaring Khrushchev a "blabbermouth" and pointedly demanding "that abundance you promised." The following June, Moscow central planners made a desperate attempt to spur agricultural production by raising retail food prices by up to 35 percent. Widespread protests resulted. "Meat! Meat! Raise our pay," chanted workers as they stormed out of factories. Red Army troops were sent to suppress spontaneous demonstrations, including a particularly violent episode in Novocherkassk in the Rostov Oblast, where workers wrote slogans such as "Use Khrushchev for sausage meat!" on factory walls. Machine guns shut down the Novocherkassk protests, leaving twenty-two dead and many more wounded.[46]

By October 1964, Khrushchev had been utterly discredited. Rivals inside the Kremlin fostered a perception that he was inept at foreign policy, the loser of the Cuban Missile Crisis who had also worsened relations with communist China. Perhaps most embarrassing, however, Soviet officials were compelled to take the humiliating step of purchasing grain from the United States in late 1963, all but acknowledging America's victory in the Farms Race. Khrushchev was unceremoniously removed from office by his archrival Leonid Brezhnev and sent to live out the rest of his days as a pensioned non-person in his countryside dacha. Food shortages were by no means the sole reason for Khrushchev's downfall, but they certainly mattered tremendously for a man who had staked so much of his political career on corn-fed communism. *All corn—no bread* was, according to memoirist and food writer Anya von Bremzen, "everyone's curse for *Kukuruznik.* . . . Russians could forgive many things, but the absence of wheat bread made them feel humiliated and angry."[47]

When not tending the corn planted in his kitchen garden, Khrushchev spent much of his time until his death in 1971 composing essays accusing his former subordinates of failing to deliver the food that consumer socialism required. "We have not achieved the abundance we desire," Khrushchev wrote, as he witnessed persistent grain, meat, egg, and dairy shortages. "Our leaders today are 'shining like stars' with all sorts of impressive [agricultural statistics], but meanwhile the shelves in our stores are empty." Clever consumers avoided government food stores, knowing that black-market sellers charged twice the government-controlled price for goods but at least had food to sell. For Khrushchev, consumers' reliance on illegal capitalist food retailers brought "great shame on our collective-farm system," but it did not suggest a need to privatize the farm or food economy à la Tito's Yugoslavia. More careful management of the collective farm system at the regional level, perhaps even deployment of robots in farm fields, would be appropriate socialist paths to farm productivity. What was certainly not needed to provision the Soviet kitchen, according to Khrushchev, was an American-style distribution network anchored by supermarkets. Instead, perhaps a Bulgarian-style peddler system, in which farmers delivered their produce directly to town squares via wagon, would best meet the needs of Soviet consumers. "They say," wrote the aging and widely ignored pensioner in May 1970, "distribution is done that way in France."[48]

Four years after Khrushchev's ouster, the Soviet Committee on Science and Technology contracted with an Italian firm to construct more than a dozen Western-style supermarkets in major Russian cities. Appropriately, the Italian firm made its sales pitch by promoting the greater efficiency in agricultural procurement allowed by the supermarket's mass buying infrastructure, rather than touting the supermarket's potential for profit. By the mid-1970s, a not-inconsequential number of Soviet citizens were introduced to their first opportunities to shop in American-style supermarkets, such as one built in Leningrad that turned three hundred thousand dollars of sales volume weekly.[49]

In contrast to Khrushchev, Marshal Tito remained largely unchallenged at the helm of the Yugoslavian federated republic until his death in 1980. And while food abundance eluded Soviet planners in the 1960s, Yugoslavian officials had reason to be optimistic. The state's supermarket industry took off in the early 1960s. An American packaging executive who traveled to Yugoslavia in 1964 reported that self-service supermarkets were "tremendously popular," suggesting that American businessmen might find a ready market for food packaging materials. Indeed, processed packaged foods became commonplace in Yugoslavia in the years following the Supermarket USA exhibit. The tonnage of canned meats produced in Yugoslavia increased 220 percent between 1957 and 1960, while items previously unknown in the communist country—ready-to-serve frozen meals, dehydrated soup mixes—began appearing on supermarket shelves.[50]

Yugoslavia's socialist supermarkets were far from revolutionizing, however. Unlike American supermarkets, the Yugoslavian stores did not exercise large-scale centralized buying power. Only state-run cooperative enterprises and farms could market foods through the supermarkets in the early 1960s. Because much of the country's meat, milk, and produce originated on small peasant farms, the cooperatives would often purchase small lots from those farmers at state-suppressed prices, then resell them at extremely high margins to supermarket buying agents. An American supermarket executive who witnessed the Vračar supermarket chain in action in the 1960s was impressed by the interior layouts of the stores but "horrified by their organization, storage, and transport system." Without a central warehouse or procurement system, the chain had to rely on buying agents—individuals who, without communicating with each other or centralized management, generally purchased foodstuffs in small lots, in cash, in chaotic wholesale markets. U.S. retailers had discovered by the 1950s how to gain extraordinary leverage on capital by buying in large lots on credit, but as of the mid-1960s Yugoslavian food retailers had not developed similar tools for controlling their supply chains.[51]

Beginning in 1965, the Yugoslavian legislature instituted a series of reforms intended to allow limited privatization of retailing and wholesaling. In December 1966, Marshal Tito explained in a state television address that it was time to "organize our commercial network in such a way as to suit best our socialist society." Privatization was intended to allow "producers of agricultural products" to make reliable long-term contracts with wholesalers and retailers, thus taming some of the chaos in the food procurement marketplace that had put "our cooperatives and agricultural farms . . . in a very difficult position." One result of the 1965–66 market reforms was that for the first time, private farmers were allowed to sell their produce directly to supermarkets. In March 1966, Tito toured the countryside and asked a group of private farmers what they were most concerned about. When one farmer suggested access to loans would be beneficial, Tito cut in: "I know what you are mostly concerned about. You are not always certain whether what you sow or produce will be purchased." One peasant "energetically" answered that yes, "this is the basic problem." Tito then announced that to "settle this problem," the state would embark on a campaign to build the infrastructure needed for a supermarket-driven supply chain. Cold-storage warehouses seemed particularly necessary, because at the time Yugoslavian beef producers were largely dependent on neighboring Italy's cold-storage infrastructure.[52]

Touring the countryside again in 1967, Tito informed a group of farmers that he was still "not satisfied with our commercial network." Farmers and private food marketers were, according to Tito, skimming high profits off of low-volume sales. "Incomes," the president declared, "should be earned by a bigger turnover in goods, by bigger sales," but unlike American supermarketers, Yugoslavian retailers and wholesalers were content to sell "smaller quantities of goods but with a high profit margin and increased prices." The official communist paper *Borba* likewise editorialized in 1968 that "the logic of a modernly-organized market is persistently knocking at the gates of our economic policy." The writer Rade Vujović saw some hope in a plan of the Association of Agricultural Estates to build supermarket-style stores in major cities; Vujović imagined that when "such big stores start operating, it will be hard for the small trade which still keeps to usurious logic to 'remain afloat.'"[53]

The number of supermarkets in Yugoslavia doubled within eight years of the legislative reforms of 1965–66. Yet the transformative effects on agricultural practices long desired by communist officials largely failed to materialize. Socially owned farms did increase their production, in some cases moving into markets long dominated by peasant producers. For example, in the late 1950s and early 1960s, socially owned farms uprooted old fruit trees, planting in their stead "high quality varieties" in an attempt to muscle in on peasant fruit growers and brandy processors. The majority of fruit orchards, however, remained in private hands—scattered on private peasants' house lots. Most Yugoslavian fruit—especially the ubiquitous plum—was either consumed locally, dried for storage, or distilled into brandy on-site. Production of most of the fruit, vegetables, beef, and milk consumed by Yugoslavians remained in the hands of small private producers, who marketed these essential foods primarily on a local level. "This is our shame," explained a communist official in 1962 to a group of agricultural experts who had expected socialist farms to displace private farms from the economy.[54]

From the perspective of some U.S. policy makers, the private farmers of Yugoslavia seemed a soft target in the 1960s. Secretary of Agriculture Orville Freeman toured Yugoslavia in 1963 as part of a monthlong junket through Eastern Europe. Upon his return Freeman suggested that improved harvests in the region were an important step toward world peace, but went on to remind the world that the United States was winning the Farms Race. "I have returned with a number of strong convictions," noted Freeman, "none more firmly reinforced than the demonstrated superiority of the family farm system of agriculture based on private ownership of the land." Congressman Edward Derwinski (R-IL) proposed in 1964 that PL 480 ("Food for Peace") funds be converted into direct loans to peasants in Yugoslavia and Poland. "A basic weakness in all communist countries," explained Derwinski, "is the independence of the farmer and his stubbornness to bow to the collectivization of farms." If the peasants received U.S. loans, "we would be supporting free enterprise," but if communist leaders rejected the offer, "the world would then see that communist governments do not have the interest of their own citizens at heart." Such a calculus offers insight into why Titoists preferred to build cold-storage warehouses and allow privatization of retailing rather than extend credit to private farmers. The needs and desires of urban consumers remained among Tito's top priorities in the 1960s, but so did the Communist Party's long-standing attempt to reduce the peasants' political and economic clout. As it turned out, Derwinski's suggestions were not adopted; the United States continued to sell agricultural surpluses to Yugoslavia via the provisions of PL 480 in 1964—essentially keeping Tito's regime afloat—rather than subsidizing Yugoslavian private farmers directly.[55]

Through the 1960s and 1970s, Yugoslavian agriculturists continued to rack up impressive production figures, particularly in comparison to Soviet Bloc states. Using American grain purchased under PL 480, Yugoslavian socialist cooperatives developed a grain-fed cattle industry that by the 1970s was shipping beef throughout Western and Eastern Europe. Yet still as of the mid-1970s private farms continued to account for most of the country's food production: 98 percent of the country's plums, 71 percent of apples, 82 percent of milk, and 80 percent of meat consumed in Yugoslavia. Private farmers owned most of the country's tractors. Some peasants earned reputations as "dinar millionaires," including a number of plum growers with lucrative brandy distilleries. According to a 1966 *New York Times Magazine* piece, the successes of private farmers gave weight to a favored witticism: "What is the shortest joke in Yugoslavia? . . . Socialism."[56]

Dissatisfaction with the country's communist leadership deepened when food shortages in the late 1970s and early 1980s exposed the uncertainty of Yugoslavian food supplies. The onset of a full-blown economic crisis in 1982, accompanied by spiraling inflation and sporadic bread riots throughout the 1980s, contributed to a slow unraveling of the socialist state. Farmers abandoned socialist farms, often turning to subsistence agriculture as farm prices plummeted. Historians continue to debate the proximate causes of the Yugoslavian federation's collapse into genocidal warfare in the early 1990s, although most agree that structural economic troubles—not just ethnic-nationalist tensions unleashed by the death of Tito—contributed to its citizens' disavowal of the socialist regime.[57]

Reflecting on "the banality of everyday life" in communist Eastern Europe, the Croatian novelist Slavenka Drakulić proclaimed in 1991 that communism "failed because of distrust, because of a fear for the future." Consumers in her native Yugoslavia, in the Soviet Union, in the Soviet Bloc states, simply could not maintain faith "in a system that was continuously unable to provide for its citizens' basic needs." Yet, Drakulić's firsthand account of everyday life under late communism struck a more complex note that may have been difficult for triumphalist American observers to understand at a time when communist governments were toppling throughout Eastern Europe. "If communism didn't fail on bread or milk," Drakulić elaborated, "it certainly failed on strawberries." In other words, state socialism not only could, but did, provide for citizens' basic needs. By raising consumers' expectations of what the state could and should provide, however, Communist Party leaders made food—its price, its availability, its symbolic weight—into a potentially destabilizing force for their regimes. Drakulić recounted a trip in the 1980s to a Manhattan supermarket, where she "just stared" at mounds of strawberries. What made her slack-jawed was not their abundance, however, nor the fact that it was midwinter. "This sight was not a miracle," Drakulić remembered; "we somehow expected it." What was stunning for Drakulić was that shoppers in the store could afford to buy the strawberries.[58]

The aftermath of Supermarket USA and the Kitchen Debate might suggest that the United States "won" the Farms Race. In both cases, the United States declared its brand of consumer capitalism, grounded in "free enterprise" and individual choice, superior to communists' attempts to feed their citizens with socialized agriculture and state-run food stores. Yet the divergent Yugoslavian and Soviet experiments with socialist food provisioning from the 1950s through the 1960s suggest an alternative interpretation. From the Eastern European viewpoint, the Farms Race was not a competition between capitalism and socialism to be measured solely in terms of quantity of food produced. Instead, the matter of how best to provide abundant food to socialist citizens was always inherently and explicitly intertwined with crucial questions of sovereignty and political legitimacy. In the United States, supermarket promoters successfully touted the "supermarket revolution" as a product of "free enterprise" even as they depended on massive state support for their industrial agricultural supply chains. In communist Europe, no such sleight-of-hand was possible. Yet, even in the avowedly capitalist United States, the relationship between farmers, consumers, the state, and supermarkets could not be summed up as free enterprise working invisible economic miracles. The Cold War Farms Race infiltrated American domestic food politics, too, if not always so explicitly as it did in communist Europe.[59]

5

Food Chains and Free Enterprise

"I think it is significant," announced Erwin D. Canham in a speech in Kansas City just weeks after Nikita Khrushchev's 1959 visit to the United States, "that Mr. Khrushchev spent some of his precious time in America looking at Iowa corn and hog farms." As president of the U.S. Chamber of Commerce, Canham interpreted Khrushchev's visit to Iowa in the accustomed terms of the Farms Race, as a demonstration of capitalism's superiority to socialism. The Soviet leader had been awed, Canham sensed, by the "magnificent abundance" of American industrial agriculture "because the Soviet Union has a tough farm problem on its worksheet." Yet as Canham and his Kansas City audience knew, the United States faced its own seemingly intractable farm problem. While Soviet farms did not produce enough food to meet the citizens' demands, American farms apparently were producing too much. Farm prices were falling and family-owned farms were disappearing. In Canham's eyes, the Soviet and American farm problems had the same root cause: both nations relied too heavily on state intervention in the agricultural marketplace. American farm policies since the New Deal had attempted to "limit the abundance" of industrial agriculture, but for Canham it was time for government to roll back its New Deal–era farm supports and force the American farmer to "go along with the changes which are inevitable in our type of economic order." It was not government policies, but "agribusiness men" who were responsible for Iowa's agricultural productivity, declared Canham. The rise of agribusiness was for Canham inevitable, and only "free enterprise" and efficient marketing of abundant foodstuffs could solve America's farm problem.[1]

Canham's confidence that America's farm surplus problem could be so easily resolved by "free enterprise" suggested a shallow understanding of just how hotly contested the nature of the farm and food marketplace remained in the United States in the 1950s and 1960s. In the rhetoric of the Farms Race, America's highly productive privately owned farms, along with the extraordinary abundance on U.S. supermarket shelves, were concrete indicators of the West's inevitable victory in the economic contest of the Cold War. Yet the realities of life in rural America, as family after family fled the countryside after World War II, indicated that the model was far from perfect. The rise of agribusiness entailed a dramatic concentration of economic power in the U.S. farm economy, giving some farmers the sense that the *free* in "free enterprise" did not apply to them. Furthermore, although the agribusiness bargain exchanged farmer autonomy for efficient distribution of foods to consumers, there were nonetheless those who questioned just how "sovereign" the consumers on the end of these industrial supply chains were. Rhetorically the battle lines of the Farms Race were starkly drawn, but on the ground in the United States, the nature of the assumed victory might have seemed Pyrrhic to critics of the agribusiness food chain.

The American family farm became a symbolic flashpoint in the Farms Race of the 1950s and 1960s. The Minnesota senator Hubert Humphrey was a particularly vocal proponent of the family farm as both a symbolic and a material response to the perceived threat of communism. In January 1957 Humphrey introduced a resolution on

National Family Farm, Food, and Fiber Policy, declaring that legislative protection of the American family farm would not only ensure American consumer abundance but would also be "an important step toward strengthening democracy throughout the world . . . and an effective roadblock to the inroads of communism." Family farmers—independent, landowning, productive, free—were enlisted as foot soldiers in the broader economic battle of the Cold War. The Texas congressman William R. Poage in 1960 suggested that Congress adopt a policy to "promote, foster, and perpetuate the family system of agriculture against all forms of collectivization whatsoever." According to Poage, "independent family farms" were the "beginning and foundation of free enterprise in America." Their demise might entail the collapse of capitalism itself. Later that year John F. Kennedy campaigned for president in key electorally contested states in the Midwest by calling for a revision of American farm policy under the umbrella term "Food for Peace," directly uniting domestic farm policy with anticommunist foreign policy in militarized terms: "We will not accept the peace of foreign domination."[2]

One reason Democratic politicians sounded a militaristic call for protection of the American family farm in the late 1950s was that it seemed to be disappearing, and rapidly at that. Fifteen years after the end of World War II, the proportion of the U.S. population living on farms had dropped by half. The farmers who stayed on the land dramatically increased the size and technological sophistication of their operations. One consequence was an astounding increase in U.S. agricultural productivity. The annual growth rate of agricultural productivity had held steady at around 1 percent from 1880 to 1940, but it tripled in the decade after 1940 and remained extraordinarily high for the rest of the twentieth century. More grain, more milk, more meat, more eggs, more fruit and vegetables—the incredible output of

American farmers made food remarkably affordable for consumers. The price of abundance, however, was fewer and fewer people living on farms.[3]

Statistics do not effectively capture the social and emotional consequences of the rapid postwar industrialization of U.S. agriculture. Increased reliance on technology allowed for more efficient production, but it also meant that farmers no longer needed to rely as much on "changing works"—that is, swapping field and housework duties with neighbors to accomplish labor-intensive tasks such as harvesting, shucking, preparing meals for work crews, and so on—which in turn meant that the farmers who remained on the land after World War II were increasingly isolated. As one farmer summed it up, the decline of changing works made farming into a job involving "a lot of hours alone on the tractor." The sense of loss, the feeling of being compelled by market forces to give up land held in the family for generations, was no doubt extraordinarily difficult for the 3.4 million farmers and their families who exited American agriculture between 1940 and 1969. The loss must have been especially painful for the nearly six hundred thousand African Americans who lost their farms in the period; ownership of land had been among the most essential markers of economic independence—a source of both tremendous pride and intergenerational resilience—in the decades after the abolition of slavery.[4]

In the context of the Farms Race, the deracination of the American countryside posed a real quandary. How could the American family farm be an effective symbol of U.S. economic superiority if it was disappearing? Democrats and Republicans tended to have opposing answers to this question. Democrats in the wake of the New Deal pushed for continuation of price supports and production controls that would keep farm families on the land at taxpayer expense. Republicans called for either gradual or dramatic removal of these supports to promote the freedom to farm (in the phrase of two-term Secretary of Agriculture Ezra Taft Benson). Yet for all the apparent disagreement, one thing was beyond question on either side of the political aisle: food for urban consumers had to be as cheap as possible. The primary question was how to coordinate the farm and food marketplace to maintain stability in the countryside without driving up the price consumers paid for their food.

Liberals could imagine a variety of ways in which government policies could confront this quandary in the 1940s and 1950s. Some found inspiration in Western Europe, where social democratic policy makers in countries including Sweden, Denmark, and Great Britain experimented with a variety of policy instruments for maintaining farm incomes while taming urban consumers' food costs. Consumer price controls, rationing, and heavy subsidies were all, at least in theory, also on the policy table in the United States. Even in Western European countries with strong social democratic parties, however, such compromises between rural and urban constituents were never easy to maintain. In 1949, Secretary of Agriculture Charles F. Brannan introduced a plan that, had it been implemented, might have brought 1950s American farm and food policy more in line with the Scandinavian approach. The Brannan Plan envisioned heavy government intervention into both the farm end and the consumer end of the food economy. Farm prices—particularly for those high-value products in highest demand at the time, such as meat and dairy products—would be artificially raised to a level deemed necessary to preserve the family farm. Consumer food prices would be kept in check, thought Brannan, through a mixture of subsidies and government-sponsored sales of surplus products. Though strongly supported by the liberal National Farmers Union, the Brannan Plan was strenuously opposed by the larger American Farm Bureau Federation and soundly defeated by congressional conservatives. The Brannan Plan's demise is often interpreted as a sign of the growing power of conservativism in post–World War II American politics, but it should also be understood as an indication of the extraordinary difficulty of developing appropriate policies for effectively and fairly coordinating food supply and demand in an industrial economy.[5]

Beginning in 1955, conservatives had a one-word answer to the quandary: *agribusiness.* In October of that year, the Harvard Business School professor John H. Davis coined the term to describe vertically integrated organizations that coordinated the production and marketing of food and fiber. Rather than leave coordination of the farm marketplace to either government policy makers or market forces, Davis suggested, such power should be delegated to corporations. Having served a stint as assistant secretary of agriculture in the Eisenhower administration before landing at Harvard, Davis explicitly intended his neologism as an intervention in contemporary farm policy debates. As Davis explained in a speech to a group of marketing specialists and policy makers, a complete rollback of government farm price supports would be counterproductive. Low prices would discourage farmers from investing in new technologies for increased production. Short-term savings for taxpayers would thus be passed on to consumers in the form of increased costs for food over the long term. Furthermore, Davis explained, the inherent risks of agricultural production—seasonality of production, fickleness of markets, uncertainty of weather—meant that farmers needed a mechanism for stabilizing prices lest the entire countryside collapse into economic chaos. For Davis the free enterprise solution to this problem was agribusiness: "If we are to reduce the role of government on the farm front, we will have to do so by transferring to agribusiness that responsibility for basic price stability which is now borne by government."[6]

The supermarket was one of Davis's favorite examples of an efficient agribusiness. Speaking to an organization of grocers, Davis extolled American supermarkets in patriotic terms: "In no other country that I know of is there anything that equals the modern American food store in its efficiency of operation, size and variety of stock carried, and volume of business done each day." But Davis intended to do more than stroke the egos of the assembled retail grocers; he sought to impress upon them the crucial role they could play in uprooting federal government intervention in the farm and food marketplace. "If you believe in free enterprise," Davis implored the food retailers, "then the farm problem is your concern too." The business methods of mass distribution could obviate the need for government intervention in the farm economy, making free enterprise a reality in the countryside.[7]

But exactly how "free" individual farmers would be in an economy dominated by agribusinesses was never entirely clear in Davis's formulation, or in the more elaborate versions he developed with the economist Ray A. Goldberg at Harvard Business School. Indeed, an interviewer for a farm magazine enlisted the rhetoric of the Farms Race to put Davis on the spot in November 1957. Replacing government support for farm prices with agribusiness coordination held an obvious appeal, admitted the interviewer. But would the turn to agribusiness make the American farmer "a mere cog in the machine as now exists in Russia?" The coordinated machinery of free enterprise, as the journalist rightly noted, might enmesh landowning farmers—the independent citizens lauded and beatified by every American politician since Thomas Jefferson—in consolidated webs of power disturbingly similar to those experienced on Soviet state farms. The farm price supports advocated by Democratic politicians and policy makers since the New Deal might be a cost to taxpayers, but they provided a positive freedom for millions of individual landowning farmers who might not otherwise be able to take part in the nation's food marketplace. Replacing the coordinating mechanism of government oversight with the marketing machinery of vertically integrated agribusiness corporations might indeed stabilize farm incomes but at the potential cost of introducing a new, subtly powerful authority in the American countryside. As John F. Kennedy put it in his 1960 campaign speech in Des Moines, a farmer "without meaningful bargaining power in the marketplace" would gain nothing if farm prices collapsed, while agribusinesses would always "stand to profit."[8]

The long-term results of the "Chicken of Tomorrow" contest offer perhaps the best example of how the coordinating mechanisms of agribusiness transformed the nature of "free enterprise" in the American countryside. As explained in Chapter 1, A&P's sponsorship of the "Chicken of Tomorrow" contest in the mid-1940s initiated a dramatic transformation of the nation's poultry economy. With their enormous buying power, chain supermarkets, including A&P, called into being a tightly coordinated industrial supply chain devoted to providing American consumers with cheap chicken. Among the most important links in that supply chain in the 1950s were so-called integrators: firms that coordinated every stage of transforming chickens from embryos into plastic-packaged supermarket commodities. The power of these integrators to dictate terms of production to farmer-growers, effectively controlling their livelihoods via elaborately constructed contract and credit arrangements, had raised serious questions about the eclipse of free enterprise in chicken country by the 1950s.[9]

A special subcommittee of the House Small Business Committee held a series of hearings in 1957 to probe precisely this question. Chaired by the Missouri Democratic representative Charles H. Brown, the congressional subcommittee aimed to uncover the causes of a sudden collapse in broiler prices in the previous year that was forcing bankruptcy on farmer-growers in Georgia, Delmarva Peninsula, and northern Arkansas. In the process of investigating the situation, the subcommittee heard testimony from chicken growers, integrators, and USDA personnel. The testimony of three individuals in particular illustrates the variety of ways in which the structures of agribusiness entailed something other than economic freedom.

Nelson Lewis, an independent chicken farmer in Delmarva, provided one viewpoint. Lewis informed the subcommittee that he had been raising chickens since the 1930s, but in the face of recent transformations in the industry he was selling off all his chicken houses. According to Lewis, the core of the problem was that "Government money commenced setting up a man from the cradle to the grave. . . . I mean, give him a hatchery, give him the chicken business, give him a dressing plant, give him chickens for to lay the eggs—the whole setup." Lewis believed that the "free enterprise" environment which drew him to chickens in the 1930s had been replaced by a world in which "doctors, lawyers, shoe salesmen" were getting free government money to drive hard-working country folk like himself out of business. When pressed to provide examples of where this alleged "Government money" was coming from, Lewis demurred, but he nonetheless insisted that the agricultural welfare state was somehow to blame for rampant overproduction (and thus low prices) of broilers. The little guy, it seemed to Lewis, couldn't compete in a rigged market.[10]

A rather different take came from Hermon Miller, director of the poultry division of the USDA's Agricultural Marketing Service. Like Lewis, Miller was concerned that free enterprise was not working as it should in the modern broiler industry. But Miller insisted that the real problem was not anything government had or had not done, but was a product of integrator firms—feed dealers, especially—who were disobeying the law of supply and demand. In Miller's reading, the root of the problem lay in the terms of the contracts binding farmers in the system. Feed dealers offered credit on easy terms to farmers, enabling them to purchase the houses, hatchlings, and feed needed to produce market-ready broilers. In return, farmers signed contracts ensuring that the feed dealers would not only buy all those chickens at a set price but would exercise significant managerial control over how the chickens were raised. Numerous representatives noted that this situation seemed like a "sharecropper" arrangement. But for Miller, the problem with this system was not the stricture placed on the independence of the farmer-grower but the inverse: farmers were sheltered from any market risk by these presigned contracts, and so had no incentive to respond to cues from the marketplace. When chickens were in oversupply, farmer-growers had no reason to cut back on their production. The contracting system resulted in highly efficient production, Miller noted, but it also distorted the workings of the market.[11]

A third view came from an acknowledged master of poultry integration, Jesse Jewell of Gainesville, Georgia. Since the 1930s Jewell had been at the forefront of transforming broiler production using the credit-driven contracting system to set up local farmers as poultry growers. Jewell thus developed a system for selling cheap chicken to retailers while simultaneously creating a market for his chicken feed, not to mention servicing the debt of north Georgia farmers desperate to get out of cotton. Jewell insisted to the assembled representatives in 1957 that his success was a result of "free enterprise," and so was the success of the chicken growers in north Georgia, who, for the first time in their lives, could afford automobiles and send their kids to decent schools. Like the others testifying, however, Jewell occasionally acknowledged that things were not what they used to be. In a series of surprising comments, Jewell insisted that chicken growers under contract not only were not "share-croppers"; they were in fact "freer than I am." Growers were "free as the birds of the air themselves right now because they can grow or not grow." But his integrating business? "I can't get out." Indeed, Jewell went on to claim that his firm was taking the brunt of the blow when it came to low chicken prices, and it did so in part to ensure that con-tracted farmer-growers wouldn't simply fly their coops (as the indepen-dent grower Nelson Lewis was doing in Delmarva).[12]

But if Jewell was really taking the hit (as he claimed) or, as Hermon Miller suggested, was sheltering contract growers from the forces of supply and demand, why did he allow farmers to keep producing too many chickens? Perhaps Jewell felt a sense of moral obligation to the previously dirt-poor farmers in north Georgia. But his repeated insistence that what his congressional grillers called sharecropping was a form of modern contract-based agribusiness suggests that he was not motivated by a sense of paternalism. An offhand comment Jewell offered in his testimony suggests the real reason for everyone's sense that free enterprise was not a reality in the chicken market. Toward the end of his testimony, Jewell noted that in any given week, the A&P supermarket chain might order "250 truckloads" of chickens. If Connecticut or Delmarva integrators were charging a cent more per bird than Georgia integrators, A&P would place the order in Georgia. If Georgia's price was higher than in Arkansas, the order would go to Arkansas. No matter where the chain store's order was placed, all other markets would quickly fall in line with their prices. Jewell didn't call it such, but what he was witnessing was monopsony power in action.[13]

In the case of the 1957 complaints of chicken growers, the unspoken and unrecognized problem of centralized supermarket buy-ing power was the root cause of the universal sense that agribusiness curtailed freedoms in the poultry marketplace. Independent growers like Nelson Lewis were being driven out of business not by government loans to lawyers and bankers but by the chain stores' unrelenting search for cheap chickens. Jesse Jewell and other integrators were indeed squeezed: on the one side by their need to keep providing all those cheap chickens in huge volumes to supermarket purchasing agents, and on the other by their inability to exercise similar concentrated buying power over growers outside their specific regions. Neither growers nor integrators were operating according to the law of supply and demand; they were operating according to the law of demand alone, and that law was being written by chain-store supermarkets.

The consequences were profound. The chicken industry followed the advice of the House Small Business Committee's final report, which suggested that integrators consolidate their operations to gain economic power. Jewell, in fact, foresaw the future when he testified. When asked how he intended to weather the economic storm created by collapsing chicken prices, Jewell declared that the only solution was to get even bigger, so that "we will not be affected by these ups and downs of the markets." Jewell did exactly that in the 1960s, as did his competitors—especially the feed firm Ralston-Purina and, increasingly in the 1970s and beyond, processing firms such as Perdue Farms and Tyson Foods, with their innovations in further-processed chicken (such as frozen breaded chicken patties). All these firms sought to develop concentrated, nationwide buying power of their own, putting them on more even footing with their chain-store buyers in the marketplace. "Get big or get out" was the mantra among chicken integrators in the postwar period. (The phrase "get big or get out," remembered as a pithy summary of American farm policy in the postwar period, is often attributed to Richard Nixon's secretary of agriculture Earl Butz; tellingly, Butz served on the board of directors of Ralston-Purina before and after he worked in the Nixon adminis-tration.)[14]

Another consequence was that the Nelson Lewises of the industry—the independent growers who sold their chickens to the highest bidder rather than participate in contract production—were swept out of the poultry business entirely in the 1960s. For growers who continued to contract (or sharecrop?) with poultry integrators, the incessant demand for more and cheaper chickens required investment in ever-larger poultry houses, which entailed spiraling cycles of debt. Particularly in the upcountry of north Georgia, home to a deeply cher-ished tradition of populist agitation, such a marked transition from a sense of independence to powerless dependence was a deep blow.[15]

More broadly, the agribusiness approach to poultry established the key structures of modern contract farming, and in doing so re-framed what "freedom to farm" meant in the United States. The cover of a 1958 USDA report on contract farming offers a graphical entry point (figure 12). We see Corporate Man in a suit, sitting at a desk with his back turned to us. From Corporate Man's desk radiate dotted lines, each extending to a link in a supply chain. The five linked ele-ments are superimposed with representations of key components of the modern poultry supply chain: a feed mill, a sack of chicken feed, a farmer gazing blankly at a tightly caged chicken, hanging dressed chicken carcasses, and finally a supermarket. Corporate Man, sitting at an oddly empty desk, is not himself attached to the chain, yet the pulses of his power (symbolized by the dotted lines) seem both re-sponsible for the chain's existence and yet instantly detachable, as if on a whim he could shut the whole thing down. The farmer seems lost in thought, perhaps mulling the fine print in the contract he has signed with an integrator firm; perhaps he senses he has as little say

Figure 12 A 1958 USDA publication visually presents the contract production of poultry as a chain, with the farmer beholden to an all-seeing suited figure at a desk.
(U.S. Department of Agriculture, *Contract Farming and Vertical Integration in Agriculture*, Agriculture Information Bulletin no. 198 [Washington, D.C.: USDA, 1958].)

about his ultimate fate as the caged chicken. The textual recommendations in the report itself present a similarly dark picture, suggesting that the only way for American farmers to maintain a semblance of autonomy in the contract-driven agribusiness model is to join a cooperative, bringing strength in numbers to bear on a market tilted in favor of the biggest players. Family farming, paradoxically, required collective action to survive the agribusiness era.[16]

Where and for whom did Corporate Man work? Most likely in a procurement office for a national supermarket chain such as A&P. His ability to call up 250 truckloads of dressed chickens at any given moment and at a place of his choosing would have been the source of Corporate Man's power. But supermarket chain-store buyers procured much more than chicken, and as their systems of mass purchasing grew in scale and scope in the 1950s the systematic impacts on the farm and food marketplace became ever more apparent. Among those most concerned were the owners of independent retail grocery stores and small regional chains. Many of these retailers belonged to the National Association of Retail Grocers, which in 1959 published a pamphlet declaring that a "cold war" was "going on in the consumer market" as national supermarket chains swallowed up their competitors. "Those who win this contest at the retail level," warned the retailers in an effort to paint the issue as a matter of national economic security, "will have enormous advantages in extending their power backward over food manufacturing, processing and farm production as well." Whether or not the scramble to create mass buying power through mergers and acquisitions qualified as a cold war, the pace of consolidation was indeed hectic through the 1950s. As one business analyst put it in 1961, all food chains shared a "dilemma—acquire or expire." Between 1949 and 1958, 83 supermarket companies acquired 315 other companies. Medium-size chains (as measured by sales volumes) were the most acquisitive, seeking not only to remove the competition of smaller firms from the market but also to build a retail network of sufficient size to warrant a large-scale wholesale buying operation that could compete with the largest national supermarket chains in the procurement realm. Such chains could exercise significant market power as both buyers and sellers at a regional level, even if their share of grocery store sales was minuscule at the national level.[17]

Cooperative buying groups and voluntary associations had enabled regional chains to exercise the same sort of concentrated buying power as the largest national supermarket chains by the end of the 1950s. The largest included Topco Associates (created in 1948), Cooperative Food Distributors of America (1936), and the Independent Grocers Alliance (IGA; 1926). By joining such a group, medium-size supermarket chains could gain the benefits of large-scale purchasing power without having to acquire retail competitors. Donald P. Lloyd of Cooperative Food Distributors of America explained to a congressional committee in 1959 that his group represented twenty-seven thousand retailers, providing them with ninety-six wholesale warehouses for procuring foodstuffs. Unlike a traditional wholesaler, however, the Cooperative ran its operations not for profit but "to get the benefit of mass purchasing power for our individual retailer members." Independent retailers effectively contracted out supply-chain management to such buying groups or voluntary associations, driving independent grocery wholesalers out of business in the process. Such consolidation of buying power—whether achieved through internal expansion, mergers and acquisitions, or buying groups or voluntary associations—meant that by the end of the 1950s American supermarkets taken as a collective unit had secured a dominant position in determining how food products would be produced, which ones would be produced, and where and when they would be bought and sold.[18]

Willard F. Mueller, an agricultural economist at the University of Wisconsin, Madison, spent much of his time in the 1950s and 1960s analyzing the increasing power of supermarket chains to dictate the terms of food production. In a 1958 article in the *Journal of Farm Economics*, Mueller examined the role of supermarkets in shaping the processed fruit and vegetable trade and found that contract production had transformed the industry. Where once supermarket buyers might have used price alone to determine the quality of produce that would end up on store shelves, by the late 1950s large-scale buyers had developed complex specifications that could be met only through contractual arrangements. Price by itself no longer conveyed all relevant information to buyers or sellers of processed fruits or vegetables. Mueller and his co-author, Norman Collins, further argued that John H. Davis's claims for the farm-price stabilizing impact that contractual arrangements could have were "extravagant." Farmers who produced for supermarkets might or might not gain from contractual arrangements as opposed to open marketing of their produce, but Mueller and Collins argued that there was "nothing inherent to vertical integration that guarantees such stability."[19]

Angus McDonald of the National Farmers Union was among those who would have agreed with Mueller's assessment. Supermarkets, as McDonald saw it, were among the key institutions contributing to the rapid dissolution of the family farm. Testifying before the Senate Judiciary Committee in 1957, McDonald drew attention to the findings of the Department of Justice's 1946 investigation of A&P, particularly the operations of its produce-buying subsidiary, Atlantic Commission Company (ACCO). "ACCO used its tremendous buying power," declared McDonald, "to depress and control prices of farm commodities." A&P's control of produce buying through ACCO "indirectly wiped out thousands of farmers," forcing them to sell at prices lower than their businesses could bear. According to McDonald, similar practices had only multiplied after A&P divested itself of ACCO in 1954 under federal antitrust pressure. Supermarket chains such as Safeway continued to pursue strategies for using consolidated buying power to bring farm prices down, particularly in the beef cattle industry. The American farmer who remained in business in the era of supermarkets, McDonald concluded, was becoming an "economic slave" to "giant monopolies."[20]

Not all farmers would have accepted McDonald's strident language. Yet American farmers in the late 1950s could clearly see that the rise of supermarkets entailed dramatic changes in the way food products were produced and sold. A 1960 USDA investigation into fresh fruit and vegetable procurement by chain stores noted the outsized importance of fresh produce for the marketing strategies of retail firms. Having a clearly defined customer base was crucial to any supermarket's competitive position in its local market, and the type of fresh produce a chain carried was essential for defining that customer base. Chains seeking a broad base of buyers would "try to offer the lowest general price level," while those cultivating higher-income buyers relied on the visual appeal of brightly colored, aesthetically uniform produce. An important consequence of this system was that field buyers for chain stores were driven by a need to know well ahead of time that they would have the desired quality of produce available at specified times, allowing the retail managers to plan effective merchandising strategies. Consequently, different chain-store buyers were not really competing against each other in an open market for, say, apples; each chain's buyer was seeking a particular range of apples produced according to a narrow range of specifications determined by the chain store's merchandising strategy. A buyer for a single chain store could thus have an exceptionally broad impact on hundreds or even thousands of produce growers. As another report for the *Journal of Marketing* noted in 1958, farmers were no longer "growing for an 'open' market which will take whatever product happens to be offered but rather for a market where the buyer has considerable discretion over the terms of purchase." Ralph A. Nemanick, a lettuce grower from Watkinsville, California, put the matter more bluntly to a panel of congressional investigators in 1959: "In the Salinas-Watsonville lettuce empire, where once 50 buyers vied for choice lots and brands and paid commensurate prices, less than a dozen of those buyers now call the tune." As a result, "obnoxious, often brutal policies now prevail" and "the producer has little alternative but submitting" to the demands of a handful of chain-store buyers.[21]

Alternatives were limited for farmers in part because no effective policy response seemed available. Even if broad political support had existed in Congress for strengthening the Robinson-Patman Act, enforcement of its anti-oligopsony provisions would have required costly efforts from a powerful Federal Trade Commission to uncover specific cases of illegal behavior on the part of chain-store buyers. Both the broader public and antitrust bureaucrats preferred to focus on the more easily comprehended issue of monopoly power. Still, enough farmers seemed upset by the apparent limits to free enterprise being imposed by chain stores in the farm and food marketplace that in 1964 President Lyndon Johnson seized an opportunity. With consumer food prices mounting steadily even as farm prices continued to slide, Johnson responded positively to a recommendation from his secretary of agriculture, Orville Freeman. In March 1964 Freeman outlined for the president the economic challenges facing America's farmers, noting that despite their world-beating productivity, many U.S. farmers were struggling to stay in business. Supermarkets seemed a significant part of the problem: "The food retailer, once the tail end of the food marketing chain, is rapidly becoming the dominant influence in the food industry." Johnson, aware that cultivating populist fervor among rural white voters could only help his election chances in a year when he was prioritizing the passage of civil rights legislation, called on Congress in March to establish a commission to investigate the nation's food system.[22]

What emerged was the National Commission on Food Marketing, which spent two years gathering evidence and hearing testimony.

Senator George McGovern of South Dakota announced that he was "convinced that chainstore buying practices, contract feeding and vertical integration have been used to depress farm prices." Agribusiness, in other words, was systematically destroying the family farm, a viewpoint shared by the Wyoming rancher Courtenay Davis when he suggested that "food chains" had "repealed the laws of supply and demand in the marketing of beef." Farmers offered example after example of how the buying practices of large chain stores constrained their freedoms in the marketplace. In its final report on the topic of food retailing, the Commission agreed with many of the farmers' criticisms, noting that national chain stores appeared to be using their power in procurement to make up for lackluster performance in retailing in comparison to more agile and innovative independent retailers. Angus McDonald of the National Farmers Union, upon reading the 1966 report, was surprised to find his viewpoint largely supported by the findings of the Commission, which "repeatedly emphasized . . . that farmers, even when organized into cooperatives, suffer from a lack in bargaining power."[23]

But two years of investigation and thousands upon thousands of pages of reports produced essentially no legislative response. Orville Freeman ruefully acknowledged that, despite unearthing a stunning range of anticompetitive business practices, the Commission had nonetheless sent its final reports to Congress with the overall message that "the food marketing system is generally competitive and sound." Yet even if no significant new legislation emerged, the Federal Trade Commission was emboldened to pursue a more aggressive stance against supermarket mergers and acquisitions in the mid-to-late 1960s. In direct response to the National Food Marketing Commission's recommendations, the FTC declared in early 1967 that it would seek to prevent any further consolidation in the retail food business. Yet such actions were predicated not upon a desire to support the viability of family farms but on the wish to preserve the viability of small food stores—in no small part because the policy tools of antimonopoly were significantly more robust than those pertaining to oligopsony. This point was driven home by the Supreme Court's 1966 decision in *Von's Grocery*, which enabled the FTC to prevent mergers in food retailing without proving that such mergers substantially reduced competition. In other words, the FTC could pursue antitrust action justified only by a general claim that helping small retailers stay in business was inherently desirable. Thus, even the invigorated antitrust action that emerged in the wake of the National Commission on Food Marketing had little to do with the Commission's most damning claims about supermarket oligopsony power.[24]

When the U.S. Chamber of Commerce president Erwin Canham insisted in 1959 that American farmers had to "go along with the changes which are inevitable in our type of economic order," he had in mind the agribusiness approach exemplified by poultry integrators and chain supermarkets. Implicit in such a statement was a declaration that consumer abundance, not farmers' economic autonomy, was the core metric of how "free" a free enterprise system was. This moving of the rhetorical goalposts of the Cold War Farms Race was necessary if agribusiness were to serve as the basis for outcompeting the Soviet Union in food production. Like John H. Davis, Canham believed that agribusinesses did a better job coordinating the farm and food marketplace than did either governments or individual farmers. Agribusinesses internalized the functions of open markets within the boundaries of vertically integrated corporations. In thus contravening the "free market," agribusinesses provided a mechanism for maintaining economic stability in the countryside while keeping food affordable for consumers. Yet the agribusiness approach entailed a relative lack of concern for the livelihoods of small farmers unable to succumb to the demands of a strictly regimented market, a market defined in large part by the desires and wants of consumers as channeled through the supermarket.

Even if supermarket capitalism did not deliver "freedom to farm," it surely was expected to deliver both choice and abundance to American consumers. Hence the sting of Richard Nixon's jab at Nikita Khrushchev during the 1959 Kitchen Debate: "To us, diversity, the right to choose . . . is the most important thing." The ultimate winner of the Farms Race, in such a formulation, would be determined by the array of foods available for consumer citizens, not by the degree of autonomy afforded to those who produced the food. In this realm, supermarkets clearly delivered, as depicted on the January 3, 1955, cover of *Life* magazine, a special issue devoted to food and "mass luxury." Enormous hams, package upon package of vegetables and fruits and mixes and sauces—all were shown crammed tightly into a shopping cart, leaving just enough room to fit a child. Pushing the cart—and, implicitly, propelling the entire "mass luxury" economy represented by its contents—was a female consumer. Readers could see only her hands and forearms on the magazine's cover, yet disembodiment made her hands seem all the more powerful, the physical agents through which consumer choice manifested itself in specific purchases. Supermarket shopping was apparently so easy that the woman could push the loaded cart, complete with child, with just one hand, her winter gloves and coat still on because the trip through the aisles was effortless and speedy. Yet as the text of the *Life* cover makes clear, what seemed like a light touch on the handle of the cart could scale up quickly—"a $73 billion market basket"—in a mass-consumption economy, implying tremendous power in those begloved, choosy fingers.[25]

The ability of consumers to satisfy their wants and needs had been a topic of serious and popular debate for centuries before the Cold War, but the economic competition between West and East after World War II gave the issue a swordlike edge. As the sociologist Don Slater has explained, "Consumer sovereignty was the most popular Cold War wedge between east and west," allowing Western commentators to decry state socialism as a failed system that prevented individuals from satisfying "even the most trivial of their desires." Such thinking gained force during the Cold War not only because America's economy was so obviously effective at satisfying desires trivial and otherwise, but also because consumer sovereignty offered a robust defense of liberalism itself. Liberal democracy, premised on popular will, had given rise to fascism in multiple nations. Once the Allies had secured victory in World War II, the question remained as to how citizens could be trusted to build democracy without succumbing to demagoguery. The answer, for a broad range of Western political theorists during the Cold War, was a vision of liberal citizens as "rational actors." In this framework, supported by reams of technical studies in game theory, individuals pursued their own interests in all matters, and optimal social outcomes would naturally result—but only if enough choices were available to those actors. Hence citizenship in Cold War–era liberal democracies was increasingly defined by the range of choices available to a nation's consumers—with purchasing decisions made in a supermarket directly comparable to decisions made at the ballot box. As the American economist George H. Hildebrand put it in 1951, "The opportunity for consumers to have a broad measure of self-government is part of the liberal idea itself. . . . Consumer sovereignty and the liberal system therefore stand or fall together."[26]

What better representation of American consumer sovereignty than a modern supermarket? "I can think of no better way [of] penetrating the Iron Curtain with our philosophy of life than the supermarket," explained Max Mandell Zimmerman, founder of the Super Market Institute, testifying before Congress in a 1957 hearing investigating rising food costs. Though typical of Zimmerman's rhetorical excesses as one of the nation's leading supermarket propagandists, such a statement had real substance within the context of the Cold War. As an article in the trade publication *Super Market Merchandising* explained in 1955, the "philosophy" to which Zimmerman referred was "that the consumer was entitled to be served at the lowest costs." This sense of entitlement was the product of a "great revolution in distribution," which "could be made as powerful a weapon in the arsenal of Western democracy as any to be found." What made the American supermarket a weapon, however, was not simply the philosophy of consumer entitlement; after all, Khrushchev's rise to power in the Soviet Union was built in no small part on repeated promises that his brand of state socialism would provide Soviet consumers with a wide range of goods at the lowest possible costs. But the uneven dialectic between the material and the ideal, the reality and the rhetoric, was the source of the American supermarket's potency. As the National Association of Food Chains head John A. Logan declared in 1958, "Self-service is a form of economic democracy" because individual consumers could make their own choices in a self-serve supermarket and in doing so they put the lie to "Communist promises of a fuller life." The supermarket could "penetrate" the Iron Curtain, then, with its material proof of consumer sovereignty. It was as if David Riesman's farce "The Nylon War," in which American planes strafe the Soviet Union with light consumer goods, were a work of nonfiction. Such thinking clearly informed the exhibits at the 1962 International Food Congress Expo, which sought to "provide the Free World [with] a potent weapon of contrast" by erecting, among other displays, a four feet in diameter "Living Salad Bowl" and a "tree of sausages."[27]

Such rhetoric was clearly intended more for domestic American audiences than for foreign. If the supermarket was the materialized embodiment of consumer sovereignty, what sort of political economy were American consumers building with their choices? At its most fundamental level, the notion of "consumer sovereignty" entailed a proscribed role for the state in regulating, subsidizing, or otherwise administering the economy. This, indeed, was the central political thrust behind the economist William Hutt's coinage of the phrase in his *Economists and the Public* (1936). If consumers, through their informed purchasing decisions, could force producers to deliver goods efficiently at the lowest possible price, then coercive powers over the economy would inhere in the hands of individual citizens rather than in the bureaucracies of a central state. The antistatist framing of consumer sovereignty explains why members of the Austrian school of economics, especially Ludwig von Mises and Friedrich Hayek—both deeply concerned about the threat to liberty posed by strong states—would be among the most prominent post–World War II promoters of the notion.[28]

Although few professional economists of the time were as taken with the formalized notion of consumer sovereignty as were Mises and Hayek, business leaders seeking to roll back the regulatory apparatus of the post–New Deal state adopted the concept wholesale. In a 1947 pamphlet outlining the "American Competitive Enterprise System," the U.S. Chamber of Commerce explained that the third of five "major characteristics" of American "free competitive enterprise" was consumer sovereignty: "The consumer, through his freedom of choice, directs production—determines what is to be produced, in what quantities, and in what form and quality and at what price." Contrary to then-popular understandings of powerful corporations administering the economy, insisted the Chamber of Commerce, "business managers and their employees are the servants of the consumers." Although New Dealers had insisted that consumers could not exercise meaningful power in the marketplace without the backing of a robust state, free market propagandists of the postwar period declared that only consumers, not regulators, could function as rational actors in the modern marketplace. One broad consequence of the conservative adoption of consumer sovereignty was a slow revolution in antitrust policy, as conservative economists began arguing from the 1940s on that concentrated economic power—whether oligopoly or oligopsony—was not in and of itself a public policy concern if consumer prices remained low and the range of choices available to consumers remained unconstrained. Though such thinking was slow to take root in either the academy or policy circles in the 1950s, by 1966 the ideas had solidified well enough to allow the legal and economic theorist Robert Bork to declare that "consumer welfare" was and always had been the sole purpose of American antitrust policy. The marked contrast with the Supreme Court's decision in *Von's Grocery* would become ever more apparent in the 1970s, when Bork's ideas, alongside those of the Chicago legal theorist Richard Posner, would hold increasing sway.[29]

For American supermarket promoters in the 1950s and 1960s, the notion of consumer sovereignty served as a defense against charges that the rapid consolidation of food retailing in the period was a matter of policy concern. Public disquiet over inflation, especially in regard to food prices, dominated much of the domestic economic political scene of the 1950s and early 1960s. This context led John A. Logan to feed press releases to major newspapers pointing out that chain supermarkets operated on exceptionally thin profit margins, generally around 1 percent net on sales. In November 1956 many of the nation's supermarket chains engaged in a gimmick, giving customers a penny attached to a note explaining that the chains' profit margins amounted to one cent on a dollar of sales. One member of the food industry explained that the impetus behind the campaign was to demonstrate that "the housewife today is buying freedom as well as food" because that one-cent profit margin was a result of a business structure that provided choice, convenience, and quality unattainable in the era before supermarkets. Or, as a professor of marketing at Northwestern University testified before the National Commission on Food Marketing in 1965, "Not the exploiter and not the robber baron but the *consumer* is king today. . . . Business has no choice but to discover what he wants and to serve his wishes, even his whims." Within the framework of consumer sovereignty, consolidated economic power was a natural, indeed necessary, result of consumer choices. To call upon antitrust enforcers to intervene would be to undermine the inherent democracy of consumer capitalism.[30]

Supermarket promoters remained insistent about consumer sovereignty in the 1950s and 1960s in part because many Americans, including influential liberal economists, refused to believe the idea held much water. Perhaps most important was the critique advanced by the Harvard economist John Kenneth Galbraith in his 1958 opus *The Affluent Society.* American capitalism prioritized the production of private goods over public goods, explained Galbraith. "The care and refreshment of the mind, in contrast with the stomach, was principally in the public domain," so whereas supermarkets were stuffed to the rafters with affordable packaged foods, America's universities were "severely overcrowded and underprovided." But against those who would claim that such an outcome was a natural result of consumer sovereignty, Galbraith insisted that "consumer wants are created by the process by which they are satisfied," and thus "the consumer makes no such choice [between public and private goods]." In addition to Galbraith's broad critique of conservative economists' failures to address the social costs of individualistic consumerism, many liberal economists offered a narrower critique of consumer sovereignty. If economies of scale in a mass-production economy pushed producers to cater to the lowest common denominator, was an individual consumer really able to make much choice? The tyranny of the majority made all products essentially similar. Furthermore, without laws and government regulations to protect the consumer from fraud, deception, or suppression of information about possible alternatives, consumer sovereignty was a hollow concept. Thus, as the economist Abba Lerner summed up in a 1972 essay, conservatives' faith in the notion of consumer sovereignty was a weak basis upon which to build an antistatist ideology.[31]

The point about whether consumers had much choice in an American supermarket resonated more widely in popular culture in the 1950s and 1960s. Though shoppers had been growing accustomed to giant self-service food stores since the 1930s, the rapid spread of the supermarket format in the 1950s, along with a significant increase in average store size by the early 1960s, had brought renewed attention to the question. By 1966 supermarkets were selling nearly three-quarters of the nation's retail foods, and of the twenty largest retail firms in the nation that year, ten were supermarket chains. The number of products carried in an average supermarket had more than doubled in the two previous decades, as the normative size for new stores ballooned to twenty thousand square feet. Supermarkets dominated the American consumer experience, as they were increasingly located as anchor stores in suburban shopping-center developments. The question of just how much choice was available in these suburban megaliths was addressed forcefully in a 1960 essay by the poet and literary critic Randall Jarrell, "A Sad Heart at the Supermarket." With the supermarket standing in metaphorically for the entirety of American mass consumerism, Jarrell noted that "we no longer need worry about having food enough to keep from starving." Yet for Jarrell, supermarket capitalism had "merely exchanged man's old bondage for a new voluntary one. But *voluntary* is wrong: the consumer is trained for his job of consuming as the factory worker is trained for his job of producing." Consumers were not sovereign rational actors but disciplined automatons, childlike in their insistent grabbing for material goods. Jarrell might have approved of a Michael Ramus cartoon in *Life*. Appearing in the same issue (January 3, 1955) whose cover suggested a shopper in a supermarket could effortlessly attain "mass luxury," Ramus's cartoon depicts a chaotic, even dangerous scene. Children exhaust their mothers with demands while male shoppers wander aisles in bewilderment. The accompanying caption explains that "much buying is done on impulse," as store managers have craftily placed syrup next to pancake mixes, and meat counters are at the rear of the store to force customers to pass as many shelves as possible before making their primary intended purchase.[32]

The food historian Ann Vileisis has argued that the reason mid-twentieth-century American shoppers had no real choice in the supermarket was that they had entered into a "covenant of ignorance" with the food industry. According to Vileisis, "Housewives did not want to be bothered with knowing details" about their food in the 1950s and 1960s, preferring instead to accept advertisers' claims that processed packaged foods were convenient and economical. Such an interpretation suggests that consumers were indeed sovereign, rationally and intentionally choosing a food system built on willful acceptance of misleading claims about convenience and healthfulness and affordability. Yet public pronouncements by consumers and their advocates in the 1960s suggest otherwise. When Congress considered establishing the National Commission on Food Marketing in response to President Johnson's request in 1964, one invited witness was Esther Peterson, assistant secretary of labor and special assistant to the president for consumer affairs. Peterson read a letter from a mother in Maryland to the committee: "Most important to me as a food shopper, of course, is the nonsense that goes on in the supermarket." The woman demanded "a fair chance to decide which product I want," suggesting that labels were intentionally confusing. A woman from Pennsylvania wrote to Peterson that supermarkets were "emotionally exhausting" because of "the increasing practice by the food companies of raising the costs of foods again and again with useless 'improvements.'" Peterson summarized the gist of the many letters she had received by suggesting that supermarket shoppers were far from sovereign: "Does the consumer now have less choice and a higher and more limited price range?"[33]

Many commentators during the 1960s noted that consumers' decisions in a supermarket, while they might appear to be individual choices, were in fact carefully orchestrated by store managers. The cattleman John F. Odea explained to the Senate Commerce Committee in March 1964 that "the consumer has been duped into believing that she sets the price [for fresh meat] and benefits directly in constantly lower prices." Odea insisted that "people in the business, that is, food-chain butchers" were all too aware that self-service purchasing of prewrapped meat made consumers less "price conscious on price per pound." Indeed, as the historian Roger Horowitz has shown, the development of see-through cellophane meat packaging in the late 1940s was explicitly pitched to retail butchers not as a means of empowering consumer choices but as a way for meat counter managers to control their inventory by influencing the choices that consumers would make. Three years before the National Commission on Food

Marketing was established, the social critic Marya Mannes declared that supermarkets were the "greatest exercise in planned confusion since the bazaars of Samarkand," requiring shoppers to bring "a slide rule and an M.I.T. graduate with us to the supermarket and figure out what we're buying." One woman, perhaps without access to a slide rule, decided in 1966 to do her own systematic study of her local supermarkets to determine "everything a frugal shopper could possibly do to buy the most for her dollar." She reported her results to the advocacy group Consumers Union, angrily declaring that she "could find no system to it all, no clear path to the best quality for the least money." The journalist Jennifer Cross summed up such frustrations in the *Nation* in 1966: "The retail shopper, far from being the sovereign, rational buyer that manufacturers like to make out, was bewildered and frustrated."[34]

Frustrated consumers could, of course, choose not to shop at chain supermarkets. Even at the height of the supermarket boom of the 1950s, some consumers turned to alternative retailers, such as cooperative stores run on democratic principles. As the historian Anne Meis Knupfer has documented, a number of food cooperatives managed to adopt supermarket-style techniques in the 1950s, combining the economies of scale of for-profit chains with "collective ownership, consumer education, and patronage refunds." One example was the Co-Op, run by the Cooperative Consumers of New Haven, Connecticut. Managed by professional retailers but directed by elected volunteers from the community, the New Haven Co-Op sought to build an alternative form of "economic democracy in action" premised not simply on abundance but on direct participation in store management and profit-sharing. The slate of candidates for a 1950 election, for instance, included an individual who had spent eight years working for the Tennessee Valley Authority building rural electrical cooperatives as well as a woman who declared that cooperatives offered "an immediate way in which democratic principles and procedures are carried out in practice." A candidate for the Finance Committee suggested that the crucial task of the cooperative was to provide "reasonable prices and raise the standard of living through distribution of their profits to their members." The Co-Op's reports to members in the 1950s, however, suggested that achieving both democratic participation and low prices was a significant challenge; the cooperative could not match the volume of sales achieved at for-profit chain stores. By the early 1970s the New Haven cooperative, although still in existence, had been forced to drop its profit-sharing scheme in order to keep prices down.[35]

A new crop of cooperative food stores emerged in the late 1960s to cater to members of the counterculture who sought what they understood to be an even deeper form of consumer sovereignty. Rejecting the entire agribusiness structure that made modern supermarkets possible, counterculture patrons of the new breed of cooperatives looked for minimally processed foods produced on small organic farms. Up to ten thousand such co-ops opened between 1969 and 1979, often located in college towns. Beyond building an alternative food production and distribution system, many of the new co-ops worked to create a form of "participatory democracy" in which owner-members consumed not just goods but also information about the ecological benefits of organic agriculture. Although these cooperatives urged their members to buy in bulk to reduce reliance on wasteful packaging, the cooperatives themselves often struggled to buy in enough quantities to achieve economies of scale. These food cooperatives never posed a serious challenge to mainstream supermarkets' dominance of food retailing. Yet they can be interpreted as part of a broader movement—appealing to many mainstream middle-class Americans as well as members of the youthful counterculture—to use informed consumption as a tool, however limited, to reject the centralization of corporate power in the postwar American economy. As the historian Thomas Jundt has argued: "With so much that seemed beyond their control, citizens could at least decide what and what not to buy." At the same time, consumer activists who took the "sovereign" aspect of consumer sovereignty to heart were, as the historian Lawrence Glickman has shown, consistently vilified by conservative business leaders who "contrasted *consumer choice* with the *consumer movement*"; consumer choice was acceptable and in fact necessary, as long as it did not directly threaten the prerogatives of business leaders or result in new regulations.[36]

Most American shoppers at midcentury, however, were not looking for participatory democracy when they entered a supermarket. Most wanted affordable food, reliable quality, and a wide array of fresh and processed foods under one roof. Supermarkets were so successful at meeting these expectations by the 1960s that many consumers had developed a sense of entitlement akin to what Max Mandell Zimmerman of the Super Market Institute had labeled the "philosophy" of American supermarketing. But when food prices suddenly ballooned in the spring of 1973 due to a complex set of events—including a rash of droughts in Europe and Asia, a decline in American cattle numbers, and President Nixon's devaluation of the dollar—thousands of supermarket shoppers felt betrayed. Spontaneously organized consumer boycotts emerged across the nation, with groups such as "Until Prices Drop" and "Fight Inflation Together" refusing to purchase at their local supermarkets until prices came down. In New York, a group of housewives rallied on Broadway carrying signs reading "Devalue Pot Roast, Not Dollars." Many hoped that collective action would force the Nixon administration to introduce effective price controls; as thirty-seven hundred signatories to an "Until Prices Drop" petition to

President Nixon put it, "We strongly object to being the helpless victims of the 'let the public be damned' attitude demonstrated by the present administration."[37]

The Nixon administration's responses, however, indicated just how deeply the conservative notion of consumer sovereignty had permeated the structures of farm and food policy making. Undersecretary of Agriculture J. Phillip Campbell, speaking at an Oklahoma City press conference on the food price crisis, suggested that rational shoppers should, rather than band together to seek collective action or political responses, simply "back out of the marketplace and the cost would go down." When pressed by journalists on whether he saw the rampant price increases as a threat to the consumer's ability to put food on the table, Campbell said, "I feel she's doing all right the way she is, I hope she keeps on." Irate letters from consumers quickly flooded Campbell's office as well as that of Secretary of Agriculture Earl Butz, many pointing out that a "choice" not to shop for food was no choice at all. "I would suggest," seethed Carol R. Chambers, "that the *only* marketplace no one can abandon is the grocery store." Ruth Wade claimed to be "amused" by Campbell's "asinine statement," but informed him that she "would like to quit buying but it would be a pretty difficult sacrifice for my two children." Mrs. James J. Powers, in a similar letter, added a snide postscript thanking Campbell sarcastically for "letting us spend our money as we see fit."[38]

The 1973 consumer boycotts were the last mass protest action of the twentieth century to seriously question the conservative vision of consumer sovereignty in the food marketplace. In the decades that followed, the American food distribution system, constructed on an agribusiness foundation that prioritized efficiency and abundance over individual autonomy for either farmers or shoppers, increasingly penetrated the global food economy. Whether this was a triumph for "free enterprise" in the broader Cold War Farms Race depended on one's viewpoint. The Texas populist Jim Hightower declared in *Eat Your Heart Out,* his 1975 blast at agribusiness, that the free market of supermarket capitalism "in the real world . . . means that farmers and consumers alike surrender essential decision-making power over supplies of basic foodstuffs to oligopolistic food firms." By contrast, the U.S. Chamber of Commerce published a pamphlet in 1974 explaining that the American "food system is predicated on continual reorganization of production by more efficient methods," and "although many farmers have been forced out of agriculture, those who are competitive enough to remain have realized a satisfactory level of family living." Consumers concerned about the price shocks of the early 1970s, according to the Chamber of Commerce, seemed to have forgotten that the share of their income spent on food had been sharply declining since the early 1950s, and in any case "there are too many forces pushing for larger sized [farm] units to achieve economies of scale to attempt to reverse this economic trend by legislation."[39]

Such claims of the inevitability of the agribusiness approach might have seemed at odds with arguments premised on consumer choice as the driving force behind economic consolidation in the farm and food economy. Was the rise of agribusiness due to fate or free will? But rather than address such a tricky question, many public figures of the 1970s instead chose to shift the rhetoric of the Farms Race. By the mid-1970s a new discourse of American "food power" on the global stage had emerged to describe American capitalism's agricultural arsenal in the Cold War.

Food Power and the Global Supermarket

Even as some American farmers and consumers continued to question just how free the enterprise of American food production and distribution had become by the end of the 1960s, some politicians and businessmen continued to aggressively promote the arsenal of American-style food abundance on the world stage. Such a stance fit well with the shifting ground of the Cold War itself. During the presidencies of John F. Kennedy and Lyndon B. Johnson, perceptions of a "hungry world" of potentially radical peasants in postcolonial regions of the global South made American-style agriculture and food provisioning ever more attractive as a weapon that could turn the communist tide. The framing of American food abundance as a product of free enterprise, however, meant that many of the most important battles in the late stages of the Cold War Farms Race were waged not by public agencies but by private firms.

Indeed, from the 1960s into the 1980s, American transnational agribusiness corporations assumed the mantle of crusaders, demonstrating U.S. farm and food power to the world. In earlier decades of the Farms Race, U.S. farmers were called upon to feed the hungry world as a counterrevolutionary project with a humanitarian veneer. By the late 1970s, however, politicians and businessmen who touted the notion of American "food power" were increasingly declaring their intent to rewrite the rules of global food production and trade on entirely profit-driven terms. Building on Cold War–inspired modernization and development projects initiated in the 1940s, 1950s, and 1960s, U.S.-based transnational agribusinesses in the 1970s, 1980s, and 1990s—including the International Basic Economy Corporation (IBEC), the former linseed-oil manufacturer turned global commodities giant Archer Daniels Midland, and the Ozarks-based retail chain Walmart—constructed a world in which private corporations, including supermarkets, emerged as the primary institutional mechanisms for regulating and coordinating global food chains. As distribution-driven agro-capitalism took command, the world's farmers became embedded in a tightly regulated web of contract-driven agriculture.

In the high-level atmosphere of Cold War diplomacy and foreign policy, the rhetoric of the Farms Race became increasingly militant in the 1960s and 1970s. References to food as a weapon had been bandied about in U.S. agricultural and foreign policy circles since World War I. But when John F. Kennedy entered the White House in 1961 having announced his intention of uniting domestic and foreign farm policy under the umbrella of "Food for Peace," Farms Race discourse paradoxically developed an even sharper edge. Orville Freeman, Kennedy's choice for secretary of agriculture, declared in January that he would work to use American "agricultural abundance as an instrument to encourage economic growth in underdeveloped areas of the world, as one of our greatest weapons for peace and freedom." The influence of modernization theory on the Kennedy administration's approach to agricultural policy on the world stage was expressed with even greater clarity by Kennedy himself in May, when the president delivered an urgent request to Congress calling for a massive investment in foreign development projects. In the same speech in which Kennedy challenged the nation to land a man on the moon, the president declared the less-developed nations of the world to be "the great battleground for the defense and expansion of freedom today." Asia, Latin America, Africa, and the Middle East were, Kennedy claimed, "the lands of the rising peoples," a carefully chosen phrase meant to instill both optimism and fear. Indeed, Kennedy explained, "adversaries of freedom" were actively seeking to cultivate alliances with those "rising peoples." Creating the U.S. Agency for International Development (USAID) to "provide generously of our skills, and our capital, and our food to assist the peoples of the less-developed nations" would bring the fight against communism to the ground even as America pushed for extraterrestrial dominance in the Space Race. Such phrasing began to resonate more widely in the early 1960s, such as when the moderate Republican senator George Aiken of Vermont delivered a commencement address at Goddard College titled "Food—America's Most Potent Weapon." "People cannot be starved into democracy," intoned Aiken, but "they can be starved into dictatorships." Citing the example of American food aid to Yugoslavia in 1950 as evidence of "the value of food as a weapon to be used in ideological or social conflicts," Aiken suggested that Yugoslavia, despite its communist leadership, was nonetheless a "free nation" because of U.S. grain deliveries.[1]

The rapid decline of wheat production in the Soviet Union's Virgin Lands campaign in the early 1960s opened a wider wedge for Farms Race thinking to guide foreign policy in the Kennedy administration. In October 1963 a trade delegation from the Soviet Union approached U.S. grain trading firms with a proposal to purchase several million tons of American grains. The last commercial grain exchange between the two countries had taken place in 1917, so the proposed deal's historical significance pressed upon both superpowers. The Kennedy administration ultimately approved the deal in November, just weeks before Kennedy's assassination, clearing a path for 150 million bushels to be sold by American agribusinesses to the Soviets. Congressional debate over the proposal illustrated the extent to which Farms Race language framed the entire episode. Wisconsin Democrat William Proxmire strongly advocated the sale in the Senate. South Carolina senator Strom Thurmond asked Proxmire whether "food is an important weapon of war, just as much so as a gun?" Proxmire replied, "There is no question about it, and further there is no question in my mind that the greatest weakness in the Soviet Union, and the greatest weakness in all the Communist countries, is their inability to produce food, the utter failure of collectivized agriculture." Grain was not, in this formulation, a fungible commodity; when it came from American soil tilled by private farmers, it was impregnated with the symbolic power to demonstrate the inability of communist farms to provide the abundance promised by leaders such as Khrushchev. Thurmond opposed the grain deal, but used the same rhetorical framework: "Food is a weapon in the cold war just as much as bullets or bombs." For Thurmond, however, selling American wheat to the Soviets would allow central planners to "continue diversion of their own resources from agricultural and food-producing segments of the economy to military preparedness." Thurmond, unlike Senator Aiken, apparently believed it possible to starve the Soviets into democracy.[2]

Thurmond ended up on the losing side of this particular political battle. But perhaps the most important result of the 1963 grain deal was its clear illustration of how the abstract foreign policy goals of Kennedy's Food for Peace initiative might also produce profits for American agribusiness corporations. The American firms Continental Grain and Cargill, two of the largest grain trading firms in the world, were the primary architects and beneficiaries of the grain deals approved by the White House. Indeed, after 1965 Food for Peace increasingly seemed to move in the direction of Food for Profit. President Lyndon Johnson's advisers on Food for Peace programs, especially Orville Freeman and Secretary of State Dean Rusk, pushed for changes in the program that allowed "friendly" nations to purchase American food in their own currency but made it a condition that nations who accepted U.S. food aid also had to demonstrate a willingness to adopt the chemical fertilizers and hybrid seeds of American-style industrial agriculture. President Johnson believed that requiring such "self-help measures" from recipient countries warranted a change in the name of the program to Food for Freedom, although Congress nixed the name change while nonetheless approving the "self-help" provisions in 1966. But the line between self-help and coerced enrollment in the American-dominated marketplace for chemical agricultural inputs was thin, and perhaps intentionally so. Robert Komer, a key adviser to the Johnson administration on relations with India, thought Food for Peace initiatives could be used to "force the grain revolution down the throats of the Indian Government." Such baldly aggressive declarations were relatively rare in the 1960s, but the general assumption that hybrid seeds and chemical fertilizers would feed the hungry world was as widely accepted in the mid-1960s as was the frank acknowledgment that rapid adoption of American-style agriculture might lead to painful dislocations of much of the developing world's rural poor. Behind both assumptions lay an awareness that agricultural transformation in the developing world, while it would demonstrate to the Soviets the superiority of capitalist agriculture, might open up untapped markets for American agribusiness firms into the bargain.[3]

Orville Freeman was a tireless advocate of the potential profits to be made from humanitarian action in the Farms Race. In a 1967 *Foreign Affairs* article Freeman bragged about the devastating blow the 1963 grain trade dealt to Nikita Khrushchev, not only as a general humiliation for the Soviet leader but specifically as proof of the inherent efficiency of privately owned farms. "If we were as far ahead of the Russians in the space race as we are in agriculture, we would by now be running a shuttle service to the moon," joked Freeman. But the Farms Race was not yet won, because the "newly independent peoples" of the developing world "are hungry; they want food, not slogans." According to Freeman, free enterprise alone had not made American farms the most productive in the world; American farmers had benefited from government-sponsored scientific and technological research. Thus, what "hungry countries" needed, in Freeman's logic, was chemical fertilizer, irrigation systems, and hybrid seeds. Elaborating on the point in a 1968 book, Freeman explained that the "technological revolution" of American industrial agriculture made it possible to "visualize a world without hunger." Such language marked a subtle but important transformation in Freeman's understanding of the American "food weapon" during his time in national office. In 1961 he had advocated American "agricultural abundance" as the path to a peaceful world, but in 1968 he pinned his hopes on "technological revolution." What a hungry world needed in this formulation was not food aid but industrial agriculture; Americans should be providing chemicals and machinery, not surplus agricultural commodities. By declaring the need to help developing nations feed themselves through the adoption of industrialized agriculture he was implicitly recognizing the role American multinational agrochemical, farm machinery, and grain trading corporations might play in the ongoing Farms Race.[4]

In 1972 the Soviet Union struck another major grain deal with the United States, importing twice as much grain as in 1963. In a bargain that members of the American press quickly denounced as the "Great Grain Robbery" when domestic grain and food prices instantly skyrocketed, members of the Nixon administration including Earl Butz and Secretary of State Henry Kissinger saw an opportunity to flex American might on the world stage via so-called food power. The sale of American grain, orchestrated by a handful of multinational grain-trading firms including Cargill, Continental, Bunge, and Cook, clearly benefited those corporations. Hubert Humphrey surmised that the Soviet premier, Leonid Brezhnev, was also a beneficiary of the deal because as humiliating as the grain imports might be, they nonetheless would feed herds of livestock needed to provide the meat that Soviet citizens had been satisfied to find in the stores after Brezhnev took over from Khrushchev. Humphrey, ever the farm-state senator, recognized that the deal was probably more important from the perspective of American farmers in opening up markets for feed grains than it was in diplomatic terms. Indeed, as members of the public came to the conclusion that the Great Grain Robbery had done little to advance world peace while apparently doing much to increase the profits of the grain cartel, the Ford administration suspended sales to the Soviets in 1974. Yet when crop failures in 1974 and 1975 pushed the Soviets to again seek U.S. grain purchases, Ford revived the possibility that American grain surpluses could be used as powerful diplomatic tools. By the mid-1970s, the dominant discourse in the Farms Race no longer revolved around the idea of "Food for Peace," but had been supplanted by the phrase "food power."[5]

As the United States faced multiple foreign policy crises in the 1970s ranging from the grinding defeat in Vietnam to OPEC's stunning successes in controlling global fuel prices, "food power" became a rallying cry for those who thought they had found a silver bullet to reassert U.S. economic dominance. Writing in the *New York Review of Books* in August 1975, the British historian Geoffrey Barraclough announced that the rapid rise of petroleum-rich states in the Middle East portended a "new cold war," one in which "the Third World, fortified by the new wealth of the Arab countries and their control over an essential source of energy, is going to take its revenge for centuries of colonial humiliation and tear down the existing system." But there was an "ace up the United States's sleeve," according to Barraclough, in the form of food power. To some it was a cheering notion that America's vast reserves of grain were now a geopolitical asset rather than an embarrassing reminder of what had been called a "surplus problem" for most of the twentieth century. In a 1974 report, for instance, the CIA's Office of Political Research noted that the United States accounted for three-fourths of the world's grain exports, which portended an "increase in U.S. power and influence," particularly among poorer countries dependent on U.S. food aid. Convinced that the world was entering a little ice age, the authors of the CIA report suggested that the Soviet Union and China would soon "experience shorter growing seasons and a drop in output," making way for the United States to "regain the primacy in world affairs it held in the immediate post-World War II era." A "high-level State Department official" put the matter more bluntly to *Business Week* in 1975: "We have the food, and the hell with the rest of the world."[6]

The weaponization of American grain exports took on explicitly political overtones when Senator Henry "Scoop" Jackson made food power a centerpiece of his bid for the 1976 Democratic presidential nomination. Speaking before a group of twenty-five hundred supporters in Miami Beach in March 1976, the senator from Washington State asked, "Why shouldn't we use food power?" The United States was "the most powerful nation on the face of the earth in terms of food," and "food power is more important than petroleum power." In ominous tones Jackson belied his reputation among neoconservatives as a brashly anticommunist hawk, suggesting that "the Russians would starve to death if it weren't for the United States." Such campaign-trail statements indicated the potentially wide resonance of the notion of food power in an era when neoconservatives called upon a public weary of war to reignite their jingoistic passions. The arch-neoconservative Norman Podhoretz, in a widely read piece in *Commentary* published a month after Jackson delivered his food power speech, declared that the nation's supposedly conservative Republican leaders were "less bellicose" than they should be. Podhoretz lambasted Richard Nixon and Gerald Ford for permitting grain sales to the Soviet Union "in exchange for little more than a smile from Leonid Brezhnev" as an example of the Republican Party's failure to revive its anticommunist militancy.[7]

Ronald Reagan may have provided the most interesting response to the suggestion that food power was the ace up America's sleeve. The California governor, running to replace Gerald Ford as the Republican Party's presidential nominee in 1976, appeared on NBC's *Meet the Press* in March to reject the basic principle of food power as a diplomatic weapon. "Selling," Reagan announced, "gives us the advantage. We can't just stubbornly say, 'We won't sell [our grain].'" The problem with conceiving of America's agricultural abundance as a diplomatic weapon, in Reagan's pithy assessment, was twofold: on one hand, unbridled capitalism was a far more powerful means of showing American food power to the world, while on the other, withholding American grain would only enable other nations to fill the trade vacuum while the United States vainly piled up its grain reserves. Reagan agreed with neoconservatives, of course, on the need to overcome America's lingering sense of emasculation by North Vietnam in the Vietnam War. Reagan's vision for a renewal of militant anticommunism left no room, however, for denying business opportunities to U.S. farmers and multinationals.[8]

By the late 1970s, in fact, Reagan's take on the idea of food power had become a consensus vision. Emma Rothschild, writing in *Foreign*

Affairs, called food power a "deluded" idea, rejecting the idea that "the politics of food" could be about anything other than "a politics of trade." Robert L. Paarlberg, a Wellesley College political scientist and the son of an Eisenhower-era assistant secretary of agriculture, summed up the literature on food power in 1978 with a straightforward assessment: "Food can never provide as much diplomatic leverage to an exporting nation as does oil." Manipulating grain exports was harder political work than food power advocates realized, Paarlberg noted. Even when statesmen did manage to deny exports to a particular country, some other grain-exporting nation—Argentina, Canada, Australia—would happily step in with its own offerings.[9]

Such predictions were borne out in 1980, when the Carter administration imposed a grain embargo on the Soviet Union in attempted retaliation for the invasion of Afghanistan. Carter's National Security Council acknowledged the weakness of the attempt, suggesting that at best a grain embargo was "a one-shot weapon," while the aftermath of the embargo—during which Argentina and Australia enjoyed unprecedented sales of grain to the Soviets—suggested that even that one shot was rather far off the mark. Orville Freeman responded to the perceived failures of the 1980 grain embargo by working with a United Nations group to draft a document calling on the United States to use its food abundance for "humanitarian purposes," not as a "weapon." Importantly, however, Freeman—the one-time overseer of the Food for Peace program—suggested that "humanitarian" approaches to grain exports would ultimately strengthen America's economic position in the world. American farmers stood to gain more from stabilized world food prices than from erratic swings in supply and demand, whether due to unpredictable weather patterns or to knee-jerk embargoes.[10]

Food power, in other words, was being replaced by market power as the guiding notion behind America's role in the global food-supply chain. This is not to suggest that purportedly philanthropic agricultural development projects disappeared in the 1970s. Indeed, after the USAID director William S. Gaud coined the term "Green Revolution" in 1968, development projects intended to rapidly boost agricultural yields in Asia and Latin America took on renewed urgency. Particularly under the aegis of the World Bank, headed from 1968 to 1981 by the former secretary of defense Robert McNamara, Green Revolutionaries pumped loans, chemicals, and hybrid seeds into the rural developing world. Heralded at the time as a permanent solution to global hunger, the Green Revolution—and its attendant dislocation of millions of peasant farmers, widespread application of pesticides and herbicides, and reliance on capital-intensive approaches to farming in capital-poor contexts—has ignited controversy up to the present day even as its basic assumptions have remained largely in place. Yet for all the warranted attention devoted to the Green Revolution by scholars, activists, and journalists in recent decades, it is easily forgotten that even while agricultural yields rose impressively in developing countries, in the developed countries of the West agricultural production was itself undergoing a revolution. In 1950, agriculture in the West was seven times more productive per acre than in the developing world. But in 1985, with the Green Revolution continuing full steam, the West's agriculture was thirty-six times more productive per acre than in developing countries. Importantly, those farm yields were increasingly being yoked to a new breed of transnational agribusinesses, many based in the United States, that sought global influence not to boost grain yields but to profit from sales of high-value processed foods and farm products. A global agribusiness revolution, in other words, was quietly under way even as the Green Revolution captured headlines.[11]

The rise of global agribusiness should be understood as distinct from the development campaigns of the Green Revolution. Multinational agribusinesses sought to increase the efficiency and global reach of distribution and marketing structures, profiting more from the movement of commodities across boundaries than from the efficiency of their production. The Green Revolution, by contrast, was first and foremost production-oriented, and its promoters often ignored marketing and distribution issues entirely. Green Revolutionaries sought to industrialize agriculture, viewing hybrid seeds as gateway drugs to chemical inputs and capital-intensive irrigation systems. In addition, the Green Revolution was understood as a means for transforming not just fields but farmers; farmers who did not adopt the chemical-dependent mode of industrial agriculture were explicitly intended to be forced off the land into urban-industrial "modernity." By contrast, the rise of global agribusiness aimed to transform consumption, cultivating notions of "sovereign" consumers whose purchases supported corporate power, not state governance of the food economy.

An instructive example is the International Basic Economy Corporation's shifting priorities in the 1960s and 1970s. From its inception in 1947 by Nelson Rockefeller, IBEC sought to profit from agricultural development projects intended to lower food costs to consumers in less-developed nations. Its various supermarket projects, starting in Venezuela in 1948 and spreading throughout Latin America and then into southern Europe by the 1960s, remained astoundingly profitable, but IBEC's attempts to industrialize agriculture produced far less stellar results. In the early 1960s, IBEC began a shift in strategy. Chickens, not grain, promised to be the global gold mine of the future. Or so Henry Saglio convinced a group of IBEC executives in 1960. Saglio was the driving force behind Arbor Acres, a chicken-breeding firm based in Connecticut that won multiple prizes in the 1940s Chicken of Tomorrow contests and as a result had become responsible for the genetic makeup of approximately half the world's commercial chickens by 1960.[12]

Arbor Acres chicks, particularly its White Rock hybrid crosses, were highly valued by poultry processors. Such firms, responding to supermarketers' demands, sought birds with enormous meaty breasts, efficient weight-gaining capabilities, low disease mortality, and white feathers. Relying on a team of geneticists and an ambitious sales strategy, Arbor Acres became a dominant player in the rapidly growing U.S. chicken industry in the 1950s, penetrating the "chicken triangle" of north Georgia, the poultry counties of the Delmarva region, and much of the rural Southwest. Genetics were key to its profits, not only because Arbor Acres birds appealed to processors, but also because the primary product sold by the firm—day-old chicks, which were raised by farmer-growers under strictly controlled contracts with poultry processors—could not themselves be bred with other birds without producing undesirable traits (including black feathers). There was thus a biological "lock" on the proprietary technology embedded in the chickens' genetic codes.[13]

Anxious about oversaturating U.S. markets with his biologically locked chicks, Henry Saglio looked overseas and saw in Latin America, southern Europe, and Asia the possibility of windfall profits. "A growing international market" for processed chicken meat suggested to Saglio "a profit potential which must inevitably result" from a transnational sales strategy, which he hoped would be aided by IBEC's expertise in building international businesses from scratch. IBEC and Arbor Acres consequently entered into a partnership and established poultry stations in Colombia and Venezuela. In 1962, IBEC purchased a major interest in the firm and helped establish operations in Italy, France, Austria, and Ireland. A year later, IBEC decided to buy the entire Arbor Acres enterprise, with Henry Saglio and his team maintaining managerial control. The purpose of the acquisition, according to a 1963 memo, was to initiate "a program of world coverage in chicken operations."[14]

Blanketing the world with industrial chickens fit squarely into IBEC's emerging agribusiness strategy in the 1960s. Still seeking to make impressive profits while lowering food prices in developing nations, IBEC's New York–based executives understood the radical potential of Arbor Acres' genetically manipulated birds. An article in *Connecticut Life* (probably the result of an IBEC press release) noted, "The poorer the nation, the better chicken market it becomes." Chickens whose genes had been manipulated to produce meat with extraordinary speed from remarkably little feed could transform entire food economies, not only delivering an affordable source of meat to urban consumers but also freeing up those countries' grain farmers to export their soybeans and corn for cash. And best of all from the perspective of Donald F. Meads—who became president and CEO of IBEC in January 1965—IBEC's Arbor Acres division would serve as the profit-reaping gatekeeper of the entire operation. From the moment Meads took over IBEC, the company moved with increasing haste to focus on its bottom line, all but pushing aside the anticommunist political objectives that had animated Nelson Rockefeller's original conception of the firm. Even so, the rhetorical framework of the Farms Race continued to provide justification for IBEC's move into poultry; as the *Connecticut Life* piece put it, Arbor Acres chicks were being put "squarely into international politics—as an arm of America's determination to alleviate hunger and strengthen emerging economies." Yet promoting agribusiness—processing, distribution, marketing—not agriculture, would in Meads's vision allow IBEC to profit more handsomely from rural development than had its earlier attempts at industrializing row crops. A 1966 internal memo stated the central aims of IBEC's poultry division: while holding on to existing market domination in the United States and Canada, the poultry group would aggressively "seek out all opportunities relating to the profitable development of the industry" in foreign countries, possibly including "vertical integration into allied fields such as feed production and processing plants." Agribusinesses would now serve as IBEC's opening wedge into developing countries.[15]

Brazil became one such target. Despite initial misgivings that Brazil's demand for poultry was already being met by existing firms, the appeal of its "immense market" could not be ignored. By the late 1960s IBEC had grabbed a 30-percent share of the market for meat-type chickens in the country, and was gunning for a 50-percent share by 1972. Although the firm operated with the sanction of the Brazilian government, its operations in the country and throughout much of the developing world relied heavily on private resources. Henry Saglio's original Connecticut poultry business benefited from close partnerships with state and federal agricultural officials. His first geneticist, hired in 1939, had been wooed away from the Connecticut Agricultural Extension Service, for instance. But as Arbor Acres moved into countries lacking America's extensive network of state-sponsored agricultural researchers, the poultry firm had to rely solely on a privately funded cadre of scientists and technicians. In the United States, in the wake of the Chicken of Tomorrow contests, government researchers, private agribusinesses, and land-grant universities had cooperated closely to transform chicken from an expensive Sunday treat into the nation's cheapest everyday meat. Outside the United States, however, private agribusinesses such as IBEC sought to piggyback on American state-supported research while operating at arm's length or farther from their host governments.[16]

Assuming corporate omnipotence did not always lead to auspicious results. In 1967, the New York–based IBEC executive John Uhlein suggested that Argentinians might be interested in a new process developed in Georgia that turned otherwise unmarketable chicken byproducts into salable commodities. Technology for deboning chicken necks, backs, and other low-value parts of the carcass allowed the Georgia firm to produce a "chicken slurry" that could easily be formed into hot dogs, "chicken loaf," and ball-shaped edibles. According to Uhlein, the company's canned chicken loaf, which retailed for 40-percent less than Hormel's SPAM, was "extremely tasty" and might appeal to Latin American consumers the way that deviled ham spread had in Venezuela. V. Peter Mortensen, vice president of IBEC's Argentinian operations, responded to Uhlein's suggestion by noting that SPAM was significantly cheaper than any existing processed chicken product. In any case, Mortensen continued, Argentinians refused to buy their chickens in any form other than whole, meaning that no byproducts were readily available to processors to make slurry, loaves, or even balls. Uhlein's optimism may have been shaped by his understanding of the U.S. chicken market, where poultry processors such as Holly Farms, Perdue Farms, and Tyson Foods were busily introducing American supermarket shoppers to prepackaged, brand-name chicken parts in the 1960s. But as Mortensen's dismissive response to Uhlein suggested, convincing non-U.S. consumers to adopt America's industrial food chain wholesale was going to take more than just clever marketing.[17]

The International Basic Economy Corporation was not the only U.S.-based agribusiness firm seeking bonanza profits abroad in the late 1960s and into the 1970s. Sellers of machinery, fertilizer, and processed foods pushed export programs, looking to establish beachheads of market-based food power even as diplomats debated the wisdom of wielding government-based food power. As had so often been the case in earlier decades, many American agribusinesses relied upon the Department of Agriculture for support. In the latter half of the 1960s the USDA launched a cooperative "market development" program with forty-five major commodity and farm groups seeking to cultivate consumption of American processed foods in some seventy countries. Advertising, free samples, and nutritional education projects introduced overseas consumers to everything from American soybean products to raisins. One USDA economist noted with satisfaction in a 1965 address to the National Agricultural Policy Conference that "European housewives . . . have quickly acquired a taste for U.S. frozen poultry," then went on to explain how such efforts to increase overseas meat consumption would pay off for American farmers in the form of boosted livestock feed-grain exports. But whether or not the USDA's efforts had much impact, it is clear that American agribusinesses were intent upon expanding into international markets. In 1971, for instance, Del Monte initiated a five-year, $125 million project to increase its holdings in real estate, transportation, and processing infrastructure around the world. The Texas populist Jim Hightower denounced Del Monte's transnational expansion as traitorous in a 1974 congressional hearing, noting that the firm had "moved from Hawaii to the Philippines for pineapple, a movement to Mexico for asparagus, fresh fruits, and vegetables, a movement to Kenya, all out of this country." For Hightower, such moves were indicators that "Food power today rests squarely with giant corporations."[18]

The actions of firms like Del Monte helped account for a remarkable swell in export sales of processed foods from the 1970s to the 1990s, such that, for the first time, the international processed food trade accounted for "several magnitudes" more in global sales volume than did raw agricultural commodities. A handful of large, multinational firms established themselves as the major concerns in this expanding global marketplace where branded and packaged foods, not the Green Revolution's unbranded commodities, held the key to profits. In 1974 the Harvard economist Thomas Horst suggested that U.S.

firms were becoming dominant in the foreign food-processing realm because businesses like Del Monte and Heinz (which had half its 1974 sales outside the United States) were first and foremost marketing firms. Marketing—from distribution to advertising—was both the primary source of these companies' profits and the motivating factor that pushed them into overseas operations. For U.S. firms seeking to mark their territory in the emerging global food system of the 1970s and beyond, marketing machinery was the key to power and profits.[19]

Archer Daniels Midland (ADM) provides the clearest example. Originally a two-bit linseed-oil processing firm based in Minnesota, in the mid-1960s ADM transformed itself into the self-proclaimed "supermarket to the world." Dwayne Andreas, who controlled the firm from 1965 to 1997, cultivated political friendships with Democrats and Republicans alike—among his closest friends were Hubert Humphrey and Jimmy Carter, but he also made substantial campaign contributions to Richard Nixon and Ronald Reagan—in an unabashed attempt to curry government favor. A 1968 amendment to the Food for Peace program pushed by Humphrey was one of Andreas's earliest political achievements. By creating a sudden demand for soy-fortified foods—of which ADM was the world's major supplier—the legislation catapulted the firm into global prominence. Despite facing repeated antitrust investigations and being forced to pay fines for multiple price-fixing schemes (including the one that inspired the 2009 film *The Informant!* starring Matt Damon), Andreas and his firm ruthlessly pursued worldwide dominance in the agricultural processing trade. In the 1980s ADM bought a 50-percent stake in Alfred C. Toepfer International, a purchase that secured ADM's place as one of the world's largest agricultural commodity-buying firms with transportation and logistics infrastructure spanning the globe. By the late 1980s, ADM's claims to be a "supermarket to the world" were far from empty rhetoric. With its ability to source raw materials from almost anywhere in the world and funnel them into nearly every processed food product sold on supermarket shelves, the company came to see itself "as a place where other big food people buy their groceries." The company gained fame for its advertisements on Sunday-morning political talk shows, but its extraordinary control over more concrete forms of marketing—transportation, logistics, distribution, processing—was the critical component of its success. As Dwayne Andreas knew, it was "big food people" who ran the show.[20]

Supermarkets—firms that both bought and sold "the groceries"—emerged as a central arbiter in this new economic world. In general supermarkets were late to the game of international expansion compared to other agribusinesses, with the important exception of the International Basic Economy Corporation. In the late 1960s and 1970s, IBEC continued its decades-long project of building American-style supermarkets around the world as part of its anticommunist crusade. Already well established in Venezuela, Argentina, Peru, and Italy, IBEC's supermarket division moved into El Salvador and began scouting possibilities in Spain in 1968. The following year IBEC's supermarkets rang up over $100 million in sales, with $3.9 million in profits, generated by a transnational network of forty-seven stores. A fire-bombing in Argentina had a "materially adverse effect on operations," but within two years the company's expansion was continuing unabated, with fifteen stores operating in Buenos Aires alone. The company's successes with exporting supermarkets to Latin America suggested to one business analyst in 1975 that supermarkets, if developed in a manner sensitive to local customs and consumer desires, could serve as a "tool of achieving modernization" in developing countries. This, of course, had been IBEC's plan ever since its first forays into Venezuela in 1947, although by the late 1960s the company's executives were paying more attention to the stores' bottom lines than to their potential for counterrevolutionary anticommunism.[21]

But 1975 also marked the arrival into Latin America of a much bigger player in international supermarketing than IBEC; the French food retailer Carrefour entered the Brazilian market that year. In 1982 Carrefour moved into Argentina, and by the 1990s it was spanning the globe, expanding into Eastern Europe, South and East Asia, Indonesia, Mexico, and Turkey. After quickly becoming a dominant company in French food retailing in the 1960s and 1970s, Carrefour came under pressure from the French government for taking food sales away from *Maman et Papa,* and furthermore could find few remaining domestic prospects in France's densely saturated retail system. So the company moved abroad. Its early incursions into South America proved a gold mine in the short term, but over time international profits failed to accumulate as rapidly as anticipated. Still, the company continued its global expansion campaigns, and in fact increased them after 1996, when the French government passed restrictions on the domestic growth of hypermarkets. By the end of the century the vast majority of the French company's stores were located outside France, although approximately half its sales were generated within its home country.[22]

Carrefour's transnational strategy, despite its apparent shortcomings, became a model for other major supermarket firms, including the Dutch firm Ahold, the German Metro Group, and U.S.-based Walmart. Latin America was a popular destination, but so were Eastern Europe and East Asia—any region that lacked a robust food retailing infrastructure was ripe for the picking by the 1990s. Even when profits were not forthcoming in a hypercompetitive environment beset by multiple multinational firms, supermarket executives felt compelled to expand abroad to secure market share for a presumably profitable future.[23]

If windfall profits did not accompany the rise of global supermarketing from the 1970s through the 1990s, what was the motivation? In an important sense, the oligopolistic structure of American-style supermarketing became a fundamental driver of these international expansion campaigns. Although certainly aided by "free trade" agendas emanating from the World Bank and the International Monetary Fund that liberalized foreign direct investment rules in developing countries, the rise of the global supermarket was not primarily driven by liberalized rules on foreign trade. The American supermarket's oligopolistic business model—in which a handful of big, centralized buyers operate in a world of many dispersed sellers—effectively necessitated globalization. Supermarkets relied on their centralized buying power to coordinate supply chains and stave off competition. Thus, a compulsion to continually expand the scale and scope of operations was inherent to the business model. As IBEC discovered in Venezuela in the 1940s, and as A&P and Kroger had discovered decades before them, once a distributor-retailer had built one distribution warehouse or field buying station, it effectively had to build dozens of retail stores to push groceries through the system and profit from high-volume, low-margin sales. If a firm had saturated its home market with retail stores, as Carrefour had done by the early 1970s, then it had to find new markets abroad—or else its competitors would.[24]

No corporation proved more dogged than Walmart in following this self-fulfilling logic of international expansion. Under the guidance of Sam Walton, the discount chain founded in Rogers, Arkansas, in 1962 became in the 1970s one of the most powerful retailers in the United States. With its initial focus on rural and small-town customers, Walmart confronted a significant logistical challenge—how to supply geographically dispersed stores with a high enough volume of goods to warrant deep discounts. In the late 1970s the company constructed an elaborate network of distribution centers. Connected by highways to retail outlets, the distribution centers pumped supplies with impressive efficiency to an ever-expanding collection of stores. The firm went an important step farther, relying on the recently created Universal Product Code (UPC; the barcode) along with computerized inventory management systems to pressure its suppliers into providing just-in-time, "always low price" goods on Walmart's terms. American retailing in the 1960s was generally highly fragmented, forcing many retailers to rely on price wars or unique services to attain market dominance. With the UPC and computerized logistics systems in the 1970s, however, retailers including Walmart increasingly found themselves empowered to dictate to suppliers what would be sold, when it would be sold, and at what price. Although crude in comparison to the highly sophisticated supply-chain management that Walmart would develop in later decades, by 1973 the firm had a centralized computer system in Bentonville, Arkansas, that was carefully tracking sales at twenty-two stores.[25]

The power of the information embedded in a universal barcode was apparent to the supermarketers who originally promoted its development. During a 1974 Senate symposium on the history and future of the UPC, the Kroger vice president Jack Strubbe declared the primary purpose of the code was to reduce labor costs by enabling higher productivity among checkout clerks. A consultant from McKinsey and Company likewise stressed that notion, although he hinted as an aside that "transaction information" gained from analyses of millions of purchases might allow retailers to have more control over product lines and pricing strategies. Included in the symposium's recorded testimony, however, was a survey of food manufacturers and processors, who announced that the UPC was nothing more than a tool for supermarkets to "exert . . . more and more control over the production and processing of foods."[26]

When Walmart moved into groceries beginning in the 1980s, it used its sophisticated supply-chain management to upend the supermarket industry in ways that A&P and Kroger executives could only have dreamed of in previous decades. Intriguingly, Sam Walton first considered the possibility of entering the grocery trade after a visit to Brazil, where he witnessed Carrefour's hypermarkets in action. When another French retailer, Euromarché, opened a hypermarket in Cincinnati, Walton decided it was time to launch his firm farther from its rural base and into the nation's suburbs. After luring top executives from existing supermarket firms, Walmart made its first foray into supermarketing in late 1987 with a store outside Dallas. As it had done with underwear and toothpaste, Walmart relied on its rural distribution centers to shuttle foodstuffs at utmost haste over the highways that led to its suburban supermarkets. By the end of the 1990s, the company's supply-chain management capabilities positioned it as the dominant supermarket in the United States. Between 1996 and 2001, the number of Supercenters—essentially hypermarkets that combined food and general merchandise sales—grew by 20 percent each year. A "new food economy" was the result, according to the food marketing expert Jean Kinsey, in which "independent producers and marketing firms" were now subject to "a set of integrated and highly managed supply chains." Walmart's competitors in the grocery field had to adopt similar supply-chain management or face elimination. Major supermarketing firms such as Kroger and Safeway pursued aggressive consolidation strategies in the 1990s, and the industry had become increasingly oligopolistic by the turn of the century.[27]

Walmart's geographic expansion and its move into groceries made launching out into international markets increasingly attractive to its top executives. It is tempting to see something more than mere coincidence in the fact that Walmart's International Division was created in the same year—1994—as the implementation of the North American Free Trade Agreement (NAFTA). By liberalizing trade and foreign investment rules among the United States, Canada, and Mexico, NAFTA undoubtedly made it easier for U.S.-based firms such as Walmart to cross borders. Yet pursuing "free trade" was not the agenda for Walmart's executives in 1994; as then-CEO David Glass explained to his managers, "We need to be the absolute dominant retail-wholesale club, the operator in all of North America[,] whatever it takes." Glass's suggestion of a "need" to be dominant could be attributed to a hypercompetitive managerial culture at Walmart—and the evidence of just such a culture has been well documented—but at a more fundamental level it speaks to the ways in which Walmart's structure essentially compelled it to grow, first from the rural Ozarks, then to the rural South and Midwest, then to American suburbs, and then across national boundaries. Indeed, as the historian Nelson Lichtenstein points out, Walmart's initial foray into Canada was effectively "an organic outgrowth of the company's expansion into the upper Midwest, New York State, and the Pacific Northwest." With distribution centers already positioned within short tractor-trailer driving distance of potential Canadian locations, Walmart's executives—or, for that matter, those at competing firms such as Costco—would have to have been asleep at the wheel not to make the cross-border leap.[28]

Market power was both the motivation for and the result of Walmart's international transformation. Over the course of the 1990s Walmart moved even farther afield, pursuing joint ventures and contract arrangements in China, Mexico, Indonesia, and Brazil alongside its wholly owned operations in Argentina and Puerto Rico. Summing up the situation, trade paper *Discount Store News* noted in 1997 that the company was "playing for strategic positioning on a global scale." Because it was "already a master of worldwide sourcing," the company's executives were "determined to seize the initiative internationally on the retailing side." Walmart's struggles to export its retail format outside North America have been the subject of much study, including its disastrous 1997 German campaign, its unimpressive performance in Japan, and its sometimes comical efforts to merge Ozark capitalism with Chinese retailing. Neither Walmart nor any other retailer is omnipotent; regulatory structures, well-supported labor unions, and cultural differences between managers and targeted customers can clearly throw a wrench into even the best-oiled corporate marketing machinery. But to focus solely on Walmart as a retailer when it is in fact a distributor-retailer can lead us astray—as *Discount Store News* noted in 1997, the firm's international move was a result not primarily of a retail strategy but instead of an effort to bring its mastery of "worldwide sourcing" to bear on as much of the globe as it could link up to its distribution network. Perhaps Walmart's managers were not always the most adept retailers, but they were unquestionably world leaders in tightening the strictures of the global supply chains that fed their stores around the world.[29]

As U.S.-based multinationals aggressively pursued global market power from the 1970s on, the political, quasi-military impetus behind the Farms Race increasingly gave way to a purely economic race for control of global supply chains. As a consequence, transnational supermarkets effectively became central gatekeepers in the world of global agribusiness. With their centralized buying power, transnational supermarkets increasingly engaged in worldwide food sourcing practices that defied the existence of nation-states. The kind of "food power" that American foreign policy makers dreamed of (briefly) in the 1970s was in effect placed in the hands of transnational supermarkets and their agribusiness suppliers. Through partnerships, mergers and acquisitions, interlinked inventory management systems, licensing arrangements, and contractual agreements, transnational food corporations developed centralized coordination tools that made national efforts at agricultural supply management seem pitifully ham-fisted in comparison. As the work of global commodity-chains analysts suggests, in an economic world driven by buyers rather than by producers of goods, the practice of "governance" becomes decentralized as much as it becomes privatized. Retailer-distributors, who derived their profits not from economies of scale or Fordist production efficiencies but from efficient marketing, came to "act as strategic brokers" in linking producers to consumers. The rules of the global supply chain, in other words, came increasingly to be written dynamically, privately, and transnationally. Government-structured trade rules, tariffs, and subsidies remained part of the regulatory environment, but so did retailers' contractual specifications to suppliers.[30]

Take, for example, the extraordinary success of U.K. food retailers in wielding oligopsony power to transform food chains in the 1980s and beyond. From the mid-1950s until the era of Margaret Thatcher, the Ministry of Agriculture, Fisheries, and Food (MAFF) was responsible for most regulatory policies affecting farmers, food processors and retailers, and consumers. Much as in the United States, agricultural concerns—determined in the British case by the National Farmers Union—dominated MAFF's priorities. Regulatory oversight of retailers did not extend into antitrust, however; the exceptional concentration of U.K. supermarketing in the 1960s and 1970s was in part a result of a consciously hands-off approach by Britain's regulatory commissions, which permitted and even abetted the rapid consolidation of food retailing in the hands of a few players. But in Margaret Thatcher's 1980s, Britain's dominant food retailers, Tesco and Sainsbury's, capitalized on an even more self-conscious withdrawal of the regulatory state. Key aspects of British food regulatory oversight—including food safety, agricultural pricing, and environmental impacts—were effectively left up to private corporations. What could be understood as deregulation was in reality a form of re-regulation, a shift in governance power from public to private institutions.[31]

As Thatcherites reduced MAFF's authority in the 1980s, British food retailers moved into the power vacuum. For British farmers, one consequence was a push to join marketing cooperatives as food retailers wielded their buying power to demand reliable supplies at prices and quality levels determined not by state agencies but by the retailers themselves. Such practices were not entirely a result of Thatcherism. For decades before Thatcher's rise to power, for instance, British retailers had used specifications and contracts to create—essentially from scratch—an industrialized chicken suited precisely to U.K. supermarket chain demands, without requiring the kind of state support of technical research enjoyed by U.S. supermarkets during the 1940s Chicken of Tomorrow campaigns. But in the 1980s Tesco and Sainsbury's went farther still, tightly coordinating British agricultural production and developing contractual relations with farmer cooperatives in continental Europe. Continued expansion brought U.K. retailers into Africa in the 1990s, where, as the geographer Susanne Freidberg has shown, supermarket produce buyers did to Zambian green bean growers what they had done to British chicken producers. Through carefully policed contractual arrangements that forced Zambian farmers to accustom themselves to a corporate vision of "continuing improvement," British supermarket agents constructed a vertically integrated, foreign-financed (white-run) agribusiness that provided Tesco and Sainsbury's shoppers with fat, blemish-free green beans airlifted nightly into Great Britain.[32]

Many, if not most, of the world's farmers have experienced the power of multinational supermarkets since the 1980s. Contracts and specifications provide transnational food corporations with power, a power that is amplified greatly by the extraordinary mobility of agricultural sourcing. In a 1993 essay, John Woodhouse, president of institutional food supplier Sysco, highlighted what he saw as a sharp break between the food-supply chains of the 1970s and of his own time. In the 1970s, Woodhouse noted, a company like Sysco looked abroad for only two kinds of food products: "the dirty and undesirable labor-intensive products, like raising and cultivating mushrooms, or harvesting pineapples," and foods that could grow only in specific climatic or soil conditions not available in the United States (bananas, mangoes). Yet by the 1990s, Woodhouse continued, Sysco could easily turn to Mexico or Central America for most of its frozen broccoli and peas. Rather than import underpaid migrant workers to California to pick and pack the produce, Sysco moved the plants south. The packing operations were "disassembled . . . put on barges, shipped down to the West Pacific Coast ports of Mexico and Central America, trucked into the interior, and set up," where "low wage rates and the labor you can utilize" provided Sysco with "just as superior a product" at much lower prices. Woodhouse's description of the process of capital flight made no room for the voices of the Central American workers or farmers whose lives must have been transformed by the sudden arrival of quick-freezing plants, though presumably his openly self-congratulatory rhetoric could easily have been interpreted as a veiled threat to put the plants on barges yet again if cheaper labor could be found elsewhere.[33]

Peripatetic sourcing in fact became the norm in the era of the global supermarket. British retailers were especially innovative; in 1990

Tesco created an "exotic fruit" team to scout out potential suppliers of mangoes, avocadoes, papayas, and so forth that could be sold at high margins. Applying specification-buying practices in contractual relations with farmers in the global South, U.K. retailers set all the important ground rules on the farm—including everything from soil-preparation techniques to specific amounts and timing of fertilizer and pesticide applications. Importantly, such reliance on contract farming allowed the British retailers to pay growers only for the fruits that fit their needs, rather than for the number of hours worked. And those needs were elaborately specified, including rules on the fruits' weight, firmness, blemishes, and precise dates of delivery. Other European supermarket chains followed suit, as when the Dutch firm Ahold established contractual relations with Guatemalan farmers in the 1990s. One cooperative of small-scale Guatemalan farmers operating under the Spanish acronym Asumpal informed a *New York Times* reporter in 2004 that in the beginning, sales of produce to Dutch supermarkets seemed promising. But as Ahold's executives ratcheted up expectations—calling for the farmers to install greenhouses, drip irrigation, and pest-control protocols to ensure more consistent volumes and quality—the cooperative was unable to keep up and lost its contract. "Supermarkets and their privately set standards," suggested the *Times* report, "loom larger for many farmers than the rules of the World Trade Organization." Or, as a spokesman for the Ahold chain openly acknowledged, "We punish farmers very hard if they don't deliver what we order."[34]

At the height of the Farms Race from the 1940s to the 1960s, American organizations promoting agricultural "modernization" around the globe declared that feeding the hungry world was the politically just and economically rewarding thing to do. By the 1990s, supermarket-driven agricultural modernization in developing countries was clearly focused on the latter half of that equation. Supermarkets sourcing exotic fruit or frozen baby peas from the global South undoubtedly helped some farmers raise their living standards; in Guatemala, for instance, the *New York Times* found one group of small farmers whose "freshly painted homes and well-clothed children" were a result of exporting baby vegetables to U.S. supermarkets rather than to local Dutch-owned stores. But such instances of localized success could also be read as highlighting the stunning mobility of agricultural supply chains. Were those U.S. buyers to find cheaper baby vegetables in another locale, the fresh paint on those Guatemalan farmers' homes might fade as they scrambled to find a new buyer— only to discover that there are, in fact, just a handful of big buyers in the oligopolistic world of agribusiness.[35]

The economist C. Peter Timmer has suggested that supermarket-driven agricultural supply chains exemplify Joseph Schumpeter's concept of "creative destruction." In Timmer's view, Schumpeter's phrase carries more positive than negative connotations. As development tools, Timmer argues, "Supermarkets are simply a vehicle for the transmission of new information and communication technologies into developing countries," with the power to "boost productivity in rich countries and poor alike." Although in the short- and medium-term time frame supermarkets' demands on global South farmers might result in "a highly unequal process of economic growth," in the long run those farmers will be better prepared to parlay their new-found skills into higher-paying urban nonfarm jobs. Such notions seem strikingly similar to the arguments of modernization theorists in the 1950s and 1960s. In those earlier decades, the Cold War–inflected worldview of Walt Rostow and Norman Borlaug ("father of the Green Revolution"), among others, drove the promotion of agricultural development as a tool for shocking the world's recalcitrant peasants into urban-industrial capitalism.[36]

The similarities raise an important question—should the rise of the global supermarket and the multinational agribusiness supply chain of the late twentieth century be understood as a departure from the economic contests of the Cold War or as a product of those contests? Debates over the periodization of the economic contours of the Cold War have produced an impressive body of scholarship. Recent works focusing on the specific relationships among development ideology, modernization theory, and the Cold War, for instance, have suggested that the core concepts of "modernization" were well in place decades before the Cold War began and continued to influence the actions of nongovernmental organizations for decades after the Cold War "consensus" splintered in the 1970s. Others have called into question the very idea of the Cold War, suggesting that the economic transformations of the mid- to late twentieth century owed more to the triumph of "rational choice liberalism" or the logic of "globalization" than to any specific confrontation between the superpowers.[37]

In this book, I have attempted to navigate a somewhat different course from these primarily intellectual and diplomatic histories. While much of what I call the Farms Race was a product of rhetoric and ideology, the concrete embodiments of that rhetoric—the farms, supermarkets, and agribusiness corporations that actually ran the race—suggest that the Cold War can and should be understood as fundamentally an economic contest over living standards. Sometimes that war was waged with words and symbols, as with the verbal sparring between Richard Nixon and Nikita Khrushchev at the 1959 Kitchen Debate, but far more often the battles took place in farm fields, in shopping carts, and in corporate offices. The American supermarket could be touted as an exportable agent of "free enterprise" in the Cold War only after it had been built upon the structure of state-supported industrialized agriculture. Likewise, in the late twentieth century, the supermarket could be seen as an agent of neoliberal globalization only because of the oligopsonistic business practices that supermarketers had developed over the course of the Cold War. When viewed from the ground up, the economic Cold War did not determine the shape of the post–Cold War economic world. But neither can the patterns laid down during the Cold War be divorced from the multinational corporation-dominated economic world that emerged in the years after the Soviet Union's demise.

Epilogue

The Indian prime minister Manmohan Singh announced in 2011 that for the first time, multinational supermarkets, including Walmart and Tesco, would be allowed to pursue business in his country. For several years Walmart had been knocking on India's door, urging political leaders to overturn long-standing legislation intended to protect family-owned small-scale retailers from foreign competition. As part of the push to reform India's restrictions on foreign direct investment in retailing, Walmart had engaged in a technical assistance campaign—we could view it as a "private Point Four" program (echoing a term often applied to Nelson Rockefeller's International Basic Economy Corporation)—meant to help farmers meet the demands of a supermarket-driven supply chain. When Singh opened the gates to multinational supermarkets, Walmart already had the beginnings of an industrial agricultural supply chain in place, and it was ready to demonstrate how its food distribution system could raise farm prices while bringing consumer costs down.[1]

The power, ambition, and reach of Walmart's approach to the grocery business would have astounded the mid-twentieth-century executives of A&P. In the 1940s, A&P relied on a teletype network to convey information to and from its centralized buying headquarters through its decentralized purchasing network; Walmart today relies upon supercomputer-driven data centers running algorithms of indescribable complexity, transmitting data by fiber-optic cable and satellites through a purchasing and distribution system of unprecedented scale and scope. Even at A&P's height of success it was far from a major multinational corporation, and in fact A&P did not even try to compete in several important regions of the United States; Walmart by contrast is today omnipresent in American retailing and is one of the world's largest multinational corporations, with substantial retail operations in more than two dozen countries. If it is hard for some to imagine a Walmart in Delhi, it would be far harder still to envision an A&P there.

The example of Walmart's entry into India suggests several ways in which the contemporary world of global agribusiness differs substantially from the age of the Cold War Farms Race. First, Walmart launched its campaign in India from the farmscape forward—starting from its strategic position of strength in supply-chain management—not from the retail box backward into the farmscape. This was canny public relations in a country dominated by a large and democratically engaged rural citizenry, but it also provides a marked contrast to the struggles that midcentury supermarket chains such as A&P faced as they sought to convince farmers of the benefits of concentrated buying power. Walmart's courting of India was furthermore framed by an open embrace of agricultural development as a nonideological tool for economic growth, quite unlike the rhetoric of the Cold War era, when agricultural development was widely understood as a weapon against communism—especially the imaginary but fearsome communism that modernization theorists assumed the peoples of developing nations would adopt if they remained hungry. Finally, the fact that India's political leaders capitulated to the demands of a handful of multinational retailer-distributors seems to suggest that the sovereignty of nation-states—crucial to the politics of the Cold War era—might in the twenty-first century be withering under the relentless drive of neoliberalism's globalizing forces.

Yet for all the change apparent in the post–Cold War era of economic globalization, deep continuities can also be traced from the world of the midcentury Farms Race through to the rise of the post-1990s global supermarket. Walmart, like A&P before it, would not be able to profitably deploy its sophisticated techniques of supply-chain management were it not for the significant government investments in agricultural productivity that enable its business model. Neoliberalism, if it even warrants its own appellation as a historic trend, depends as much upon the exercise of state power as did the construction of an industrialized agricultural supply chain in the early twentieth century. Walmart needs the same kind of state investments in chemical agriculture, confined animal feeding operations, and biological interventions in plant and animal organisms that enabled the successes of A&P, Kroger, and Safeway in earlier decades. Neoliberalism, like liberalism, derives from state power, though the latter pretends to ignore government influence while the former rejects it ideologically if not in practice. "Free enterprise," consistently placed within ironic scare quotes throughout this book, was a fiction perpetrated most forcefully during the Cold War, when the pretense of a laissez-faire "weak state" was crucial for staking out a moral high ground against communist centralized planning, yet was actively denied in practice by powerful government agents and corporate allies intent upon firing figurative torpedoes against the foundations of communism.[2]

Even when economic development is framed as an apolitical exercise, as Walmart did in early-twenty-first-century forays into Indian food retailing, no objective observer could deny that such actions were inherently political exercises of power. As the anthropologist James Ferguson presciently noted in his 1990 examination of the "anti-politics machine" of economic development in Lesotho, the claims of being "apolitical" that are often touted by both public and private enterprises engaged in rural development schemes seem to follow a remarkably repetitive cycle. The purported goals of development—to produce rural economic stability, promote the rise of middle-class consumerism, and justify the existence of nation-states that have guided those economic outcomes—often seem to result in the entrenchment of existing economic and political power structures.[3]

As I have gone to some lengths to illustrate, the globalizing practices of multinational agribusinesses did not emerge from an inherent logic of capitalist enterprise. Supermarkets were invented in the United States, where they benefited from state support for their supposedly "free enterprise" business model. Beginning with Nelson Rockefeller's forays into Venezuelan food distribution in 1947, that business model was exported with the explicit aim of profiting from deploying the "weaponry" of the Farms Race. A decade later, Supermarket USA airlifted ten thousand square feet of consumer capitalism into Yugoslavia with much the same motivation. Though the path from the Farms Race to the post–Cold War global supermarket was neither straight nor direct, the ideological apparatus and concrete actions of midcentury economic Cold Warriors undoubtedly paved the way for the rise of multinational agribusinesses.

A deep irony thus seems infused into the contemporary global food system. Expanding consumer choice and protecting producer autonomy were the primary justifications for the actions of American businesses and government policy makers in the Cold War Farms Race. The structures of today's world food marketplace that have been built upon those Cold War foundations, however, seem in many ways to constrain the ability of farmers and consumers to make choices.

Consider contemporary Venezuela. A robust network of modern supermarkets continued to operate in Venezuela long after IBEC sold its retail operations there in the 1970s. As of 2015, the country had more than 1,500 privately owned supermarkets. But the mere existence of American-style food retailers has never produced the economic stability imagined by IBEC executives during the Cold War. Venezuela's economy is still anchored by petroleum exports, and its supermarkets remain heavily dependent upon imported foodstuffs. Government price controls, rationing, and subsidies instituted under the populist leaders Hugo Chávez and Nicolás Maduro have helped to keep staple foods affordable for average Venezuelans in retail shops. In 2015, in fact, the Food and Agriculture Organization upheld Venezuela as a case study in achieving "food sovereignty" by effectively eliminating hunger nationwide. But particularly during times of low world oil prices, those state policies also contribute to shortages that regularly force consumers to endure excruciating waiting times to purchase packaged staple products sold by large domestic agribusinesses, including Polar (the country's largest food company). Critics of Chávez and Maduro, both domestically and abroad, have repeatedly seized upon these shortages in recent years as evidence of government incompetence or even malfeasance. At the same time, Venezuela is effectively self-sufficient in its production of fruits and vegetables, which are primarily grown by small-scale farmers and distributed in the country's street markets or in its more than 160,000 small-scale *Madre-y-Padre* abastos and bodegas. To exercise choice and autonomy in the contemporary Venezuelan food economy thus requires that both consumers and farmers navigate an extraordinarily complex, psychologically draining marketplace, in which government policy makers and private enterprises struggle—sometimes directly against each other—to effectively coordinate food supplies in an intensely politicized economic environment. It is certainly not the case that the mere existence of large supermarkets and vertically integrated agribusinesses has either revolutionized or counterrevolutionized the nation's food economy.[4]

In the formerly socialist countries of central and eastern Europe, meanwhile, capitalist supermarkets likewise anchor agrifood systems in which consumer choice and producer autonomy remain deeply contested. After the end of the Cold War, private supermarkets rapidly spread throughout these regions. Some domestic chains flourished, such as Konzum in Croatia, Bosnia and Herzegovina, and Serbia, and Magnit in Russia. Western European chains, however, also made significant inroads, including German firms (Metro Group, Lidl, Aldi), Dutch Interspar (SPAR), and the United Kingdom's Tesco. Fierce competition among both domestic and foreign chains has led to a proliferation of retail formats. Increasingly prominent has been the streamlined sourcing strategy of discounters such as Lidl and Aldi, which stock between one thousand and three thousand lines in their stores, in stark contrast with the more than fifty thousand offerings generally carried by hypermarkets. The new breed of discount retailers pursue hyper-focused, sophisticated supply-chain management techniques, driving aggressively hard bargains on price and quality with suppliers. For consumers who remember the shortages and queues of the socialist era, the propagation of multinational supermarkets selling a tremendous array of different food products at a wide range of price points no doubt offers a strong sense of autonomy and choice. Among some central and eastern European farmers, however, the expansion of multinational retailers and their tough approach to supply-chain management has increasingly sparked protests in recent years. Farmers convinced that foreign supermarkets are to blame for dropping food prices have helped convince legislators in countries including Poland, Hungary, Slovakia, and Romania to implement special taxation, packaging, and local procurement requirements on foreign retailers, in apparent contravention of European Commission rules on trade liberalization. Multinational agribusiness is now a fact of life in the formerly socialist states of central and eastern Europe, but the extent to which that can be interpreted as a victory of "free enterprise" remains deeply uncertain.[5]

Many citizens in the supermarket's home country of the United States also continue to question the consequences of agribusiness-driven food systems that depend on industrialized agriculture. Perhaps most notable has been the rise of the local-food movement, evidenced by a rapid proliferation since the mid-2000s of urban farmers' markets, Community Supported Agriculture schemes, city community gardens, and even front-yard farming. Locavores see the supermarket-driven food chain as a destroyer of small-scale rural economies, a standardizer of the taste and aesthetic variety of various foods, and a threat to environmental sustainability and animal welfare. Supermarket chains ranging from Walmart to Whole Foods have responded to such criticisms by implementing sustainability schemes within their supply-chain management practices, and in some cases have significantly increased their reliance on local suppliers. Supermarket critics will rightly point out that such practices are often overhyped and misleading; so-called local food products sometimes travel hundreds of miles before arriving at a store. Critics of the local-food movement, meanwhile, can also rightly point out that locavorism is generally most easily practiced by affluent consumers, and all too often relies upon assumptions that women must disproportionately bear the moral responsibility and added workload of finding and buying such food. It is far from possible to resolve this debate in a brief epilogue. But it is worth noting that both proponents and opponents of supermarket-anchored food systems tend to rely on similar assumptions about consumer choice and sovereignty. Locavores suggest in words and deeds that only individual consumers have the power to break the "logic" of the industrial agrifood system, while agribusiness defenders suggest that corporations are simply delivering on the aggregate demands of billions of individual consumers. Both sides, in other words, seem to have so thoroughly accepted the Cold War Farms Race's rhetorical proclamations of American food as a product of free enterprise and consumer sovereignty that our contemporary political discourse continues to be impoverished, devoid of policy proscriptions robust enough to move beyond easily caricatured dichotomies. Long after the formal end of the Cold War, our language about food systems is still permeated by the problematic assumptions of a bygone era.[6]

Finally, it is worth considering the very real possibility that the post–Cold War era of globalization will someday seem as absurd as the 1950s propaganda film featuring the incredulous British socialist losing his political bearing in an American supermarket. Walmart is currently open for business in India, but so far the company operates only a handful of wholesale (not retail) stores. Tesco, the supermarket chain that for decades pursued internationalization just as aggressively as Walmart and Carrefour, recently announced plans to pull back to its home base in the United Kingdom. In feuds with the European Union, Russian leader Vladimir Putin has urged citizens to reject Western food supplies and rely instead on local, organic, patriotically Russian farms. As of this writing, the announcement by high-tech firm Amazon that it would acquire the Whole Foods supermarket chain pushed more than one journalist to spout hyperbolic claims of a coming "revolution" in food retailing; terms such as "bloodbath," "grocery war," and "conquering army" have been bandied about wantonly. Supermarkets continue to be instruments of incredible power in the world's agricultural landscapes and food marketplaces, but, as has always been the case, that power remains a product of human choices and actions. We might hope that in the future those choices and actions could be framed in something other than militaristic terms.[7]

Notes

Abbreviations

IBEC International Basic Economy Corporation Records
   J Series: IBEC-J
   R Series: IBEC-R

NARA-II National Archives and Records Administration II, College Park, Md.
   RG 489, Entry 22, Records of the Office of International Trade Fairs
   (RG 489, Entry 22)
   RG 16, Entry 17, Records of the Secretary of Agriculture, General Cor-
   respondence (RG 16, Entry 17)

RAC Rockefeller Archive Center, Sleepy Hollow, N.Y.
   Nelson A. Rockefeller Papers, Series A, Record Group 4 (RG 4-A)
   Nelson A. Rockefeller Papers, Series B, Record Group 4 (RG 4-B)

RFERLRI Records of Radio Free Europe/Radio Liberty Research Institute, Buda-
   pest, Hungary
   Open Society Archives (OSA)
   Subfonds 2, East European Research and Analysis Department, Series 1,
   Subject Files Relating to the Bloc (Subfonds 2, Series 1)
   Subfonds 7, U.S. Office, Series 8, Subject Files Relating to Yugoslavia
   (Subfonds 7, Series 8)
   Subfonds 8, Publications Department, Series 3, Background Reports
   (Subfonds 8, Series 3)

Introduction

1. *America's Distribution of Wealth,* prod. National Education Program, film, 12 min., 1955, available at http://www.archive.org/details/Americas1955 (accessed April 20, 2010).

2. Piggly Wiggly Southern, Inc., *Free Enterprise,* dir. Hal Geer, 16 mm. film, 15 min., 1975, Herman E. Talmadge Collection, Audiovisual Materials, UC 0225, Richard B. Russell Library for Political Research and Studies, Athens, Ga.

3. Victoria de Grazia, "Changing Consumption Regimes in Europe, 1930–1970: Comparative Perspectives on the Distribution Problem," in *Getting and Spending: European and American Consumer Societies in the Twentieth Century,* ed. Susan Strasser, Charles F. McGovern, and Matthias Judt, 59–83 (Cambridge: Cambridge University Press, 1998), 59. On the "artificial division" between production and consumption in much recent historical work, see Gary S. Cross and Robert Proctor, *Packaged Pleasures: How Technology and Marketing Revolutionized Desire* (Chicago: University of Chicago Press, 2014). Historical studies of supply chains remain relatively rare, but some notable recent works that refuse to divorce production from consumption include Richard P. Tucker, *Insatiable Appetite: The United States and the Ecological Degradation of the Tropical World* (Berkeley: University of California Press, 2000); Mark R. Finlay, *Growing American Rubber: Strategic Plants and the Politics of National Security* (New Brunswick, N.J.: Rutgers University Press, 2010); Bartow J. Elmore, *Citizen Coke: The Making of Coca-Cola Capitalism* (New York: Norton, 2014); Gregory T. Cushman, *Guano and the Opening of the Pacific World: A Global Ecological History* (New York: Cambridge University Press, 2013). One historical study that directly acknowledges the role of supermarkets in shaping agricultural practice is Fernando Collantes, "Food Chains and the Retailing Revolution: Supermarkets, Dairy Processors and Consumers in Spain," *Business History* 58, no. 7 (2016): 1055–76.

4. "Grocer Sees Food Winning Cold War," *New York Times,* Aug. 13, 1953, 15.

5. W. W. Rostow, "Marx Was a City Boy; or, Why Communism May Fail," *Harper's,* Feb. 1955, 30.

6. On American supermarkets, see especially Tracey A. Deutsch, *Building a Housewife's Paradise: Gender, Politics, and American Grocery Stores in the Twentieth Century* (Chapel Hill: University of North Carolina Press, 2010); Marc Levinson, *The Great A&P and the Struggle for Small Business in America* (New York: Hill and Wang, 2011); James M. Mayo, *The American Grocery Store: The Business Evolution of an Architectural Space* (Westport, Conn.: Greenwood Press, 1993); Richard S. Tedlow, *New and Improved: The Story of Mass Marketing in America* (New York: Basic, 1990); Sharon Zukin, *Point of Purchase: How Shopping Changed American Culture* (New York: Routledge, 2004); Adam Mack, "Good Things to Eat in Suburbia: Supermarkets and American Consumer Culture, 1930–1970" (Ph.D. diss., University of South Carolina, 2006); William Applebaum, *Super Marketing: The Past, the Present, a Projection* (Chicago: Super Market Institute, 1969). International studies of supermarket business history include Gareth Shaw, Louise Curth, and Andrew Alexander, "Selling Self-Service and the Supermarket: The Americanisation of Food Retailing in Britain,

1945–1960," *Business History* 46 (Oct. 2004): 568–82; Andrew Alexander et al., "The Co-Creation of a Retail Innovation: Shoppers and the Early Supermarket in Britain," *Enterprise & Society* 10 (Sept. 2009): 529–58; Bridget Williams, *The Best Butter in the World: A History of Sainsbury's* (London: Ebury Press, 1994); Joanna Blythman, *Shopped: The Shocking Power of British Supermarkets* (London: Fourth Estate, 2004); Kim Humphery, *Shelf Life: Supermarkets and the Changing Cultures of Consumption* (Cambridge: Cambridge University Press, 1998).

7. On the Cold War as economic contest, see David C. Engerman, "The Romance of Economic Development and New Histories of the Cold War," *Diplomatic History* 28 (Jan. 2004): 24–54; Alfred E. Eckes, Jr., and Thomas W. Zeiler, *Globalization and the American Century* (New York: Cambridge University Press, 2003); Joel Isaac and Duncan Bell, eds., *Uncertain Empire: American History and the Idea of the Cold War* (New York: Oxford University Press, 2012); Nick Cullather, "The War on the Peasant: The United States and the Third World," in *The Cold War in the Third World*, ed. Robert J. McMahon, 192–207 (New York: Oxford University Press, 2013); Kenneth Osgood, *Total Cold War: Eisenhower's Secret Propaganda Battle at Home and Abroad* (Lawrence: University Press of Kansas, 2006); Laura A. Belmonte, *Selling the American Way: U.S. Propaganda and the Cold War* (Philadelphia: University of Pennsylvania Press, 2008); Jacqueline McGlade, "More a Plowshare than a Sword: The Legacy of US Cold War Agricultural Diplomacy," *Agricultural History* 83 (Winter 2009): 79–102; Zachary Karabell, *The Leading Indicators: A Short History of the Numbers That Rule Our World* (New York: Simon and Schuster, 2014); Geir Lundestad, *The Rise and Decline of the American "Empire": Power and Its Limits in Comparative Perspective* (New York: Oxford University Press, 2012); William M. McClenahan, Jr., and William H. Becker, *Eisenhower and the Cold War Economy* (Baltimore: Johns Hopkins University Press, 2011). On supermarkets and "Americanization," see Emanuela Scarpellini, "Shopping American-Style: The Arrival of the Supermarket in Postwar Italy," *Enterprise & Society* 5 (Dec. 2004): 625–68; Victoria de Grazia, *Irresistible Empire: America's Advance Through Twentieth-Century Europe* (Cambridge: Harvard University Press, 2005), 376–415; Shaw et al., "Selling Self-Service"; Rachel Bowlby, *Carried Away: The Invention of Modern Shopping* (New York: Columbia University Press, 2001). Entry points to the substantial literature on Americanization include Jessica C. E. Gienow-Hecht, "Always Blame the Americans: Anti-Americanism in Europe in the Twentieth Century," *American Historical Review* 111 (Oct. 2006): 1067–91; Matthias Kipping and Ove Bjarnar, eds., *The Americanisation of European Business: The Marshall Plan and the Transfer of U.S. Management Models* (London: Routledge, 1998); Jan Logemann,

Trams or Tailfins? Public and Private Prosperity in Postwar West Germany and the United States (Chicago: University of Chicago Press, 2012); Emily S. Rosenberg, *Spreading the American Dream: American Economic and Cultural Expansion, 1890–1945* (New York: Hill and Wang, 1982); Olivier Zunz, *Why the American Century?* (Chicago: University of Chicago Press, 1998); William H. Marling, *How "American" Is Globalization?* (Baltimore: Johns Hopkins University Press, 2006); Mona Domosh, *American Commodities in an Age of Empire* (New York: Routledge, 2006).

Chapter 1. Machines for Selling

1. "The Great A&P," *Fortune*, Nov. 1947, 102.

2. Godfrey M. Lebhar, *Chain Stores in America, 1859–1959* (New York: Chain Store Publishing, 1959); Susan V. Spellman, *Cornering the Market: Independent Grocers and Innovation in American Small Business* (Oxford: Oxford University Press, 2016); Richard S. Tedlow, *New and Improved: The Story of Mass Marketing in America* (New York: Basic, 1990), 214–26; Marc Levinson, *The Great A&P and the Struggle for Small Business in America* (New York: Hill and Wang, 2011), 211, 257; Jonathan J. Bean, *Beyond the Broker State: Federal Policies Toward Small Business, 1936–1961* (Chapel Hill: University of North Carolina Press, 1996), 17–36; Carl G. Ryant, "The South and the Movement Against Chain Stores," *Journal of Southern History* 39 (May 1973): 207–22; Joseph Palamountain, *The Politics of Distribution* (Cambridge: Harvard University Press, 1955).

3. Federal Trade Commission, *Chain Stores, Final Reports on the Chain-Store Investigation, S. Doc. 4,* 74th Cong., 1st sess., 1935, 16; Robert J. Thornton, "How Joan Robinson and B. L. Hallward Named Monopsony," *Journal of Economic Perspectives* 18 (Spring 2004): 257–61; Joan Robinson, *The Economics of Imperfect Competition* (London: Macmillan, 1933), 211–31. As Robinson knew, instances of pure monopsony—in which only one buyer dominates an entire market—are rare; government military procurement during wartime is the most obvious example: see Mark R. Wilson, *Destructive Creation: American Business and the Winning of World War II* (Philadelphia: University of Pennsylvania Press, 2016). Far more common is oligopsony, in which several large buyers set market conditions; for an excellent historical analysis of oligopsony in action see Barbara Hahn, *Making Tobacco Bright: Creating an American Commodity, 1617–1937* (Baltimore: Johns Hopkins University Press, 2011).

4. Daniel Scroop, "The Anti-Chain Store Movement and the Politics of Consumption," *American Quarterly* 60 (Dec. 2008): 925–49; Nancy Beck Young, *Wright Patman: Populism, Liberalism, and the American Dream* (Dallas: Southern Methodist

NOTES TO PAGES 11-16

University Press, 2000); Gabrielle Esperdy, *Modernizing Main Street: Architecture and Consumer Culture in the New Deal* (Chicago: University of Chicago Press, 2008), 37–44; Bean, *Beyond the Broker State,* 40–41; Tedlow, *New and Improved,* 214; Federal Trade Commission, *Chain Stores, Final Reports on the Chain-Store Investigation.*

5. Federal Trade Commission, Schedule for Chain Stores, Great Atlantic and Pacific Tea Co., June 15, 1929, Box 113, Folder Gre 3, RG 122, FTC Records, PI 7 Entry 7, Economic Investigations File, National Archives and Records Administration II (hereafter NARA-II), College Park, Md.; Walter Page Hedden, *How Great Cities Are Fed* (Boston: D. C. Heath, 1929), 196; Levinson, *Great A&P,* 104.

6. Clarence Saunders, U.S. Patent 1242872A, "Self-Serving Store," Oct. 9, 1917, 1, 2, 3. Tracey A. Deutsch, *Building a Housewife's Paradise: Gender, Politics, and American Grocery Stores in the Twentieth Century* (Chapel Hill: University of North Carolina Press, 2010), 13–42; Helen Tangires, *Public Markets and Civic Culture in Nineteenth-Century America* (Baltimore: Johns Hopkins University Press, 2003); Rowena Olegario, *A Culture of Credit: Embedding Trust and Transparency in American Business* (Cambridge: Harvard University Press, 2006); Lisa C. Tolbert, "The Aristocracy of the Market Basket: Self-Service Food Shopping in the New South," in *Food Chains: From Farmyard to Shopping Cart,* ed. Warren J. Belasco and Roger Horowitz (Philadelphia: University of Pennsylvania Press, 2009), 179–95. For an insightful analysis of how self-service spread throughout the trade, see Franck Cochoy, "'How to Build Displays That Sell': The Politics of Performativity in American Grocery Stores," *Journal of Cultural Economy* 3 (July 2010): 299–315.

7. Tedlow, *New and Improved,* 226–35; Charles F. Phillips, "The Supermarket," *Harvard Business Review* 16 (Winter 1938): 190–91.

8. William I. Walsh, *The Rise and Decline of the Great Atlantic & Pacific Tea Company* (Secaucus, N.J.: L. Stuart, 1986), 47–49; House Committee on Ways and Means, *Excise Tax on Retail Stores, Vol. 1, Hearing,* 76th Cong., 3d sess., March 27–30, April 1–5, 8–11, 1940; Levinson, *Great A&P,* 198–226.

9. Roland Marchand, "Suspended in Time: Mom-and-Pop Groceries, Chain Stores, and National Advertising During the World War II Interlude," in *Produce and Conserve, Share and Play Square: The Grocer and the Consumer on the Home-Front Battlefield During World War II,* ed. Barbara McLean Ward (Hanover, N.H.: University Press of New England, 1994), 117–39; "Food Prices of Chains and Independents Since GMPR," n.d. [March 1943], Box 71, Food Prices in Chain and Independent Stores Folder, RG 188, Office of Price Administration Records, Entry 129, Food Programs Branch, Division of Research, Subject Files, NARA-II.

10. So much has been written about the A&P antitrust case that this note could easily consume an entire book's worth of space. Among the best introductions to the case are Levinson, *Great A&P,* 220–34; M. A. Adelman, "The Great A&P Muddle," *Fortune,* Dec. 1949, 122–25, 178–80; Joel B. Dirlam and Alfred E. Kahn, "Antitrust Law and the Big Buyer: Another Look at the A & P Case," *Journal of Political Economy* 60 (April 1952): 118–32.

11. Shane Hamilton, "Supermarkets, Free Markets, and the Problem of Buyer Power in the Postwar United States," in *What's Good for Business: Business and American Politics Since World War II,* ed. Kim Phillips-Fein and Julian Zelizer, 177–94 (New York: Oxford University Press, 2012).

12. The best studies of government influence over the industrialization of U.S. agriculture include Deborah K. Fitzgerald, *Every Farm a Factory: The Industrial Ideal in American Agriculture* (New Haven: Yale University Press, 2003); Steven Stoll, *The Fruits of Natural Advantage: Making the Industrial Countryside in California* (Berkeley: University of California Press, 1998); Alan L. Olmstead and Paul W. Rhode, *Creating Abundance: Biological Innovation and American Agricultural Development* (New York: Cambridge University Press, 2008); A. Hunter Dupree, *Science in the Federal Government: A History of Policies and Activities* (Baltimore: Johns Hopkins University Press, 1986); Alan I. Marcus, *Agricultural Science and the Quest for Legitimacy: Farmers, Agricultural Colleges, and Experiment Stations, 1870–1890* (Ames: Iowa State University Press, 1985); Pete Daniel, *Breaking the Land: The Transformation of Cotton, Tobacco, and Rice Cultures Since 1880* (Urbana: University of Illinois Press, 1985); Kendra Smith-Howard, *Pure and Modern Milk: An Environmental History Since 1900* (New York: Oxford University Press, 2013); Timothy Johnson, "Nitrogen Nation: The Legacy of World War I and the Politics of Chemical Agriculture in the United States, 1916–1933," *Agricultural History* 90 (Spring 2016): 209–29; Paul K. Conkin, *A Revolution Down on the Farm: The Transformation of American Agriculture Since 1929* (Lexington: University Press of Kentucky, 2008). On growth rates in the agricultural sector, see Sally H. Clarke, *Regulation and the Revolution in United States Farm Productivity* (Cambridge: Cambridge University Press, 1994); Bruce L. Gardner, *American Agriculture in the Twentieth Century: How It Flourished and What It Cost* (Cambridge: Harvard University Press, 2002); Conkin, *Revolution Down on the Farm,* 97–98. On the ways in which federal government power developed in "hidden" forms in the late nineteenth century, putting the lie to claims of "laissez-faire," see Brian Balogh, *A Government Out of Sight: The Mystery of National Authority in Nineteenth-Century America* (New York: Cambridge University Press, 2009).

13. Great Atlantic & Pacific Tea Company, *You—and Your Company!* (New York: Great Atlantic & Pacific Tea Company, 1944), 16.

14. James E. Boyle, "The Chain Store and the Farm Cooperative," *Chain Store Progress* (Sept. 1930): 3; Frederick quoted in "Chain Store Buying and the Farmer," *Chain Store Progress* (April 1931): 3. For a probing perspective on the long-term consequences of standardization of the food chain, see Deborah K. Fitzgerald, "Eating and Remembering," *Agricultural History* 79 (Fall 2005): 393–408.

15. William Cronon, *Nature's Metropolis: Chicago and the Great West* (New York: Norton, 1991), 97–147; Olmstead and Rhode, *Creating Abundance*, 28–43.

16. Deborah K. Fitzgerald, "Farmers Deskilled: Hybrid Corn and Farmers' Work," *Technology and Culture* 34 (April 1993): 324–43; Shane Hamilton, *Trucking Country: The Road to America's Wal-Mart Economy* (Princeton: Princeton University Press, 2008), 64; Smith-Howard, *Pure and Modern Milk*, 12–66.

17. "Great A&P," 104, 107 (emphasis added). For more on the challenge of maximizing profits in a decentralized retail system, see James M. Mayo, *The American Grocery Store: The Business Evolution of an Architectural Space* (Westport, Conn.: Greenwood Press, 1993), 77.

18. "Great A&P," 249–50.

19. A&P, *You—and Your Company!*, 33.

20. It is impossible to pinpoint the exact locations of all A&P retail stores at this time; these data were never publicized or archived, and even if they had been they would have changed constantly: one of A&P's key business strategies was to hold only short-term leases on their retail buildings, allowing stores to move location regularly as the population shifted. What I am mapping as A&P stores, then, is based on statewide aggregate data of A&P store locations as reported in company documents from the period, correlated to cities with more than fifty thousand residents in 1949. The dots representing stores should thus be interpreted as highly likely locations—there may have been others, and some of the "stores" depicted probably did not exist in these places. Still, the overall pattern of distribution is accurate enough to allow for ArcGIS's proximity analysis tools to indicate significant patterns. Proximity was calculated using ArcGIS's "near tables" analysis engine.

21. L. O. Kunkel, *Wart of Potatoes: A Disease New to the United States*, Circular 6, Office of Cotton Truck and Forage Crop Disease Investigations (Washington, D.C.: USDA, Bureau of Plant Industry, 1919); Freeman A. Weiss and Philip Brierley, *Factors of Spread and Repression in Potato Wart*, Technical Bulletin 56 (Washington, D.C.: USDA, 1928); R. E. Hartman and R. V. Akeley, "Potato Wart in America," *American*

Potato Journal 21 (Oct. 1944): 283–88; Jude Ejikeme Obidiegwu, Kerstin Flath, and Christiane Gebhardt, "Managing Potato Wart: A Review of Present Research Status and Future Perspective," *Theoretical and Applied Genetics* 127, no. 4 (2014): 763–80; "Agricultural Bioterrorism Protection Act of 2002: Listing of Biological Agents and Toxins and Requirements and Procedures for Notification of Possession," 67 *Federal Register* 155 (Aug. 12, 2002), 52383–89.

22. B. L. Wade, "Breeding and Improvement of Peas and Beans," *USDA Yearbook of Agriculture, 1937* (Washington, D.C.: GPO, 1937), 251–82.

23. William H. Friedland and Amy Barton, "Tomato Technology," *Society,* Sept./Oct. 1967, 34–42; Deborah Barndt, *Tangled Routes: Women, Work, and Globalization on the Tomato Trail,* 2d ed. (Lanham, Md.: Rowman and Littlefield, 2008); Barry Estabrook, *Tomatoland: How Modern Industrial Agriculture Destroyed Our Most Alluring Fruit* (Kansas City: Andrews McMeel Publishing, 2011).

24. Further explorations of the dietary consequences of the supermarket-driven approach to standardization include Ann Vileisis, *Kitchen Literacy: How We Lost Knowledge of Where Food Comes from and Why We Need to Get It Back* (Washington, D.C.: Island Press, 2008); Michael Pollan, *The Omnivore's Dilemma: A Natural History of Four Meals* (New York: Penguin, 2006).

25. Dirlam and Kahn, "Antitrust Law and the Big Buyer," 128–29; A&P, *You—and Your Company!,* 40.

26. A&P, *You—and Your Company!,* 16; Paul Ingram and Hayagreeva Rao, "Store Wars: The Enactment and Repeal of Anti-Chain-Store Legislation in America," *American Journal of Sociology* 110 (Sept. 2004): 460; William Greer, *America the Bountiful: How the Supermarket Came to Main Street* (Washington, D.C.: Food Marketing Institute, 1986), 92–94.

27. Greer, *America the Bountiful,* 94; Douglas G. McPhee, *A Business Approach to Farm Surpluses* (Washington, D.C.: National Association of Food Chains, 1939), 18, 53; "Unlike Taxes," *Time,* Jan. 31, 1938, 54.

28. Stoll, *Fruits of Natural Advantage,* 45; Charles Postel, *The Populist Vision* (Oxford: Oxford University Press, 2007), 103–33; Charles Collins Teague, *Fifty Years a Rancher* (Los Angeles: Ward Ritchie Press, 1944), 176; Victoria Saker Woeste, *The Farmer's Benevolent Trust: Law and Agricultural Cooperation in Industrial America, 1865–1945* (Chapel Hill: University of North Carolina Press, 1998).

29. Karl C. Seeger, A. E. Tomhave, and H. L. Shrader, *The Results of the Chicken-of-Tomorrow 1948 National Contest* (Newark: University of Delaware Agricultural Experiment Station, July 1948), Box 9, John L. Skinner Papers, American Poultry

Historical Society, National Agricultural Library, Special Collections, Beltsville, Md. (hereafter APHS); "A&P Poultry Handbook for Markets," Aug. 20, 1947, Box 3, A&P Manuals Folder, Howard C. Pierce Papers, APHS; H. L. Shrader, A. E. Tomhave, and Karl C. Seeger, "The Chicken-of-Tomorrow Story" (n.d. [1948?]), Box 1, John E. Weidlich Papers, APHS; Committee for Improving Meat-Type in Poultry, Minutes of Meeting of Chairmen of Sub-Committees on Breeding, Market-Type, Procedure and Awards, Lexington, Ky., Sept. 4, 5, 1945, Box 1, John E. Weidlich Papers, APHS. On the broader context of the "Chicken of Tomorrow" project, see Roger Horowitz, *Putting Meat on the American Table: Taste, Technology, Transformation* (Baltimore: Johns Hopkins University Press, 2005), 103–28.

30. William Boyd, "Making Meat: Science, Technology, and American Poultry Production," *Technology and Culture* 42 (Oct. 2001): 657; "History of Arbor Acres," n.d. [Oct. 1963?], Microfilm Reel J-78, International Basic Economy Corporation Records, J Series (hereafter IBEC-J), Rockefeller Archive Center, Sleepy Hollow, N.Y. (hereafter RAC).

31. Advertisements quoted in John Williams Andrews, "U.S. vs. A&P: Battle of Titans," *Harper's*, Sept. 1950, 65 ; "Edison on Selling and Advertising Patent Goods," *Printer's Ink*, Sept. 8, 1910, 3–4, quoted in Susan Strasser, *Satisfaction Guaranteed: The Making of the American Mass Market* (New York: Basic, 1989), 203.

32. Charles F. McGovern, *Sold American: Consumption and Citizenship, 1890–1945* (Chapel Hill: University of North Carolina Press, 2006). On A&P's decline, see Tedlow, *New and Improved*, 249–58; Levinson, *Great A&P,* 247–57.

Chapter 2. The Farms Race Begins

1. Henry A. Wallace, "The Price of Free World Victory," speech delivered to the Free World Association, New York City, May 8, 1942, reprinted in Henry A. Wallace, *Democracy Reborn* (New York: Reynal and Hitchcock, 1944), 190; Franklin D. Roosevelt, Annual Message to Congress on the State of the Union, Jan. 6, 1941, https://fdrlibrary.org/documents/356632/390886/readingcopy.pdf/42234a77-8127-4015-95af-bcf831db311d (accessed October 12, 2017); Elizabeth Borgwardt, *A New Deal for the World: America's Vision for Human Rights* (Cambridge: Harvard University Press, 2005), 157.

2. Witherow quoted in John C. Culver and John Hyde, *American Dreamer: The Life and Times of Henry A. Wallace* (New York: Norton, 2000), 279–80; Henry Luce, "The American Century," *Life*, Feb. 17, 1941, 64, 65. Alan Brinkley emphasizes the commonalities between Luce and Wallace in *The Publisher: Henry Luce and His*

American Century (New York: Knopf, 2010), 269–73, but does not address the significance of food for both figures.

3. Robert H. Haddow, *Pavilions of Plenty: Exhibiting American Culture Abroad in the 1950s* (Washington, D.C.: Smithsonian Institution Press, 1997); Walter L. Hixson, *Parting the Curtain: Propaganda, Culture, and the Cold War, 1945–1961* (New York: St. Martin's, 1997); Laura A. Belmonte, *Selling the American Way: U.S. Propaganda and the Cold War* (Philadelphia: University of Pennsylvania Press, 2008); Kenneth Osgood, *Total Cold War: Eisenhower's Secret Propaganda Battle at Home and Abroad* (Lawrence: University Press of Kansas, 2006); Andrew L. Yarrow, "Selling a New Vision of America to the World: Changing Messages in Early U.S. Cold War Print Propaganda," *Journal of Cold War Studies* 11 (Fall 2009): 3–45; Ruth Oldenziel and Karin Zachmann, eds., *Cold War Kitchen: Americanization, Technology, and European Users* (Cambridge: MIT Press, 2009); Greg Castillo, *Cold War on the Home Front: The Soft Power of Midcentury Design* (Minneapolis: University of Minnesota Press, 2010); Zachary Karabell, *The Leading Indicators: A Short History of the Numbers That Rule Our World* (New York: Simon and Schuster, 2014).

4. It should be noted at the outset that I do not intend this chapter to be a comprehensive survey of all the agriculture- or food-related components of the Cold War. Perhaps most obvious, in this chapter I do little to explore the important agricultural transformations in newly postcolonial nations in South Asia, Southeast Asia, or Africa. Some excellent works in this vein include Benjamin Siegel, "'Self-Help Which Enobles a Nation': Development, Citizenship, and the Obligations of Eating in India's Austerity Years," *Modern Asian Studies* 50 (May 2016): 975–1018; Akhil Gupta, *Postcolonial Developments: Agriculture in the Making of Modern India* (Durham, N.C.: Duke University Press, 1998); Nick Cullather, *The Hungry World: America's Cold War Battle Against Poverty in Asia* (Cambridge: Harvard University Press, 2010). On Cold War–era Chinese agriculture, see Sigrid Schmalzer's magnificent *Red Revolution, Green Revolution: Scientific Farming in Socialist China* (Chicago: University of Chicago Press, 2016). For a detailed analysis of Cold War–era foreign policies related to food and agriculture, see Bryan L. McDonald, *Food Power: The Rise and Fall of the Postwar American Food System* (Oxford: Oxford University Press, 2017).

5. Helen Zoe Veit, *Modern Food, Moral Food: Self-Control, Science, and the Rise of Modern American Eating in the Early Twentieth Century* (Chapel Hill: University of North Carolina Press, 2013), 58; Emily S. Rosenberg, *Spreading the American Dream: American Economic and Cultural Expansion, 1890–1945* (New York: Hill and Wang, 1982), 77; *Report of the Secretary of Agriculture, 1945* (Washington, D.C.: GPO, 1946),

1. One could also argue, as Avner Offer has done, that conflicts over access to food helped spark the outbreak of the First World War: Avner Offer, *The First World War: An Agrarian Interpretation* (Oxford: Oxford University Press, 1989).

6. Sarah T. Phillips, *This Land, This Nation: Conservation, Rural America, and the New Deal* (Cambridge: Cambridge University Press, 2007), 191; David Ekbladh, *The Great American Mission: Modernization and the Construction of an American World Order* (Princeton: Princeton University Press, 2009), 38. Numerous agricultural historians have portrayed New Deal farm policies as inherently and intentionally inequitable, particularly for landless southern farmers, although a new generation of scholars has attempted to offer more sympathetic interpretations of New Dealers' intentions. Key works in the critical vein include Pete Daniel, *Breaking the Land: The Transformation of Cotton, Tobacco, and Rice Cultures Since 1880* (Urbana: University of Illinois Press, 1985); Jack Temple Kirby, *Rural Worlds Lost: The American South, 1920–1960* (Baton Rouge: Louisiana State University Press, 1987). Key works in the sympathetic vein include Jess Gilbert, *Planning Democracy: Agrarian Intellectuals and the Intended New Deal* (New Haven: Yale University Press, 2015); Tore C. Olsson, *Agrarian Crossings: Reformers and the Remaking of the US and Mexican Countryside* (Princeton: Princeton University Press, 2017).

7. Olsson, *Agrarian Crossings;* Jonathan Harwood, "Peasant Friendly Plant Breeding and the Early Years of the Green Revolution in Mexico," *Agricultural History* 83 (Summer 2009): 384–410; Jonathan Harwood, "Global Visions vs. Local Complexity: Experts Wrestle with the Problem of Development," in *Rice: Global Networks and New Histories,* ed. Francesca Bray, Peter A. Coclanis, Edda L. Fields-Black, and Dagmar Schaefer, 41–56 (New York: Cambridge University Press, 2015); Jonathan Harwood, *Europe's Green Revolution and Others Since: The Rise and Fall of Peasant-Friendly Plant Breeding* (London: Routledge, 2012). For a study that emphasizes the peasant-unfriendly aftermath of the Mexican Agricultural Program, see Deborah K. Fitzgerald, "Exporting American Agriculture: The Rockefeller Foundation in Mexico, 1943–53," *Social Studies of Science* 16 (Aug. 1986): 457–83. For a broader view of how the Rockefeller Foundation became an important partner in U.S. Cold War foreign policy agendas, see Inderjeet Parmar, *Foundations of the American Century: The Ford, Carnegie, and Rockefeller Foundations in the Rise of American Power* (New York: Columbia University Press, 2012), 97–220.

8. Fitzgerald, "Exporting American Agriculture," 477; Uma Lele and Arthur A. Goldsmith, "The Development of National Agricultural Research Capacity: India's Experience with the Rockefeller Foundation and Its Significance for Africa,"

Economic Development and Cultural Change 37 (Jan. 1989): 305–43; Glenn Davis Stone and Dominic Glover, "Disembedding Grain: Golden Rice, the Green Revolution, and Heirloom Seeds in the Philippines," *Agriculture and Human Values* 34, no. 1 (2017): 87–102; Cullather, *Hungry World,* 102–7, 159–79.

9. "The Rocky Roll," *Time,* Oct. 6, 1958, 17. The tennis anecdote comes from John H. Perkins, *Geopolitics and the Green Revolution: Wheat, Genes, and the Cold War* (New York: Oxford University Press, 1997), 148.

10. "Nelson Aldrich Rockefeller," Oct. 1948, Box 14, Folder 85, Nelson A. Rockefeller Papers, Series A, RG 4 (hereafter RG 4-A), RAC; Rosenberg, *Spreading the American Dream,* 206–209; Ekbladh, *Great American Mission,* 73.

11. Claude C. Erb, "Prelude to Point Four: The Institute of Inter-American Affairs," *Diplomatic History* 9 (Fall 1985): 254; Kathleen A. Nehls, "Red-Tape Fraternities: State-Building in the Age of Associationalism" (Ph.D diss., University of Georgia, 2015); Daniel Immerwahr, *Thinking Small: The United States and the Lure of Community Development* (Cambridge: Harvard University Press, 2015).

12. "Venezuela," n.d. (1942?), Box 1693, Folder 9, RG 229, Records of the Office of Inter-American Affairs, Entry 147, Records of the Department of Basic Economy, Food Supply Division, Project Files, NARA-II; Nelson A. Rockefeller to Diógenes Escalante, June 12, 1943, ibid.; "Food Production Program in Venezuela," Feb. 15, 1944, Folder 11, ibid.

13. Melvyn P. Leffler, "The American Conception of National Security and the Beginnings of the Cold War, 1945–48," *American Historical Review* 89 (April 1984): 357, 364.

14. "United Nations Conference on Food and Agriculture: Text of the Final Act," *American Journal of International Law* 37 (Oct. 1943): 163; Amy L. S. Staples, *The Birth of Development: How the World Bank, Food and Agriculture Organization, and World Health Organization Changed the World, 1945–1965* (Kent, Ohio: Kent State University Press, 2006).

15. Mordecai Ezekiel, "A Physical Plan for a World of Plenty," *Free World,* Jan. 1945, 27–30, Box 38, Folder 15, Mordecai Ezekiel Papers, Franklin D. Roosevelt Presidential Library and Museum, Hyde Park, N.Y. For more on Ezekiel's role in postwar development thinking, see Nils Gilman, *Mandarins of the Future: Modernization Theory in Cold War America* (Baltimore: Johns Hopkins University Press, 2003), 39–43. On the international postwar roles of New Dealers, see Phillips, *This Land, This Nation,* 242–84; Jason Scott Smith, "The Liberal Invention of the Multinational Corporation: David Lilienthal and Postwar Capitalism," in *What's Good for Business:*

Business and American Politics Since World War II, ed. Kim Phillips-Fein and Julian Zelizer (New York: Oxford University Press, 2012), 107–22.

16. *Congressional Record,* 79th Cong., 2d sess., 92:2, Feb. 19, 1946, p. 1454, cited in Susan Levine, *School Lunch Politics: The Surprising History of America's Favorite Welfare Program* (Princeton: Princeton University Press, 2008), 82; George C. Marshall, "The Marshall Plan Speech," June 1947, the George C. Marshall Foundation, at http://marshallfoundation.org/marshall/the-marshall-plan/marshall-plan-speech/ (accessed July 1, 2016); Melvyn P. Leffler, "The Cold War: What Do 'We Now Know'?" *American Historical Review* 104 (April 1999): 516–18; Jacqueline McGlade, "More a Plowshare than a Sword: The Legacy of US Cold War Agricultural Diplomacy," *Agricultural History* 83 (Winter 2009): 82; Emanuele Bernardi, "Political Stability, Modernization and Reforms During the First Years of the Cold War," in *Agriculture in Capitalist Europe, 1945–1960: From Food Shortages to Food Surpluses,* ed. Carin Martiin, Juan Pan-Montojo, and Paul Brassley, 44–63 (London: Routledge, 2016).

17. Michael Goldman, *Imperial Nature: The World Bank and Struggles for Social Justice in the Age of Globalization* (New Haven: Yale University Press, 2005), 56–57; Nick Cullather, "The War on the Peasant: The United States and the Third World," in *The Cold War in the Third World,* ed. Robert J. McMahon (New York: Oxford University Press, 2013), 192–207. On the 1948 presidential campaign, see Culver and Hyde, *American Dreamer,* esp. 465–570.

18. Chester Bowles, "America's Food in a Hungry World," *Super Market Merchandising* (June 1948): 159, 161, 162. On Bowles and the Office of Price Administration, see Meg Jacobs, *Pocketbook Politics: Economic Citizenship in Twentieth-Century America* (Princeton: Princeton University Press, 2005).

19. Harry S Truman, "Inaugural Address," Jan. 20, 1949, *Public Papers of the Presidents of the United States, Harry S Truman, 1949* (Washington, D.C.: GPO, 1966), 112–16; Cary Reich, *The Life of Nelson A. Rockefeller: Worlds to Conquer, 1908–1958* (New York: Doubleday, 1996), 427–28, 430; Erb, "Prelude to Point Four," 249; Benjamin H. Hardy to Mr. [Francis] Russell, "Use of U.S. Technological Resources as a Weapon in the Struggle with International Communism," Nov. 23, 1948, Box 1, Benjamin H. Hardy Papers, Harry S Truman Library, Independence, Mo.

20. Hardy, "Use of Technological Resources," 1, 2.

21. House Committee on Foreign Affairs, *International Technical Cooperation Act of 1949 ("Point IV" Program), Part 1, Hearings,* 81st Cong., 1st sess., Sept. 27, 28, 30, Oct. 3–7, 1949, 79, 82, 83; "Legislative Background of Point Four Program, Memorandum

Prepared in the Department of State, Jun. 20, 1950," in *Foreign Relations of the United States, 1950, National Security Affairs: Foreign Economic Policy, Volume 1*, ed. Neal H. Petersen, John P. Glennon, David W. Mabon, Ralph R. Goodwin, and William Z. Slany, Document 304 (Washington, D.C.: GPO, 1977).

22. Stanley Andrews, Oral History Interview by Richard D. McKinzie, Alamo, Texas, October 31, 1970, Oral History Collection, Harry S Truman Library, Independence, Mo., 32–34, 31, 42.

23. International Development Advisory Board, *Partners in Progress: A Report to the President*, March 1951, Box 10, Folder 10, Series III, National Foreign Trade Council, Inc. Records, Series III, Hagley Museum and Library Archives, Wilmington, Del.; Harry S Truman to Nelson Rockefeller, March 11, 1951, in The American Presidency Project, ed. John T. Woolley and Gerhard Peters, http://www.presidency.ucsb.edu/ws/?pid=14032 (accessed July 6, 2016); Ekbladh, *Great American Mission*, 299n109.

24. Nick Cullather, "Development? It's History," *Diplomatic History* 24 (Fall 2000): 651; Ekbladh, *Great American Mission*, 101; Alfred E. Eckes, Jr., and Thomas W. Zeiler, *Globalization and the American Century* (New York: Cambridge University Press, 2003), 137–42. On the broader questions of "empire" vs. "hegemony," see Charles S. Maier, "Alliance and Autonomy: European Identity and U.S. Foreign Policy Objectives in the Truman Years," in *The Truman Presidency*, ed. Michael J. Lacey (Cambridge: Cambridge University Press, 1989), 273–98; Charles S. Maier, *Among Empires: American Ascendancy and Its Predecessors* (Cambridge: Harvard University Press, 2006).

25. Joanna L. Grisinger, *The Unwieldy American State: Administrative Politics Since the New Deal* (New York: Cambridge University Press, 2012), 202–203.

26. Senate Committee on Foreign Relations, *Nomination of John Foster Dulles, Secretary of State-Designate, Hearings*, 83d Cong., 1st sess., Jan. 15, 1953, 29, 30; Senate Committee on Foreign Relations, *Mutual Security Act of 1953, Hearings*, 83d Cong., 1st sess., May 5–8, 11–16, 18–19, 23, 25, 27, 29, 1953, 100, 101; House Committee on Foreign Affairs, *Selected Executive Session Hearings of the Committee, 1951–56*, Vol. 10: *Mutual Security Program, Part 2, Mutual Security Act of 1953, Hearings*, 83d Cong., 1st sess., May 18, June 2, 1953, 74.

27. Reorganization Plan No. 7 of 1953, 67 Stat. 639; Paul P. Kennedy, "Concept and Scope of Point 4 Viewed as Undergoing Shift," *New York Times*, Sept. 24, 1953, 1, 12; Phillips, *This Land, This Nation*, 279–80; Senate Committee on Foreign Relations, *Mutual Security Act of 1953, Hearings*, 16; Michael E. Latham, *The Right Kind of Revolu-*

tion: Modernization, Development, and U.S. Foreign Policy from the Cold War to the Present (Ithaca: Cornell University Press, 2011), 42–43; Andrews, Oral History Interview, 71.

28. Dwight D. Eisenhower, Remarks at the Convention of the National Association of Retail Grocers, June 16, 1954, American Presidency Project, http://www.presidency.ucsb.edu/ws/?pid=9924 (accessed February 27, 2007); David E. Hamilton, *From New Day to New Deal: American Farm Policy from Hoover to Roosevelt, 1928–1933* (Chapel Hill: University of North Carolina Press, 1991).

29. Victoria Saker Woeste, *The Farmer's Benevolent Trust: Law and Agricultural Cooperation in Industrial America, 1865–1945* (Chapel Hill: University of North Carolina Press, 1998); Shane Hamilton, "Agribusiness, the Family Farm, and the Politics of Technological Determinism in the Post–World War II United States," *Technology and Culture* 55 (July 2014): 563–64; Senate Committee on Agriculture and Forestry, *Agricultural Adjustment Act of 1949, Hearings*, 81st Cong., 1st sess., July 7, 11–15, 18, 19, 1949, 179.

30. Senate Committee on Appropriations, *Agricultural Appropriations for 1955, Hearings*, 83d Cong., 2d sess., March 23–26, 29–31, April 9, 12, 14–16, 19, 26–30, May 3–5, 1954, 729.

31. House Committee of the Whole House, *Agricultural Trade Development and Assistance Act of 1954*, 83d Cong., 2d sess., Rpt. 1776, June 9, 1954, 5, 6; *Congressional Record*, 83d Cong., 2d sess., June 15, 1954, vol. 100, pt. 6, pp. 8287, 8291.

32. Trudy H. Peterson, *Agricultural Exports, Farm Income, and the Eisenhower Administration* (Lincoln: University of Nebraska Press, 1979), 46–48; John H. Davis, "Goals of Farm Policy in a Free Society," address before the National Farm Forum, Des Moines, Iowa, Feb. 19, 1955, Subject File GB2.320, Harvard Business School, Baker Library Historical Collections, Cambridge, Mass., 3. I shall discuss the implications of Davis's neologism further in Chapter 5.

Chapter 3. *Supermercado* USA

1. Bernardo Jofre to H. W. Bagley, Sept. 11, 1956, Microfilm Reel J-65, IBEC-J, RAC.

2. On Rockefeller, see Cary Reich, *The Life of Nelson A. Rockefeller: Worlds to Conquer, 1908–1958* (New York: Doubleday, 1996); Richard Norton Smith, *On His Own Terms: A Life of Nelson Rockefeller* (New York: Random House, 2014). "Full belly": J. C. Moffett, *American Supermarkets in Milan or Sunflowers Grow in Italy*, report to Maxwell Graduate School, Syracuse University, New York, Jan. 15, 1960, Microfilm Series IBEC, 9, RAC. General histories of IBEC include Wayne G. Broehl, Jr., *The International Basic Economy Corporation* (Washington, D.C.: National Planning

Association, 1968); Darlene Rivas, *Missionary Capitalist: Nelson Rockefeller in Venezuela* (Chapel Hill: University of North Carolina Press, 2002); Kenneth D. Durr, *A Company with a Mission: Rodman Rockefeller and the International Basic Economy Corporation, 1947–1985* (Rockville, Md.: Montrose, 2006).

3. Amy L. S. Staples, *The Birth of Development: How the World Bank, Food and Agriculture Organization, and World Health Organization Changed the World, 1945–1965* (Kent, Ohio: Kent State University Press, 2006), 1; David Ekbladh, *The Great American Mission: Modernization and the Construction of an American World Order* (Princeton: Princeton University Press, 2009), 9. On the Cold War missions of not-for-profit agencies, see Olivier Zunz, *Philanthropy in America: A History* (Princeton: Princeton University Press, 2011).

4. Andrew Carnegie, "Wealth," *North American Review* (June 1889): 654; Nelson A. Rockefeller, Speech Before American Chamber of Commerce, São Paulo, Brazil, Sept. 16, 1948, Box 146, Folder 1586, RG 4-A, RAC; Nelson Lichtenstein, *A Contest of Ideas: Capital, Politics, and Labor* (Urbana: University of Illinois Press, 2013), 170–74.

5. C. J. Bauer, Report to the Board of Directors of the Creole Petroleum Corporation, Nov. 4, 1937, Box 66, Folder 564, RG 4-A, RAC; C. J. Bauer, Report to the Directors of the Creole Petroleum Corporation, March 2, 1938, Folder 565, ibid.; "Communism," Dec. 1946, Box 52, Folder 475, Nelson A. Rockefeller Papers, Series L, Record Group 4, RAC, quoting W. H. Lawrence, "Rise of Reds in Americas Traced to Low Pay-High Profit Economy," *New York Times*, Dec. 31, 1946, 1; Kenneth J. Kadow and John R. Camp to Nelson A. Rockefeller (hereafter NAR) and Board of Directors of IBEC, "Preview of the Venezuelan Program," Jan. 14, 1947, Box 145, Folder 1580, RG 4-A, RAC; NAR, Memorandum re Arrangements Following Trip to Venezuela, Feb. 7, 1947, Box 14, Folder 144, Nelson A. Rockefeller Papers, Series B, RG 4 (hereafter RG 4-B), RAC; NAR, Report on Trip to Venezuela, June 27, 1947, Box 27, Folder 270, RG 4-B, RAC; Rómulo Betancourt to NAR, June 26, 1947, Box 10, Folder 92, RG 4-B, RAC. On the broader context of U.S. approaches to Latin America in the Cold War, see Greg Grandin, "What Was Containment? Short and Long Answers from the Americas," in *The Cold War in the Third World*, ed. Robert J. McMahon, 27–47 (New York: Oxford University Press, 2013).

6. Certificate of Incorporation, Venezuelan Basic Economy Corporation, May 15, 1947, Box 10, Folder 92, RG 4-B, RAC; Durr, *Company with a Mission*, 19; Venezuelan Basic Economy Corporation, Press Release, Feb. 10, 1947, 1, 2, Box 14, Folder 143, RG 4-B, RAC; IBEC Policy Committee Meeting Minutes, Feb. 4, 1947, Box 12, Folder 116, RG 4-B, RAC.

7. Kenneth J. Kadow to NAR and Berent Friele, March 14, 1947, 2–3, Box 12, Folder 122, RG 4-B, RAC. During the war, Kadow left the University of Delaware to work for the Office of Inter-American Affairs in Brazil, where he directed technical assistance for commercial farmers. After the war he worked as a development consultant for Stettinius Associates, a New York firm established by former Secretary of State Edward R. Stettinius, Jr., to promote development in Liberia. See Kenneth J. Kadow, "Attacking Brazil's Food Problems," *Agriculture in the Americas* 5 (March 1945): 53–55; W. C. Brister to F. C. Owen, March 31, 1948, Box 1676, Folder B-4, RG 229, Records of the Office of Inter-American Affairs, Entry 146, NARA-II; Rodney Carlisle, "The 'American Century' Implemented: Stettinius and the Liberian Flag of Convenience," *Business History Review* 54 (Summer 1980): 175–91.

8. Dwight H. Mahan, "Report on Food Conditions in Venezuela," April 1947, Box 14, Folder 140, RG 4-B, RAC.

9. Stacy May, "Butter, Guns or Both," *Proceedings of the Academy of Political Science* 19 (Jan. 1942): 383–89; Stacy May, "Folklore and Fact About Underdeveloped Areas," *Foreign Affairs* 33 (Jan. 1955): 212–24; Stacy May to NAR, Berent Friele, and Morrison G. Tucker, April 29, 1947, Box 14, Folder 140, RG 4-B, RAC.

10. Stacy May to John R. Camp, April 1, 1947, Microfilm Reel J-81, IBEC-J, RAC.

11. José Martín, "Rockefeller, No! Reforma Agraria, Si!," *El Popular,* March 28, 1947, 16, English translation in Box 14, Folder 143, RG 4-B, RAC; Bernardo Jofre to Francis A. Jamieson, July 29, 1947, Box 14, Folder 143, RG 4-B, RAC.

12. Stacy May, Memorandum, "Interview with Anthony B. Toro, Jr.," July 19, 1947, Box 14, Folder 140, RG 4-B, RAC; Anthony B. Toro to NAR, March 30, 1949, 4, Box 8, Folder 84, ibid.

13. International Basic Economy Corporation, Press Release, Jan. 16, 1948, Box 145, Folder 1581, RG 4-A, RAC.

14. Mahan, "Report on Food Conditions in Venezuela," 4–5; International Basic Economy Corporation, Annual Report, 1950, Microfiche 0700-20-01, IBEC-J, RAC; "Cargill Report," July 23, 1947, Box 24, Folder 252, RG 4-B, RAC.

15. John R. Camp to Ted Watson, March 8, 1948, Microfilm Reel R-94, International Basic Economy Coporation Records, R Series (hereafter IBEC-R), RAC. The post–World War II assumption that Iowa should be the model for Latin American agriculture was a departure from the Rockefeller Foundation's pre–World War II work, according to Tore C. Olsson, *Agrarian Crossings: Reformers and the Remaking of the US and Mexican Countryside* (Princeton: Princeton University Press, 2017).

16. Robert P. Russell to NAR, April 1, 1948, Microfilm Reel R-94, IBEC-R, RAC; IBEC Press Release, July 26, 1947, Box 14, Folder 143, RG 4-B, RAC; Robert P. Russell to Ted Watson, April 26, 1948, IBEC-R, RAC.

17. C. T. Watson, "Brief Report on PACA Activities," July 20, 1948, Microfilm Reel R-94, IBEC-R, RAC, 1; Robert P. Russell to IBEC Executive Committee, Feb. 21, 1949, Box 7, Folder 70, RG 4-B, RAC, 1, 2; M. G. Tucker to William F. Machold, Nov. 10, 1948, Microfilm Reel R-94, IBEC-R, RAC, 1; Morrison G. Tucker, Memorandum, "Venezuelan Field Visits with DuPont Representatives," Jan. 7, 1949, Microfilm Reel R-94, IBEC-R, RAC, 4, 17.

18. C. F. Seabrook to NAR, March 12, 1949, Microfilm Reel R-95, RAC, IBEC-R. On Seabrook, see Shane Hamilton, *Trucking Country: The Road to America's Wal-Mart Economy* (Princeton: Princeton University Press, 2008), 118–19.

19. Robert P. Russell, "Revolution, the American Way," *American Magazine,* Sept. 1949, 28, 121.

20. H. A. Von Wald to E. G. Van Wagner, Feb. 17, 1951, 1, Microfilm Reel R-94, IBEC-R, RAC; IBEC Annual Report, 1953, Microfiche 0700-20-01, IBEC-J, RAC.

21. On "high modernist" agricultural industrialization projects, see James C. Scott, *Seeing Like a State: How Certain Schemes to Improve the Human Condition Have Failed* (New Haven: Yale University Press, 1998). On "low modernism," see Jess Gilbert, *Planning Democracy: Agrarian Intellectuals and the Intended New Deal* (New Haven: Yale University Press, 2015). R. J. Blas to F. E. Dominy, April 23, 1943, Box 1693, Folder 9, RG 229, Entry 147, NARA-II; F. E. Dominy, "Venezuela," Dec. 26, 1942, Box 1693, Folder 9, RG 229, Entry 147, NARA-II; Hebe M. C. Vessuri, "Foreign Scientists, the Rockefeller Foundation and the Origins of Agricultural Science in Venezuela," *Minerva* 32 (Sept. 1994): 267–96; Robert P. Russell to Merrill W. Abbey, Nov. 15, 1948, Microfilm Reel J-81, IBEC-J, RAC.

22. Venezuelan Basic Economy Corporation, Project Proposal, Compañia Anónima Distribuidora de Alimentos (CADA), July 28, 1947, Box 16, Folder 154, RG 4-B, RAC; Toro to Rockefeller, March 30, 1949, 1, Box 8, Folder 84, RG 4-B, RAC; Durr, *Company with a Mission,* 28.

23. NAR to U.S. Department of Commerce, Feb. 21, 1948; Stacy May to NAR and Thomas S. Gates, Jr., March 16, 1948; Stacy May to Morrison G. Tucker, April 28, 1948; Stacy May to John Q. Adams, July 7, 1948, all Microfilm Reel J-82, IBEC-J, RAC.

24. Flor Brennan, Memorandum, "Material Left by Mr. Armando Capriles with NAR," Nov. 17, 1948, Microfilm Reel J-83, IBEC-J, RAC, 1, 2.

25. W. F. Coles to NAR, June 27, 1949, 1, Box 32, Folder 302, RG 4-B, RAC; "'Automercado' Center Opens in Las Mercedes," *Caracas Journal*, Nov. 3, 1954, 8, Microfilm Reel J-68, IBEC-J, RAC; "Kansan Helps Venezuelans Make Changes," *Wichita Beacon*, March 7, 1968, Microfilm Reel J-83, IBEC-J, RAC; William F. Coles to John E. Lockwood, Jan. 6, 1950, Microfilm Reel J-65, IBEC-J, RAC. Boogaart would become IBEC's point man in establishing supermarkets in Italy in the mid-1950s; see Emanuela Scarpellini, "Shopping American-Style: The Arrival of the Supermarket in Postwar Italy," *Enterprise & Society* 5 (Dec. 2004): 625–68.

26. "Report on the Activities of C.A. Todos, Year 1949," March 11, 1950, Microfilm Reel J-65, IBEC-J, RAC; W. D. Bradford to IBEC Executive Committee, "Proposed Supermarket and Shopping Center, Lima, Peru," Nov. 4, 1954, Box 8, Folder 79, RG 4-B, RAC; W. D. Bradford to IBEC Investment Committee, "Proposed Supermarket and Shopping Center—Sao Paulo," Feb. 15, 1956, Box 8, Folder 77, RG 4-B, RAC; Bernardo Jofre to Francis A. Jamieson, Dec. 16, 1953, Folder 79, RG 4-B, RAC; "IBEC Realty Company, Inc.," March 20, 1962, Microfilm Reel J-10, IBEC-J, RAC; Victoria de Grazia, *Irresistible Empire: America's Advance Through Twentieth-Century Europe* (Cambridge: Harvard University Press, 2005), 407–8; IBEC Supermarket Division—Venezuela, Aug. 10, 1957, Box 8, Folder 81, RG 4-B, RAC ; "'Automercado' Center Opens in Las Mercedes," *Caracas Journal*, Nov. 3, 1954, 3, 8, Microfilm Reel J-68, IBEC-J, RAC; Excerpt from VBEC Progress Report, Aug. 1 to Aug. 31, 1951, Microfilm Reel J-65, IBEC-J, RAC.

27. Wallace D. Bradford to John E. Lockwood, Jan. 6, 1950, Microfilm Reel J-65, IBEC-J, RAC; Excerpt from VBEC Progress Report, June 15–July 15, 1950, ibid.; IBEC Annual Report, 1950, 7, 8, Microfiche 0700-20-01, IBEC-J, RAC; Louise S. Bingham to Wallace D. Bradford, Sept. 26, 1950, Microfilm Reel J-65, IBEC-J, RAC.

28. William H. Meserole, *Streamlined Wholesale Grocery Warehouses* (Washington, D.C.: Department of Commerce, 1945), 3; Robert Purcell to W. B. Dixon Stroud, May 31, 1958, Microfilm Reel 7, IBEC-IBEC, RAC; Hamilton, *Trucking Country*, 120–21; IBEC Annual Report, 1956, Microfiche 0700-20-01, IBEC-J, RAC.

29. "'Automercado' Center Opens in Las Mercedes," 1; J. Wayne Hisle to R. A. Agostini, Nov. 2, 1956, 1, Microfilm Reel J-65, IBEC-J, RAC; Richard A. Agostini to J. W. Hisle, Oct. 23, 1956, Microfilm Reel J-65, IBEC-J, RAC; IBEC Annual Report, 1957, 5, Microfiche 0700-20-01, IBEC-J, RAC.

30. Ramos quoted in Francis A. Jamieson to NAR and David Rockefeller, June 7, 1956, 2, Box 148, Folder 1617, RG 4-A, RAC; Francis A. Jamieson to Stroud, Levy, Bradford, Jan. 22, 1957, Box 8, Folder 81, RG 4-B, RAC; Bernardo Jofre to Francis A. Jamieson, Jan. 16, 1957, Box 8, Folder 81, RG 4-B, RAC.

31. IBEC Annual Report, 1960, Microfiche 0700-20-01, IBEC-J, RAC; James N. Wallace, "Private Point Four: Rockefeller Firm Aids 17 Countries, Makes Profits at Same Time," *Wall Street Journal,* July 14, 1961, 13, Box 8, Folder 81, RG 4-B, RAC; IBEC Annual Report, 1961, Microfiche 0700-20-01, IBEC-J, RAC.

32. R. O. Provost to W. D. Bradford, Feb. 15, 1961, Microfilm Reel J-68, IBEC-J, RAC; "Blast in Venezuela," *New York Times,* Feb. 15, 1961, 8; R. O. Provost to David Haweeli, Nov. 7, 1962, Microfilm Reel J-83, IBEC-J, RAC; IBEC Newsletter, Sept.–Oct. 1963, Microfilm Reel J-68, IBEC-J, RAC.

33. Hal Brands, *Latin America's Cold War* (Cambridge: Harvard University Press, 2010), 39; IBEC Newsletter, April/May/June 1965, Microfilm Reel J-83, IBEC-J, RAC.

34. "Pro-Venezuela Launches Attack on 'Automercado,'" *Caracas Daily Journal,* Nov. 15, 1962, Microfilm Reel J-68; John Anderson to Robert W. Purcell, April 6, 1965, Microfilm Reel J-83; Richard O. Provost to Donald E. Meads, May 12, 1965, all IBEC-J, RAC. Alan Knight suggests that locals' desires for American-style goods and investment opportunities made collaboration rather than resistance the dominant characteristic of U.S.-Latin American economic relations in the twentieth century. See Knight, "U.S. Imperialism/Hegemony and Latin American Resistance," in *Empire and Dissent: The United States and Latin America,* ed. Fred Rosen, 23–52 (Durham, N.C.: Duke University Press, 2008). Hal Brands, by contrast, marks the 1960s as a period of widespread business resistance to U.S. foreign direct investment and its consequent enabling of capital flight out of Venezuela: Brands, *Latin America's Cold War,* 92.

35. IBEC Newsletter, Oct./Nov./Dec. 1966, Microfilm Reel J-83; William R. B. Atkin to Rodman C. Rockefeller, Aug. 19, 1966, Microfilm Reel J-43; IBEC Annual Report, 1966, Microfiche 0700-20-01; all IBEC-J, RAC.

36. Food Products Group, Report to the IBEC Board of Directors, Dec. 13, 1966, 6, Microfilm Reel J-43, IBEC-J, RAC.

37. "Legal Opinion for the Insurance Companies Involved in the Fire Loss at the 'Minimax' Supermarkets," Oct. 3, 1969, Microfilm Reel J-36, IBEC-J, RAC; Brands, *Latin America's Cold War,* 92; Natalia Vega, "'Malvenido Mister Rockefeller': Acciones de protesta en 1969," *Rojo y Negro Revista del Centro de Documentación y Estudios Sociales* 2 (2011): 2; Ernesto Capello, "Latin America Encounters Nelson Rockefeller: Imagining the *Gringo Patrón* in 1969," in *Human Rights and Transnational Solidarity in Cold War Latin America,* ed. Jessica Stites Mor, 48–73, 51 (Madison: University of Wisconsin Press, 2013).

38. Andy Baker and David Cupery, "Anti-Americanism in Latin America: Economic Exchange, Foreign Policy Legacies, and Mass Attitudes Toward the Colossus

of the North," *Latin American Research Review* 48, no. 2 (2013): 106–30; Durr, *Company with a Mission*, 192–97.

Chapter 4. Socialist Supermarkets and "Peaceful Competition"

1. David Riesman, "The Nylon War (1951)" in Riesman, *Abundance for What?* (Garden City, N.Y.: Doubleday, 1964), 67–79.

2. "U.S. Supermarket Soon Will Invade Tito's Domain," *New York Times*, July 24, 1957, 31; Paul Hofmann, "Italian Housewives Gape at Supermarket Display," *New York Times*, June 21, 1956, 26.

3. U.S. Information Service, American Consulate, "Statement of John A. Logan," Sept. 6, 1957, Box 27, Folder 3, RG 489, Entry 22, Records of the Office of International Trade Fairs (hereafter RG 489, Entry 22), NARA-II; "U.S. Supermarket in Yugoslavia," *New York Times Magazine*, Sept. 22, 1957, 12–13; "U.S. Pavilion Attendance Figures at 1957 Fall Fairs," Oct. 9, 1957, Box 16, Folder 2, RG 489, Entry 22, NARA-II.

4. Seymour Freidin, "The Wonderful Supermarket," *New York Post*, Sept. 27, 1957, M3, Box 16, Folder 2, RG 489, Entry 22, NARA-II. Frozen foods, to be sure, would have seemed especially exotic to many Western as well as Eastern Europeans in the 1950s for whom reliable refrigeration was far rarer than in the United States. See Erik van der Vleuten, "Feeding the Peoples of Europe: Transnational Food Transport Infrastructure in the Early Cold War, 1947–1960," in *Materializing Europe: Transnational Infrastructures and the Project of Europe,* ed. Alexander Badenoch and Andreas Fickers (London: Palgrave Macmillan, 2010), 148–77. On Eisenhower's cultural diplomacy and propaganda campaigns, see Kenneth Osgood, *Total Cold War: Eisenhower's Secret Propaganda Battle at Home and Abroad* (Lawrence: University Press of Kansas, 2006); Greg Castillo, *Cold War on the Home Front: The Soft Power of Midcentury Design* (Minneapolis: University of Minnesota Press, 2010); Walter L. Hixson, *Parting the Curtain: Propaganda, Culture, and the Cold War, 1945–1961* (New York: St. Martin's, 1997); Laura A. Belmonte, *Selling the American Way: U.S. Propaganda and the Cold War* (Philadelphia: University of Pennsylvania Press, 2008); Robert H. Haddow, *Pavilions of Plenty: Exhibiting American Culture Abroad in the 1950s* (Washington, D.C.: Smithsonian Institution Press, 1997); Stephen J. Whitfield, *The Culture of the Cold War,* 2d ed. (Baltimore: Johns Hopkins University Press, 1996); Cristina Carbone, "Staging the Kitchen Debate: How Splitnik Got Normalized in the United States," in *Cold War Kitchen: Americanization, Technology, and European Users,* ed. Ruth Oldenziel and Karin Zachmann (Cambridge: MIT Press, 2009), 59–81; David Caute, *The Dancer Defects: The Struggle for Cultural Supremacy During the Cold War*

(New York: Oxford University Press, 2005); Penny M. Von Eschen, *Satchmo Blows Up the World: Jazz Ambassadors Play the Cold War* (Cambridge: Harvard University Press, 2004). Broader studies of the interrelationships between U.S. and Western European consumer culture and politics in the twentieth century include Victoria de Grazia, *Irresistible Empire: America's Advance Through Twentieth-Century Europe* (Cambridge: Harvard University Press, 2005); Jan Logemann, *Trams or Tailfins? Public and Private Prosperity in Postwar West Germany and the United States* (Chicago: University of Chicago Press, 2012); Mary Nolan, *Visions of Modernity: American Business and the Modernization of Germany* (New York: Oxford University Press, 1994); Reinhold Wagnleitner, *Coca-Colonization and the Cold War: The Cultural Mission of the United States in Austria After the Second World War* (Chapel Hill: University of North Carolina Press, 1994).

5. "U.S. Supermarket in Yugoslavia," *New York Times Magazine,* Sept. 22, 1957, 12; Office of International Trade Fairs, Industry Exhibits Division, "Report on U.S. Exhibit at Zagreb International Trade Fair," Nov. 8, 1957, Box 27, Folder 3, RG 489, Entry 22, NARA-II; D. Paul Medalie, "Final Fair Report," Oct. 5, 1957, Box 27, Folder 3, RG 489, Entry 22, NARA-II; National Association of Food Chains, Press Release, "Remarks by Clarence Randall, Special Assistant to the President, at Luncheon of NAFC," Oct. 21, 1957, Box 27, Folder 3, RG 489, Entry 22, NARA-II; William Greer, *America the Bountiful: How the Supermarket Came to Main Street* (Washington, D.C.: Food Marketing Institute, 1986), 169.

6. "Preliminary Report of Ad Hoc Group to the Inter-Agency Advisory Group for the Trade Fair Program," Dec. 8, 1954, Box 1, Folder 2, RG 489, Entry 22, NARA-II; Paul Hawk to Arnold Zempel, "Second Report of Ad Hoc Group to the Inter-Agency Advisory Group for the Trade Fair Program," Dec. 15, 1954, Box 1, Folder 2, RG 489, Entry 22, NARA-II; Jessica E. Martin, "Corporate Cold Warriors: American Business Leaders and Foreign Relations in the Eisenhower Era" (Ph.D. diss., University of Colorado, Boulder, 2006); "Trade Fairs: How to Win Friends and Customers Abroad," *Time,* July 1, 1957, 72.

7. "Suppliers Providing Equipment or Fixtures and Donating Merchandise and Supplies for the 'Supermarket U.S.A.,'" n.d. (Aug. 1957), Box 26, Folder 14, RG 489, Entry 22, NARA-II; "U.S. Marks 10 Years of Trade-Fair Exhibits," *New York Times,* Dec. 8, 1964, 65; Alison Mackenzie to Alice Murphy, May 16, 1957, Box 36, Folder 338, RG 4-B, RAC.

8. Matthias Kipping and Ove Bjarnar, eds., *The Americanisation of European Business: The Marshall Plan and the Transfer of U.S. Management Models* (London:

Routledge, 1998), 7; Dennison I. Rusinow, "Yugoslavia's Supermarket Revolution," *Reports—American Universities Field Staff* 16, no. 1 (Jan. 1969): 3; Vergil D. Reed to Harrison T. McClung, Feb. 8, 1957, Box 27, Folder 1, RG 489, Entry 22, NARA-II; Patrick Hyder Patterson, "Making Markets Marxist? The East European Grocery Store from Rationing to Rationality to Rationalizations," in *Food Chains: From Farmyard to Shopping Cart,* ed. Warren J. Belasco and Roger Horowitz (Philadelphia: University of Pennsylvania Press, 2009), 196–216.

9. H. W. Brands, *The Specter of Neutralism: The United States and the Emergence of the Third World, 1947–1960* (New York: Columbia University Press, 1989), 141–80; Lorraine M. Lees, *Keeping Tito Afloat: The United States, Yugoslavia, and the Cold War, 1945–1960* (University Park: Pennsylvania State University Press, 1997), xiii; "Food Shortages Threaten Yugoslavia's Political and Economic Survival," *Department of State Bulletin,* Dec. 11, 1950, 937–40; House Committee on Foreign Affairs, *Yugoslav Emergency Relief Assistance Act of 1950,* 81st Cong., 2d. sess., H. Rpt. 3179, 1950, 1951; House Committee on Foreign Affairs, *Yugoslav Emergency Relief Assistance Act of 1950, Hearings,* 81st Cong., 2d sess., Nov. 29, 30, 1950, 20; "Providing Foodstuffs for Yugoslavia," *Department of State Bulletin,* Jan. 22, 1951, 150.

10. John R. Lampe, Russell O. Prickett, and Ljubiša S. Adamović, *Yugoslav-American Economic Relations Since World War II* (Durham, N.C.: Duke University Press, 1990), 73–104; William Taubman, *Khrushchev: The Man and His Era* (New York: Norton, 2003), 289, 342–43, 346; Nikita Khrushchev to the CPSU CC Presidium, Oct. 6, 1956, Archive of the President of the Russian Federation, Moscow, Russia, fond 52, opis 1, delo 349, list 64–113.

11. "Theme and Content of U.S. Official Exhibits at Six Fall International Trade Fairs," April 4, 1957, Box 16, Folder 2, RG 489, Entry 22, NARA-II; Vergil D. Reed to Harrison T. McClung, Feb. 8, 1957, 2, Box 27, Folder 1, RG 489, Entry 22, NARA-II; "Script Synopsis—U.S. Exhibit Zagreb Fair, 1st Draft," May 17, 1957, Box 27, Folder 1, RG 489, Entry 22, NARA-II; Alfred Stern to William R. Traum, "Zagreb Fair—Agricultural Consultant, Prof. A. B. Hamilton," May 20, 1957, Box 27, Folder 1, RG 489, Entry 22, NARA-II; John M. Morahan, "U.S. Supermarket for Zagreb," *New York Herald Tribune,* July 24, 1957, sec. 2, p. 3; Robert Miller to William Traum, "Zagreb Fair: Questions 18 and 7," July 12, 1957, Box 26, Folder 14, RG 489, Entry 22, NARA-II; Robert Miller to William R. Traum, " 'American-Way' Super-Market Exhibits," Oct. 10, 1957, Box 27, Folder 3, RG 489, Entry 22, NARA-II; Maurice F. King to William R. Traum, "Shipping Costs for Zagreb," Aug. 23, 1957, Box 27, Folder 1, RG 489, Entry 22, NARA-II.

12. Elie Abel, "Typical American Supermarket Is the Hit of Fair in Yugoslavia," *New York Times,* Sept. 8, 1957, 1, 18; Office of International Trade Fairs, Industry Exhibits Division, "Report on U.S. Exhibit at Zagreb International Trade Fair," Nov. 8, 1957, Box 27, Folder 3, RG 489, Entry 22, NARA-II.

13. "Yugoslav Agriculture Since 1945," July 14, 1959, Box 73, Folder 3, Fonds 300, Records of Radio Free Europe/Radio Liberty Research Institute (hereafter RFERLRI), Subfonds 8, Publications Department, Series 3, Background Reports (hereafter Subfonds 8, Series 3), Open Society Archives (hereafter OSA), Budapest, Hungary; "Yugoslavia's Agriculture IV," RFE Background Report, Jan. 21, 1958, Box 72, Folder 2, Fonds 300, RFERLRI, Subfonds 8, Series 3, OSA; Joel M. Halpern, "Farming as a Way of Life: Yugoslav Peasant Attitudes," in *Soviet and East European Agriculture,* ed. Jerzy F. Karcz (Berkeley: University of California Press, 1967), 356–84; Melissa K. Bokovoy, "Peasants and Partisans: Politics of the Yugoslav Countryside, 1945–1953," in *State-Society Relations in Yugoslavia, 1945–1992,* ed. Melissa K. Bokovoy, Jill A. Irvine, and Carol S. Lilly (New York: St. Martin's, 1997), 115–38.

14. House Committee on Foreign Affairs, *Yugoslav Emergency Relief Assistance Act of 1950, Hearings,* 81st Cong., 2d sess., Nov. 29, 30, 1950, 44; Robert Mark Spaulding, " 'Agricultural Statecraft' in the Cold War: A Case Study of Poland and the West from 1945 to 1957," *Agricultural History* 83 (Winter 2009): 5–28; Nick Cullather, "The War on the Peasant: The United States and the Third World," in *The Cold War in the Third World,* ed. Robert J. McMahon (New York: Oxford University Press, 2013), 192–207.

15. Radio Free Europe, "Draft Policy Statement on Collectivization," 1963, Box 1, Folder 1, Fonds 300, RFERLRI, Subfonds 2, East European Research and Analysis Department, Series 1, Subject Files Relating to the Bloc (hereafter Subfonds 2, Series 1), OSA, 1, 3, 4; "Summary of Views and Discussion on Collectivization," Jan. 1963, Box 1, Folder 1, Fonds 300, RFERLRI, Subfonds 2, Series 1, OSA, 1.

16. "Yugoslavia's Agriculture," RFE Background Report, Aug. 3, 1957, Box 71, Folder 4, Fonds 300, RFERLRI, Subfonds 8, Series 3, OSA; W. B. Johnston and I. Crkvenčić, "Examples of Changing Peasant Agriculture in Croatia, Yugoslavia," *Economic Geography* 33, no. 1 (1957): 50–71; Frank Oražem, "Agriculture Under Socialism," *Slovene Studies* 11, nos. 1–2 (1989): 215–22; Tito quoted in Desimir Tochitch, "Collectivization in Yugoslavia," *Journal of Farm Economics* 41 (Feb. 1959): 27; "Yugo Agriculture Situation," RFE Background Report, Sept. 21, 1956, Box 70, Folder 4, Fonds 300, RFERLRI, Subfonds 8, Series 3, OSA.

17. Slobodan Stanković, "Soviet Agricultural Road Unsuitable for Yugoslavia, Skupstina Said," RFE Background Report, April 30, 1957, 1, Box 71, Folder 3, Fonds

300, RFERLRI, Subfonds 8, Series 3, OSA; "The New Yugoslav Agrarian Policy: Resolution of Federal People's Assembly on Perspective Development of Agriculture and Cooperatives," Verbatim from *Politika,* Beograd, April 28, 1957, 2, 3, 4, Box 1, Folder 2, Fonds 300, RFERLRI, Subfonds 7, U.S. Office, Series 8, Subject Files Relating to Yugoslavia (hereafter Subfonds 7, Series 8), OSA.

18. Dennison I. Rusinow, "Laissez-Faire Socialism in Yugoslavia," *Reports—American Universities Field Staff* 15 (Sept. 1967): 1–19; Stevo Julius, *Neither Red nor Dead: Coming of Age in Former Yugoslavia During and After World War II* (Ann Arbor: Medvista, 2003), 420; "Reasons for Agricultural Successes in Yugoslavia—II," RFE Background Report, Oct. 15, 1959, 3, Box 73, Folder 3, Fonds 300, RFERLRI, Subfonds 8, Series 3, OSA.

19. Department of Commerce, "American Exhibit, Zagreb International Trade Fair, 1957, De-Briefing of D. Paul Medalie," Nov. 14, 1957, Box 27, Folder 3, RG 489, Entry 22, NARA-II; National Association of Food Chains, NAFC Press Release, April 28, 1958, Box 26, Folder 14, RG 489, Entry 22, NARA-II; Milorad Jovanović to John A. Logan, April 30, 1958, Box 26, Folder 14, RG 489, Entry 22, NARA-II; Rusinow, "Yugoslavia's Supermarket Revolution," 11.

20. Organisation for European Economic Co-Operation, *The Economic Performance of Self-Service in Europe* (Paris: OEEC, 1960); Emanuela Scarpellini, "Shopping American-Style: The Arrival of the Supermarket in Postwar Italy," *Enterprise & Society* 5 (Dec. 2004); Logemann, *Trams or Tailfins?* 185–218; Mary Nolan, "Consuming America, Producing Gender," in *The American Century in Europe,* ed. R. Laurence Moore and Maurizio Vaudagna (Ithaca: Cornell University Press, 2003), 243–61; Patterson, "Making Markets Marxist?" 201–2; Katherine Pence, " 'You as a Woman Will Understand': Consumption, Gender and the Relationship Between State and Citizenry in the GDR's Crisis of 17 June 1953," *German History* 19 (June 2001): 218–52; "Food Costs Less in Hungary," *Toledo Blade,* Nov. 7, 1963, Box 10, Folder 3, Fonds 300, RFERLRI, Subfonds 2, East European Research and Analysis Department, Series 5, Subject Files Relating to Hungary, OSA. Supermarkets were not the only way to address the issue of food availability. In East Germany, for instance, efforts to "fill the 'meat gap' [*Fleischlücke*]" included the construction of a fast-food fried chicken chain and the marketing of frozen fish sticks in the 1960s: Burghard Ciesla and Patrice G. Poutrus, "Food Supply in a Planned Economy: SED Nutrition Policy Between Crisis Response and Popular Needs," in *Dictatorship as Experience,* ed. Konrad H. Jarausch (New York: Berghahn, 1999), 143–62.

21. Nikita Khrushchev to the CPSU CC Presidium, Oct. 8, 1956, fond 52, opis 1, delo 349, list 64–113, Archive of the President of the Russian Federation, Moscow;

Osgood Caruthers, "Moscow Assails Tito Farm Policy," *New York Times,* Jan. 27, 1959, 3, Box 1, Folder 2, Fonds 300, RFERLRI, Subfonds 7, Series 8, OSA. Consumer politics and state legitimation are addressed in Susan E. Reid, "The Khrushchev Kitchen: Domesticating the Scientific-Technological Revolution," *Journal of Contemporary History* 40 (April 2005): 289–316; Susan E. Reid, "Cold War in the Kitchen: Gender and the De-Stalinization of Consumer Taste in the Soviet Union Under Khrushchev," *Slavic Review* 61 (Summer 2002): 211–52; Susan E. Reid, "'Our Kitchen Is Just as Good': Soviet Responses to the American Kitchen," in *Cold War Kitchen,* 83–112.

22. Lazar Volin, "Khrushchev and the Soviet Agricultural Scene," in *Soviet and East European Agriculture,* 3; Nikita S. Khrushchev, *Stroitel'stvo kommunizma v SSSR I razvitie sel'skogo khoziaistva,* vol. 2 (Moscow: Gosudarstvennoe izdatel'stvo politicheskoi literatury, 1962–64), 126–27, quoted in Taubman, *Khrushchev,* 262; Reid, "Cold War in the Kitchen," 221, quoting John Gunther, *Inside Russia Today,* rev. ed. (1958; Harmondsworth, U.K.: Penguin, 1964), 422.

23. Taubman, *Khrushchev,* 427; "Khrushchev Sees Soviet Farm Lead," *New York Times,* May 24, 1957, 3. On the broader context of Khrushchev's charged-up rhetoric of economic competition in the mid-1950s, see David C. Engerman, "The Romance of Economic Development and New Histories of the Cold War," *Diplomatic History* 28 (Jan. 2004): 24–54.

24. Edmund Nash, "Purchasing Power of Soviet Workers, 1953," Aug. 1953, Box 7, RG 306, U.S. Information Agency Records, Entry 1003, Feature Packets, Recurring Subjects, NARA-II; Lauren K. Soth, "If the Russians Want More Meat," *Des Moines Register,* Feb. 10, 1955, in *Pulitzer Prize Editorials: America's Best Writing, 1917–2003,* 3d ed., ed. William David Sloan and Laird B. Anderson (Ames: Iowa State University Press, 2003), 137; Arch N. Booth, "Products of Free Choice," address to Chamber of Commerce of the United States, Annual Meeting, Washington, D.C., April 26, 1964, Series I, Box 25, Chamber of Commerce of the United States Records, Hagley Museum and Library Archives, Wilmington, Del.

25. Nikita Khrushchev, "To Overtake and Outstrip in the Next Years the United States of America in the Per Capita Output of Meat, Butter, and Milk," Leningrad, May 22, 1957, Foreign Broadcast Information Service, *Daily Report, Foreign Radio Broadcasts,* May 24, 1957, pp. CC5, 7, 8, 11; David C. Engerman, "South Asia and the Cold War," in *The Cold War in the Third World,* 73–74; Audra J. Wolfe, *Competing with the Soviets: Science, Technology, and the State in Cold War America* (Baltimore: Johns Hopkins University Press, 2012), 55–73; David C. Engerman, *Know Your Enemy: The Rise and Fall of America's Soviet Experts* (New York: Oxford University Press,

2011), 121; Robert M. Collins, *More: The Politics of Economic Growth in Postwar America* (New York: Oxford University Press, 2000), 46–47.

26. Jenny Leigh Smith, *Works in Progress: Plans and Realities on Soviet Farms, 1930–1963* (New Haven: Yale University Press, 2014), 228, 1, 9. Oscar Sanchez-Sibony suggests that even if Soviet "ideational discourse" prioritized competition with the United States, in reality most of the nation's economic policies in the 1960s and 1970s sought "accommodation and cooperation" with the West: Sanchez-Sibony, *Red Globalization: The Political Economy of the Soviet Cold War from Stalin to Khrushchev* (New York: Cambridge University Press, 2014), 8.

27. "Garst and Chairman Khrushchev," Radio Free Europe report, Nov. 19, 1964, Box 1, Folder 1, Fonds 300, RFERLRI, Subfonds 2, Series 1, OSA; Roswell Garst to Fred Lehman, Jim Wallace, Bob Wood, and Hugh Morrison, Nov. 2, 1955, Reel 50, Henry A. Wallace Papers, Microfilm Edition, University of Iowa Library, Special Collections, Iowa City, Iowa.

28. Agricultural gigantism, patterned after American industrial practice, was a central feature of 1920s Soviet economic policies. See Deborah K. Fitzgerald, *Every Farm a Factory: The Industrial Ideal in American Agriculture* (New Haven: Yale University Press, 2003), 157–83. On corn's place in plans for boosting meat and dairy production, see Taubman, *Khrushchev,* 305; Smith, *Works in Progress,* 163; "Conference of Farm Personnel of Northwest Provinces and Autonomous Republics," *Pravda,* Apr. 13, 1955, translated in *Current Digest of the Soviet Press,* May 25, 1955, 9, 11.

29. Smith, *Works in Progress,* 163; Volin, "Khrushchev and the Soviet Agricultural Scene," 14–15.

30. Nikita Khrushchev, June 3, 1957, interview on CBS television, Foreign Broadcast Information Service, *Daily Report, Foreign Radio Broadcasts,* June 4, 1957, BB2, BB5, BB7.

31. Ibid., BB7; Taubman, *Khrushchev,* 303–5.

32. Anatole I. Popluiko, "Comment on Lazar Volin, 'Khrushchev and the Soviet Agricultural Scene,'" in *Soviet and East European Agriculture,* 25; Nikita Khrushchev, "The Shelves in Our Stores Are Empty," in *Memoirs of Nikita Khrushchev,* vol. 2: *Reformer, 1945–1964,* ed. Sergei Khrushchev (University Park: Pennsylvania State University Press, 2006), 409. It is worth noting that the Soviet Union's foreign aid programs of the 1950s focused primarily on industrial development, not agricultural transformation, outside its own borders. See Joseph S. Berliner, *Soviet Economic Aid: The New Aid and Trade Policy in Underdeveloped Countries* (New York: Praeger, 1958), 30–55.

33. Office of the American National Exhibition in Moscow, "Excerpts of Round-table Discussion on Plans for Moscow Exhibition Held with Newspaper Correspondents in New York City," Jan. 8, 1959, 2, 5, Box 1, Folder 5, RG 306, U.S. Information Agency Records, Entry 54, Records Relating to the American Exhibit in Moscow, NARA-II. On the VDNKh, see Caute, *The Dancer Defects,* 34; Anya von Bremzen, *Mastering the Art of Soviet Cooking: A Memoir of Food and Longing* (New York: Crown, 2013), 74.

34. Office of the American National Exhibition, "Excerpts of Roundtable Discussion," 6, 7.

35. "Basic Policy Guidance for the U.S. Exhibit in Moscow in 1959," Jan. 1959, 1–2, Box 1, Folder 5, RG 306, U.S. Information Agency Records, Entry 54, Records Relating to the American Exhibit in Moscow, NARA-II; Abbott Washburn to Franklin J. Lunding, Feb. 24, 1959, Box 1, Folder 6, RG 306, U.S. Information Agency Records, Entry 54, Records Relating to the American Exhibit in Moscow, NARA-II; Mechlin Moore, "Mikoyan Goes to See Supermarket—and Buys," *Washington Post,* Jan. 7, 1959, 1.

36. Carbone, "Staging the Kitchen Debate," 70; Llewellyn E. Thompson to Department of State, Nov. 17, 1958, Box 2, Folder 2, RG 306, U.S. Information Agency Records, Entry 54, Records Relating to the American Exhibit in Moscow, NARA-II; Abbott Washburn to George Nelson, "Suggested Items for Food Exhibits in Moscow based on Interviews with State Department and USIA Personnel," March 4, 1959, Box 1, Folder 7, RG 306, U.S. Information Agency Records, Entry 54, Records Relating to the American Exhibit in Moscow, NARA-II; Barbara A. Sampson to Phil George, Feb. 25, 1959, Box 1, Folder 7, RG 306, U.S. Information Agency Records, Entry 54, Records Relating to the American Exhibit in Moscow, NARA-II.

37. Allen Wagner to Abbott Washburn, March 2, 1959, Box 1, Folder 7, RG 306, U.S. Information Agency Records, Entry 54, Records Relating to the American Exhibit in Moscow, NARA-II; Clarence Francis, Oral History Interview with Ed Edwin, 1967, Series III, No. 36, Eisenhower Administration Project, Columbia University Libraries Oral History Research Office, New York, N.Y.; Washburn to Nelson, "Suggested Items," March 4, 1959.

38. George V. Allen, Oral History Interview #2 with Ed Edwin, Washington, D.C., 1967, Series III, No. 4, Eisenhower Administration Project, Columbia University Libraries Oral History Research Office, New York, N.Y.; "Debate in Sokolniki Park," *Christian Science Monitor,* July 29, 1959, 14; Francis B. Stevens, "A New Crack in the Iron Curtain," *U.S. News and World Report,* Aug. 10, 1959, 39.

39. Vladimir Zhukov, "What the Facts Say," *Pravda*, July 28, 1959, 4, translated in *Current Digest of the Soviet Press*, August 26, 1959, 9–10; "The Two Worlds: A Day-Long Debate," *New York Times*, July 25, 1959, 3; Lynne Attwood, *Gender and Housing in Soviet Russia: Private Life in a Public Space* (Manchester, U.K.: Manchester University Press, 2010), 155; "When Nixon Took on Khrushchev," *U.S. News and World Report*, Aug. 3, 1959, 37; Amy Randall, *The Soviet Dream World of Retail Trade and Consumption in the 1930s* (New York: Palgrave Macmillan, 2008), 134–53; Gary S. Cross, *An All-Consuming Century: Why Commercialism Won in Modern America* (New York: Columbia University Press, 2000), 1–9.

40. "Two Worlds," *New York Times*, 1; Reid, "'Our Kitchen Is Just as Good,'" 83–112. For especially astute analyses of the relationship between gender roles, household technologies, and socialist state planning in non-Soviet contexts, see Karin Zachmann, "A Socialist Consumption Junction: Debating the Mechanization of Housework in East Germany, 1956–1957," *Technology and Culture* 43 (Jan. 2002): 73–99; Paulina Bren, *The Greengrocer and His TV: The Culture of Communism After the 1968 Prague Spring* (Ithaca: Cornell University Press, 2010), 159–76.

41. V. Osipov, "First Day, First Impressions," *Izvestia*, July 26, 1959, 3, translated in *Current Digest of the Soviet Press*, August 26, 1959, 7; "Unfavorable Comments on Exhibit," n.d. (Sept. 1959), Box 4, Folder 4, RG 306, U.S. Information Agency Records, Entry 54, Records Relating to the American Exhibit in Moscow, NARA-II; George V. Allen, Oral History Interview #2 with Ed Edwin, Washington, D.C., 1967, 124.

42. Arkady Perventsev, "To Be Friends We Must Know Each Other," *Trud*, Aug. 30, 1959, 4, translated in *Current Digest of the Soviet Press*, September 30, 1959, 12; Julie Hessler, *A Social History of Soviet Trade: Trade Policy, Retail Practices, and Consumption, 1917–1953* (Princeton: Princeton University Press, 2004), 286; Jenny Leigh Smith, "Empire of Ice Cream: How Life Became Sweeter in the Postwar Soviet Union," in *Food Chains*, 142–57; Smith, *Works in Progress*, 151–52.

43. Greer, *America the Bountiful*, 172–73; "Text of the Address Made by Khrushchev at Civic Dinner in San Francisco," *New York Times*, Sept. 22, 1959, 23; George Mills, "25,000 Greet Khrushchev: He Challenges U.S. to Contest in Corn and Meat," *Des Moines Register*, Sept. 23, 1959, 1, 10; Nikita Khrushchev, Speech at the Reception in the Des Moines Chamber of Commerce, Sept. 22, 1959, in *Khrushchev in America* (New York: Crosscurrents, 1960), 153, 154, 155, 157.

44. Taubman, *Khrushchev*, 427; Nikita Khrushchev, Speech Broadcast over U.S. Television, Sept. 27, 1959, in *Khrushchev in America*, 205; U. M. Trofimova, Speech

Before the Meeting of the People of Moscow in Honor of N. S. Khrushchev's Return to the Soviet Union, Sept. 28, 1959, in *Khrushchev in America*, 214.

45. Kiplinger Washington Agency, *Washington Letter*, Aug. 8, 1959, Box 1, Folder 9, RG 306, U.S. Information Agency Records, Entry 54, Records Relating to the American Exhibit in Moscow, NARA-II; Richard M. Nixon, Speech by the Vice President of the United States at the 1960 Soil Conservation Field Days, Sioux Falls, S.D., Sept. 23, 1960, The American Presidency Project, ed. John T. Woolley and Gerhard Peters, http://www.presidency.ucsb.edu/ws/index.php?pid=25434 (accessed October 20, 2009).

46. Taubman, *Khrushchev*, 480–81, 507, 516, 519–20; Reid, "Cold War in the Kitchen," 251. For a fictionalized account of the period that highlights the connections between consumer expectations of abundance and the rapid decline in Khrushchev's claim to power, see Francis Spufford, *Red Plenty: Inside the Fifties' Soviet Dream* (London: Faber and Faber, 2010).

47. Taubman, *Khrushchev*, 615–17; Central Intelligence Agency, Office of Research and Reports, "The Significance of Four Million Tons of U.S. Wheat for Food Consumption in the USSR," Oct. 15, 1963, Box 28, Folder Wheat, Theodore Sorensen Papers, John F. Kennedy Library, Boston, Mass.; Von Bremzen, *Mastering the Art of Soviet Cooking*, 147, 148.

48. Nikita Khrushchev, *Memoirs of Nikita Khrushchev*, 2:355, 412, 413, 415, 418, 417. France's central food markets, particularly Paris's Les Halles, had long been an object of derision in the West. The historian Herbert Lüthy, for instance, declared Les Halles in 1955 to be "an archaism, an economic absurdity, perhaps the most absurd legacy of centuries of French centralism. . . . Every night a whole quarter of the city is turned into a welter of fish and blood and rotting vegetable refuse." Herbert Lüthy, *France Against Herself: A Perceptive Study of France's Past, Her Politics, and Her Unending Crises* (New York: Praeger, 1955), 22. Perhaps even more ironically, Bulgarians were busy building supermarkets as Khrushchev wrote: see "Супермаркети [Supermarkets]," n.d. (June 1971?), Box 77, Fonds 300, RFERLRI, Subfonds 20, Bulgarian Unit, Series 2, Subject Card Files, OSA.

49. "Putting Supermarkets on the Steppes," *Business Week*, Sept. 20, 1969, 78, 80; Robert F. Dietrich, "No Ink at This Red Super," *Progressive Grocer* (Aug. 1975): 60–62. Supermarkets expanded much more rapidly in Russia after the collapse of the Soviet Union in 1991, as various German, Dutch, and French chains quickly moved into the region: Liesbeth Dries, Thomas Reardon, and Johan F. M. Swinnen, "The Rapid Rise of Supermarkets in Central and Eastern Europe: Implications for the

Agrifood Sector and Rural Development," *Development Policy Review* 22 (Sept. 2004): 525–56; Jeanne Whalen, " 'Hypermarkets' Herald New Phase in Retail," *Moscow Times,* Dec. 23, 1997.

50. H. H. Loeffler, "Yugoslav Trek from Farm to City Steps Up Market for Packaging Materials, Handling Equipment," *International Commerce,* Dec. 7, 1964, 9, Box 2, Folder 4, Fonds 300, RFERLRI, Subfonds 7, Series 8, OSA; D.J., "The Food Industry," *Yugoslav Survey* 3 (July 1962): 1441.

51. "Unjustifiably High Profit Margins in Agricultural Procurement," *Belgrade Privredni Pregled,* Aug. 27, 1965, 7, Box 1, Folder 3, Fonds 300, RFERLRI, Subfonds 10, Balkan Section: Albanian and Yugoslav Files, Series 3, Yugoslav Subject Files II, OSA; Rusinow, "Yugoslavia's Supermarket Revolution," 5, 11, 14, 17.

52. Milica Uvalić, *Investment and Property Rights in Yugoslavia: The Long Transition to a Market Economy* (Cambridge: Cambridge University Press, 1992); "Tito Talks on TV," *Politika,* Dec. 30, 1966, 1, Box 261, Folder 3, Fonds 300, RFERLRI, Subfonds 10, Balkan Section: Albanian and Yugoslav Files, Series 2, Yugoslav Subject Files I, OSA; Clyde R. Keaton, "Yugoslav Farm Policy Aims at Gradual Collectivization," *Foreign Agriculture,* Oct. 3, 1966, 6–7, Box 1, Folder 3, Fonds 300, RFERLRI, Subfonds 7, Series 8, OSA; "Tito at the Cooperative 'Sloga' of Trstenik," *Politika,* March 17, 1966, 1, Box 5, Folder 3, Fonds 300, RFERLRI, Subfonds 10, Balkan Section: Albanian and Yugoslav Files, Series 2, Yugoslav Subject Files I, OSA; "Lack of Cold-Storage Space," *Ekonomska Politika,* July 10, 1965, 889, Box 5, Folder 4, Fonds 300, RFERLRI, Subfonds 10, Balkan Section: Albanian and Yugoslav Files, Series 2, Yugoslav Subject Files I, OSA.

53. "President Tito Talks with Farmers," *Politika,* April 2, 1967, 1, Box 6, Folder 1, Fonds 300, RFERLRI, Subfonds 10, Balkan Section: Albanian and Yugoslav Files, Series 2, Yugoslav Subject Files I, OSA; Rade Vujović, "The Dark Region," *Borba,* May 19, 1968, 2, Box 5, Folder 6, ibid.

54. Stipe Lovreta, "Retail Trade Network's 1961–1971 Progress Described," *Belgrade Privredni Pregled,* Sept. 3, 1973, 8, Box 90, Folder 9, Fonds 300, RFERLRI, Subfonds 10, Balkan Section: Albanian and Yugoslav Files, Series 2, Yugoslav Subject Files I, OSA; Ing. A. M., "Development of Fruit Growing," *Yugoslav Survey* 3 (Jan. 1962): 1148, 1149, 1150; Dusan Pejcić, "Agriculture—'Achilles Heel' of Yugoslav Economy (II)," RFE Background Report, Sept. 13, 1962, Box 75, Folder 1, Fonds 300, RFERLRI, Subfonds 8, Series 3, OSA.

55. "A.M. Intro-Freeman," Radio Free Europe report, Aug. 22, 1963, Box 1, Folder 1, Fonds 300, RFERLRI, Subfonds 2, Series 1, OSA; "Proposes Local Currency-Farm Tie-Up," RFE Special report, Feb. 20, 1964, Box 1, Folder 1, Fonds 300, RFERLRI,

Subfonds 2, Series 1, OSA; Lampe, Prickett, and Adamović, *Yugoslav-American Economic Relations,* 69–71.

56. Lampe, Prickett, and Adamović, *Yugoslav-American Economic Relations,* 117; Clyde R. Keaton, "Yugoslavia Becoming Cash Market as Its Economy Grows," *Foreign Agriculture,* Dec. 21, 1964, 9, Box 2, Folder 4, Fonds 300, RFERLRI, Subfonds 7, Series 8, OSA; "Eastern Europe Cattle Industry Expansion," RFE report, Nov. 29, 1973, Box 2, Folder 2, Fonds 300, RFERLRI, Subfonds 2, Series 1, OSA; Zdenko Antić, "Private Sector in Yugoslav Agriculture," RFE Background Report, Dec. 4, 1969, Box 78, Folder 4, Fonds 300, RFERLRI, Subfonds 8, Series 3, OSA; Slobodan Stanković, "Yugoslavia's Agriculture Again at the Crossroads," RFE Background Report, July 30, 1975, Box 82, Folder 1, Fonds 300, RFERLRI, Subfonds 8, Series 3, OSA; David Binder, "Keeping Up with the Jovanovics," *New York Times Magazine,* April 3, 1966, 38, 52.

57. On food shortages and bread riots, see Zdenko Antić, "Serious Shortcomings in Food Supplies in Belgrade," RAD Background Report 257, Nov. 26, 1979, Box 84, Folder 1, Fonds 300, RFERLRI, Subfonds 8, Series 3, OSA; Zdenko Antić, "Discussion on Price Increases Causes Panic Buying in Yugoslavia," Aug. 21, 1981, Box 43, Folder 4, Fonds 205, Records of the Open Media Research Institute, Subfonds 4, Information Services Department, Series 80, Yugoslav Subject Files, OSA; Victoria Pope, "Yugoslavia's Leaders Fear Public Unrest as Meat, Coffee, Gasoline Become Scarce," *Wall Street Journal,* Oct. 28, 1982, 35; Robert F. Miller, "Developments in Yugoslav Agriculture: Breaking the Ideological Barrier in a Period of General Economic and Political Crisis," *Eastern European Politics and Societies* 3 (Fall 1989): 501. Significant studies that offer multicausal explanations of Yugoslavia's collapse include Susan L. Woodward, *Socialist Unemployment: The Political Economy of Yugoslavia, 1945–1990* (Princeton: Princeton University Press, 1995); John R. Lampe, *Yugoslavia as History: Twice There Was a Country,* 2d ed. (Cambridge: Cambridge University Press, 2000); R. J. Crampton, *The Balkans Since the Second World War* (New York: Longman, 2002); Dejan Djokić, ed., *Yugoslavism: Histories of a Failed Idea, 1918–1992* (Madison: University of Wisconsin Press, 2003). On the economic challenges posed by meeting consumer desires in other relatively prosperous Eastern European countries in the 1970s, see Stephen Kotkin, "The Kiss of Debt: The East Bloc Goes Borrowing," in *The Shock of the Global: The 1970s in Perspective,* ed. Niall Ferguson et al. (Cambridge, Mass.: Belknap, 2010), 80–93.

58. Slavenka Drakulić, *How We Survived Communism and Even Laughed* (New York: Norton, 1991), xii, 189, 19. Patrick Hyder Patterson, in "Making Markets Marxist?" notes that Eastern European supermarkets, by "telling customers that they are in

charge could lead them to think of themselves as in charge, and to act accordingly" (216).

59. Even when privatization of the farm and food economies of Eastern Europe *did* occur in the 1990s, the results were hardly auspicious for either consumers or farmers, in the short or long run. See Jessica Allina-Pisano, *The Post-Soviet Potemkin Village: Politics and Property Rights in the Black Earth* (Cambridge: Cambridge University Press, 2007); Rachel Sabates-Wheeler, *Cooperation in the Romanian Countryside: An Insight into Post-Soviet Agriculture* (Lanham, Md.: Lexington, 2005); Katherine Verdery, *The Vanishing Hectare: Property and Value in Postsocialist Transylvania* (Ithaca: Cornell University Press, 2003).

Chapter 5. Food Chains and Free Enterprise

1. Erwin D. Canham, "The Farmer in the Space Age," address before the Kansas City, Missouri, Chamber of Commerce, Oct. 7, 1959, Series I, Box 21, Chamber of Commerce of the United States Records, Hagley Museum and Library Archives, Wilmington, Del., pp. 1, 2, 6, 10. Andrew Godley has suggested that American-style agribusiness and Soviet-style collectivization should both be understood as "organizational responses to the problems of marketing perishable foods." Andrew Godley, "The Emergence of Agribusiness in Europe and the Development of the Western European Broiler Chicken Industry, 1945 to 1973," *Agricultural History Review* 62 (Dec. 2014): 316.

2. *Congressional Record*, 85th Cong., 2d sess., vol. 103, pt. 1, Jan. 9, 1957, p. 379; House Committee on Agriculture, *General Farm Legislation, Part 1, Hearings*, 86th Cong., 2d sess., Feb. 18–March 17, 1960, 1; Remarks of Senator John F. Kennedy, Des Moines, Iowa, Kennedy-Johnson Midwest Farm Conference, August 21, 1960, The American Presidency Project, ed. John T. Woolley and Gerhard Peters, http://www. presidency.ucsb.edu/ws/index.php?pid=74133, para. 39–40 (accessed April 17, 2009).

3. Bureau of the Census, *Historical Statistics of the United States* (1976), 457; Bruce L. Gardner, *American Agriculture in the Twentieth Century: How It Flourished and What It Cost* (Cambridge: Harvard University Press, 2002), 4–5; J. L. Anderson, *Industrializing the Corn Belt: Agriculture, Technology, and Environment, 1945–1972* (De Kalb: Northern Illinois University Press, 2008).

4. Douglas Harper, *Changing Works: Visions of a Lost Agriculture* (Chicago: University of Chicago Press, 2001), 176; Pete Daniel, *Dispossession: Discrimination Against African American Farmers in the Age of Civil Rights* (Chapel Hill: University of North Carolina Press, 2013), 6; Adrienne Monteith Petty, *Standing Their Ground:*

Small Farmers in North Carolina Since the Civil War (Oxford: Oxford University Press, 2013).

5. Anton Steen, "The Farmers, the State and the Social Democrats," *Scandinavian Political Studies* 8 (June 1985): 45–63; Vibeke Sørensen, *Denmark's Social Democratic Government and the Marshall Plan, 1947–1950* (Copenhagen: Museum Tusculanum Press, 2001), 184–218; David J. Vail, Knut Per Hasund, and Lars Drake, *The Greening of Agricultural Policy in Industrial Societies: Swedish Reforms in Comparative Perspective* (Ithaca: Cornell University Press, 1994), 91–113; Brian Burkitt and Mark Baimbridge, "The Performance of British Agriculture and the Impact of the Common Agricultural Policy: An Historical Review," *Rural History* 1 (Oct. 1990): 265–80; Virgil W. Dean, *An Opportunity Lost: The Truman Administration and the Farm Policy Debate* (Columbia: University of Missouri Press, 2006); Bruce E. Field, *Harvest of Dissent: The National Farmers Union and the Early Cold War* (Lawrence: University Press of Kansas, 1998).

6. John H. Davis, "Business Responsibility and the Market for Farm Products," Address Before Boston Conference on Distribution, Oct. 17, 1955, Box 3, Folder 78, John H. Davis Papers, National Agricultural Library, Special Collections, Beltsville, Md., 5.

7. John H. Davis, "Teamwork in the Field of Food Distribution," Address at the Annual Convention of the National Association of Retail Grocers, Chicago, Ill., June 18, 1953, Box 3, Folder 47, ibid., 9.

8. John H. Davis, "Where Do You Belong in Tomorrow's Agriculture?" *New Jersey Farm and Garden,* Nov. 1957, 18; Remarks of Senator John F. Kennedy, August 21, 1960, American Presidency Project, para. 8. For Goldberg's contributions, see John H. Davis and Ray A. Goldberg, *A Concept of Agribusiness* (Boston: Harvard Business School, 1957), and Ray A. Goldberg, *Agribusiness Coordination: A Systems Approach to the Wheat, Soybean, and Florida Orange Economies* (Boston: Harvard Business School, 1968).

9. On the rise of integrators, see Monica Richmond Gisolfi, *The Takeover: Chicken Farming and the Roots of American Agribusiness* (Athens: University of Georgia Press, 2016); William Boyd and Michael Watts, "Agro-Industrial Just-in-Time," in *Globalising Food: Agrarian Questions and Global Restructuring,* ed. David Goodman and Michael Watts (London: Routledge, 1997), 192–223; Steve Striffler, *Chicken: The Dangerous Transformation of America's Favorite Food* (New Haven: Yale University Press, 2005).

10. House Committee on Small Business, *Problems in the Poultry Industry, Part 1, Hearings,* 85th Cong., sess. 1, May 9, 10, 13, 1957, 115.

11. Ibid., 16, 21, 23.

12. Ibid., 223. In a 1987 oral history interview, the poultry entrepreneur Don Tyson (of Tyson Foods) echoed the point, suggesting that the contract system emerged when feed dealers "started softening the downs" for farmers, shielding growers from the chaos of an uncertain market while taking the majority of profits that accrued from "the ups." Oral History Interview with Don Tyson, Springdale, Ark., June 1987, interviewed by Franklin Evarts, Volume 1, The Poultry Industry in Arkansas: An Oral History, Shiloh Museum of Ozark History, Springdale, Ark., 60.

13. Ibid., 239. Alessandra Tessari and Andrew Godley have correctly pointed out that in the United Kingdom, supermarkets played a more direct, even aggressive, role in structuring the British integrated poultry business in the 1950s and 1960s. See especially Alessandra Tessari and Andrew Godley, "Made in Italy. Made in Britain: Quality, Brands and Innovation in the European Poultry Market, 1950–80," *Business History* 56 (Feb. 2014): 1–27. Likewise, Neil Wrigley has shown that U.K. supermarkets exercised oligopsony power earlier and more forcefully than U.S. supermarkets; see Wrigley, "The Consolidation Wave in U.S. Food Retailing: A European Perspective," *Agribusiness* 7 (Autumn 2001): 489–513. Helen Mercer considers the U.K. retailers' ability to "dictate terms and conditions to their suppliers" to be a "defining feature of the UK retailing environment"; see Mercer, "Retailer-Supplier Relationships Before and After the Resale Prices Act, 1964: A Turning Point in British Economic History?" *Enterprise & Society* 15 (March 2014): 133.

14. House Committee on Small Business, *Problems in the Poultry Industry, Committee Print,* 85th Cong., 2nd sess., Aug. 22, 1958, 10; House, *Problems, Part 1,* 235; Striffler, *Chicken,* 38–92.

15. Gisolfi, *The Takeover;* Monica Richmond Gisolfi, "Leaving the Farm to Save the Farm: The Poultry Industry and the Problem of 'Public Work,' 1950–1970," in *Migration and the Transformation of the Southern Workplace Since 1945,* ed. Robert Cassanello, Colin J. Davis, and Melanie Shell-Weiss (Gainesville: University of Florida Press, 2009), 64–79.

16. U.S. Department of Agriculture, *Contract Farming and Vertical Integration in Agriculture,* Bulletin no. 198 (Washington, D.C.: USDA, 1958), cover and passim. The early-twentieth-century cooperative movement in U.S. agriculture was in many ways built on the premise of building countervailing power in a marketplace defined by oligopsony and oligopoly; see H. Vincent Moses, "G. Harold Powell and the Corporate Consolidation of the Modern Citrus Enterprise, 1904–1922," *Business History Review* 69 (Summer 1995): 119–55; Charles Postel, *The Populist Vision* (Oxford: Oxford University Press, 2007); Elisabeth S. Clemens, *The People's Lobby: Organizational*

Innovation and the Rise of Interest Group Politics in the United States, 1890–1925 (Chicago: University of Chicago Press, 1997); Victoria Saker Woeste, *The Farmer's Benevolent Trust: Law and Agricultural Cooperation in Industrial America, 1865–1945* (Chapel Hill: University of North Carolina Press, 1998).

17. National Association of Retail Grocers, *The Merger Movement in Retail Food Distribution, 1955–1958* (Chicago: National Association of Retail Grocers, 1959), 3; Frank J. Charvat, *Supermarketing* (New York: Macmillan, 1961), 174, 170, 175, 178; Willard F. Mueller and Leon Garoian, *Changes in the Market Structure of Grocery Retailing* (Madison: University of Wisconsin Press, 1961), 26.

18. Mueller and Garoian, *Changes*, 35–42; House Select Committee on Small Business, *Small Business Problems in Food Distribution, Part 1, Volume 1, Hearing*, 86th Cong., 1st sess., June 22, 23, 1959, 100.

19. Willard F. Mueller and Norman R. Collins, "Grower-Processor Integration in Fruit and Vegetable Marketing," *Journal of Farm Economics* 39 (Dec. 1957): 1474, 1481.

20. Senate Committee on the Judiciary, *To Amend Section 2 of the Clayton Act, Part 2, Hearings*, 85th Cong., 1st sess., March 27–29, April 2–5, 1957, 1002, 1003, 1007, 1008.

21. William E. Folz and Alden Coe Manchester, *Chainstore Merchandising and Procurement Practices: The Changing Retail Market for Fruits and Vegetables* (Washington, D.C.: USDA, Agricultural Marketing Service, 1960), 12, 20, 24; Norman R. Collins and John A. Jamison, "Mass Merchandising and the Agricultural Producer," *Journal of Marketing* (April 1958): 361; House Select Committee on Small Business, *Small Business Problems in Food Distribution, Part 2, Volume 2, Hearing*, 86th Cong., 1st sess., Nov. 10–12, 1959, 788–89.

22. Orville L. Freeman to Lyndon B. Johnson, March 24, 1964, Box 4259, Folder 17, RG 16, Records of the Secretary of Agriculture, Entry 17, General Correspondence (hereafter RG 16, Entry 17), NARA-II, 1; Lyndon B. Johnson, "The President's News Conference at the LBJ Ranch," March 28, 1964, in *Public Papers of the Presidents of the United States* (Washington, D.C.: GPO, 1964), 430.

23. Senate Committee on Commerce, *Study of Food Marketing, Part 1, Hearing*, 88th Cong., 2nd sess., March 23–25, 1964, 11, 52; Senate Committee on Commerce, *Study of Food Marketing, Part 2, Hearing*, 88th Cong., 2d sess., April 8, 13, 16, 22, 23, 29, 30, 1964; National Commission on Food Marketing, *Organization and Competition in Food Retailing* (Washington, D.C.: GPO, 1966), 73, 333, 334; Angus McDonald, "The National Commission on Food Marketing: Legislative Analysis Memorandum #1–66," June 21, 1966, Box 4458, Folder 24, RG 16, Entry 17, NARA-II.

24. Orville L. Freeman to Charles L. Schultze, Nov. 14, 1966, Box 4458, Folder 24, RG 16, Entry 17, NARA-II; United States v. Von's Grocery Co., 384 U.S. 270 (1966); Richard J. Archer, "Techniques of Litigating Government Merger Cases," *Business Lawyer* 25 (Jan. 1970): 723–24; Rom J. Markin, *The Supermarket: An Analysis of Growth, Development, and Change,* rev. ed. (Pullman: Washington State University Press, 1968), 29; "Food Buyers and Sellers," *New Republic,* Jan. 28, 1967, 9.

25. "The Two Worlds: A Day-Long Debate," *New York Times,* July 25, 1959, 3. The cover of the January 3, 1955 issue of *Life* can be viewed online at http://www.cover-browser.com/covers/life/19.

26. Don Slater, *Consumer Culture and Modernity* (Cambridge, Mass.: Blackwell, 1997), 35–36; S. M. Amadae, *Rationalizing Capitalist Democracy: The Cold War Origins of Rational Choice Liberalism* (Chicago: University of Chicago Press, 2003), 3–4; George H. Hildebrand, "Consumer Sovereignty in Modern Times," *American Economic Review* 41 (May 1951): 33. Among works exploring the longer twentieth-century history of debates on the nature and extent of consumer power, see Kathleen Donohue, *Freedom from Want: American Liberalism and the Idea of the Consumer* (Baltimore: Johns Hopkins University Press, 2003); Charles F. McGovern, *Sold American: Consumption and Citizenship, 1890–1945* (Chapel Hill: University of North Carolina Press, 2006), esp. 155–57; Meg Jacobs, *Pocketbook Politics: Economic Citizenship in Twentieth-Century America* (Princeton: Princeton University Press, 2005); Juliet B. Schor, "In Defense of Consumer Critique: Revisiting the Consumption Debates of the Twentieth Century," *Annals of the American Academy of Political and Social Science* 611 (May 2007): 16–30.

27. House Committee on Agriculture, *Food Marketing Costs, Hearing,* 85th Cong., 1st sess., Oct. 8, 9, 1957, 111; "Looking Backwards: 25 Years of Supermarket Progress," *Super Market Merchandising* (Aug. 1955): 84; John A. Logan, "Modern Food Distribution," *Vital Speeches of the Day,* Nov. 15, 1958, 86, 85; David Riesman, "The Nylon War (1951)" in Riesman, *Abundance For What?* (Garden City, N.Y.: Doubleday, 1964), 67–79; Glenn Snyder, "Fantastic Food Show," *Progressive Grocer* (Aug. 1962): 60, 62. See also Adam Mack, "Good Things to Eat in Suburbia: Supermarkets and American Consumer Culture, 1930–1970" (Ph.D. diss., University of South Carolina, 2006), chap. 5.

28. Joseph Persky, "Retrospectives: Consumer Sovereignty," *Journal of Economic Perspectives* 7 (Winter 1993): 183–91; R. A. Gonce, "L. E. von Mises on Consumer Sovereignty," in *Perspectives on the History of Economic Thought,* vol. 3, ed. D. E. Moggridge (Brookfield, Vt.: Elgar, 1990), 136–46.

29. Chamber of Commerce of the United States, *The American Competitive Enterprise System,* Series II, Box 17, Chamber of Commerce of the United States Records, Hagley Museum and Library Archives, Wilmington, Del., 6, 9; Robert H. Bork, "Vertical Integration and the Sherman Act: The Legal History of an Economic Misconception," *University of Chicago Law Review* 22 (Autumn 1954): 157–201, cited in Patrice Bougette, Marc Deschamps, and Frédéric Marty, "When Economics Met Antitrust: The Second Chicago School and the Economization of Antitrust Law," *Enterprise & Society* 16 (June 2015): 318–19. On New Deal–era understandings of consumer "sovereignty," see Meg Jacobs, " 'Democracy's Third Estate': New Deal Politics and the Construction of a 'Consuming Public,' " *International Labor and Working-Class History* 55 (Spring 1999): 27–51. On business leaders' use of Austrian economic theory to undermine support for New Deal liberalism, see Kim Phillips-Fein, *Invisible Hands: The Making of the Conservative Movement from the New Deal to Reagan* (New York: Norton, 2009).

30. "Net of Food Chains below 1% of Sales," *New York Times,* Feb. 1, 1956, 47; James J. Nagle, "Food Chains Give Lesson on Profit," *New York Times,* Nov. 11, 1956, 186; Jennifer Cross, *The Supermarket Trap: The Consumer and the Food Industry,* rev. ed. (Bloomington: Indiana University Press, 1976), 1. On the politics of inflation in the 1950s, see Meg Jacobs, "Inflation: The 'Permanent Dilemma' of the American Middle Classes," in *Social Contracts Under Stress: The Middle Classes of America, Europe, and Japan at the Turn of the Century,* ed. Olivier Zunz, Leonard Schoppa, and Nobuhiro Hiwatari, 130–53 (New York: Sage, 2002). On advertising campaigns suggesting that "housewives" could purchase "freedom" at the supermarket, see Katherine J. Parkin, *Food Is Love: Advertising and Gender Roles in Modern America* (Philadelphia: University of Pennsylvania Press, 2006), 30–78.

31. John Kenneth Galbraith, *The Affluent Society* (Boston: Houghton Mifflin, 1958), 253, 260; Tibor Scitovsky, "On the Principle of Consumers' Sovereignty," *American Economic Review* 52 (May 1962): 262–68; Abba Lerner, "The Economics and Politics of Consumer Sovereignty," *American Economic Review* 62 (March 1972): 258–66.

32. Markin, *Supermarket,* 1, 22, 66; Edward A. Brand, *Modern Supermarket Operation* (New York: Fairchild Publications, 1963), 4; Randall Jarrell, "A Sad Heart at the Supermarket," *Daedalus* 89 (Spring 1960): 362, emphasis in original; "Shopper's Delight," *Life,* Jan. 3, 1955, 38–39, cartoon by Michael Ramus. Tracey A. Deutsch deftly explores the complications of shopping in 1950s supermarkets—primarily as exercises in constraining women's authority—in *Building a Housewife's Paradise:*

Gender, Politics, and American Grocery Stores in the Twentieth Century (Chapel Hill: University of North Carolina Press, 2010), esp. 183–207.

33. Ann Vileisis, *Kitchen Literacy: How We Lost Knowledge of Where Food Comes from and Why We Need to Get It Back* (Washington, D.C.: Island Press, 2008), 171; Senate Committee on Commerce, *Study of Food Marketing, Part 2, Hearing,* 88th Cong., 2d sess., April 8, 13, 16, 22, 23, 29, 30, 1964, 160, 161.

34. Senate Committee on Commerce, *Study of Food Marketing, Part 1, Hearing,* 88th Cong., 2nd sess., March 23–25, 1964, 60, 64; Roger Horowitz, *Putting Meat on the American Table: Taste, Technology, Transformation* (Baltimore: Johns Hopkins University Press, 2005), 139; Mannes, quoted in John J. Lindsay, "The Giant Non-Economy Size," *Nation,* Dec. 9, 1961, 472; "Fat Cats in the Food Market," *Consumer Reports,* June 1966, 306; Jennifer Cross, "Truth in Packaging: The Supermarket Caper," *Nation,* Feb. 1966, 208.

35. Anne Meis Knupfer, *Food Co-Ops in America: Communities, Consumption, and Economic Democracy* (Ithaca: Cornell University Press, 2013), 12; "Information about the Candidates," *Co-Op Bulletin,* May 4, 1950, 1–4, Box 1, Folder A, Cooperative Consumers of New Haven, Inc., New Haven Museum and Historical Society, New Haven, Conn.; Robert L. Smith, "General Manager's Report," *Co-Op Bulletin,* May 14, 1953, 2–3, Box 1, Folder B, Cooperative Consumers of New Haven, Inc., New Haven Museum and Historical Society, New Haven, Conn.; Bob Forbes, "Introduction to Co-Mart, Inc.," n.d. (1973?), Box 1, Folder O, Cooperative Consumers of New Haven, Inc., New Haven Museum and Historical Society, New Haven, Conn. For a perceptive study of how the United Kingdom's Co-Operative food chain struggled to adapt supermarket techniques in the 1950s, see Lawrence Black, "'Trying to Sell a Parcel of Politics with a Parcel of Groceries': The Co-Operative Independent Commission (CIC) and Consumerism in Post-War Britain," in *Consumerism and the Co-Operative Movement in Modern British History,* ed. Lawrence Black and Nicole Robertson (Manchester, U.K.: Manchester University Press, 2009), 33–50.

36. Warren J. Belasco, *Appetite for Change: How the Counterculture Took on the Food Industry,* 2d ed. (Ithaca: Cornell University Press, 2007), 33, 37, 87–93; Knupfer, *Food Co-Ops in America,* esp. chaps. 7, 8, and 9; Thomas Jundt, *Greening the Red, White, and Blue: The Bomb, Big Business, and Consumer Resistance in Postwar America* (New York: Oxford University Press, 2014), 3; Lawrence B. Glickman, *Buying Power: A History of Consumer Activism in America* (Chicago: University of Chicago Press, 2009), 264.

37. "Meat Retailers Say Boycott Slashed Sales but Prices Remain Tied to Wholesale Costs," *Wall Street Journal,* April 9, 1973, 4; Virginia Harris and Fern Krauss to Earl Butz, April 18, 1973, Box 5689, Folder 3, RG 16, Entry 17, NARA-II.

38. "Housewife Seen as Price Force," *Washington Post,* Feb. 24, 1973, 4; Carol R. Chambers to J. Phil Campbell, Feb. 24, 1973 (emphasis in original), Box 5689, Folder 1, RG 16, Entry 17, NARA-II; Ruth Wade to J. Phil Campbell, March 12, 1973, Box 5689, Folder 1, RG 16, Entry 17, NARA-II; Mrs. James J. Powers to J. Phil Campbell, Feb. 26, 1973, Box 5689, Folder 1, RG 16, Entry 17, NARA-II.

39. Jim Hightower, *Eat Your Heart Out: Food Profiteering in America* (New York: Vintage, 1975), 239; Chamber of Commerce of the United States, *The Changing Structure of U.S. Agribusiness and Its Contributions to the National Economy,* Series II, Box 29, Chamber of Commerce of the United States Records, Hagley Museum and Library Archives, Wilmington, Del., 1, 2, 15–16, 20.

Chapter 6. Food Power and the Global Supermarket

1. Orville L. Freeman, *World Without Hunger* (New York: Praeger, 1968), x; John F. Kennedy, "Special Message to Congress on Urgent National Needs," May 25, 1961, Speech Files, Papers of John F. Kennedy, John F. Kennedy Presidential Library and Museum, http://www.jfklibrary.org/Asset-Viewer/Archives/JFKPOF-034-030.aspx (accessed October 22, 2014), 1, 3, 4. Aiken's address is in *Congressional Record,* 87th Cong., 1st sess., vol. 107, pt. 13, Sept. 1, 1961, pp. 17913, 17914.

2. *Congressional Record,* 88th Cong., 1st sess., vol. 109, pt. 14, Oct. 1, 1963, p. 18507; *Congressional Record,* 88th Cong., 1st sess., vol. 109, pt. 19, Dec. 19, 1963, p. 25133.

3. Arvin Donley, "The Inside Story of a Groundbreaking Trade Agreement," July 2, 2013, World-Grain.com, http://www.world-grain.com/News/News%20Home/Features/2013/7/The%20inside%20story%20of%20a%20groundbreaking%20trade%20agreement.aspx?cck=1 (accessed January 12, 2016); Komer quoted in Kristin L. Ahlberg, *Transplanting the Great Society: Lyndon Johnson and Food for Peace* (Columbia: University of Missouri Press, 2008), 81–93, 111; Nick Cullather, "The War on the Peasant: The United States and the Third World," in *The Cold War in the Third World,* ed. Robert J. McMahon (New York: Oxford University Press, 2013), 192–207.

4. Orville L. Freeman, "Malthus, Marx, and the North American Breadbasket," *Foreign Affairs* 45 (July 1967): 583, 587, 592; Freeman, *World Without Hunger,* 15, 42. On the ways in which U.S. agribusinesses piggybacked onto diplomatic engagement with Spain in the 1950s to open up markets for farm inputs, see Ernesto Clar, "A World of Entrepreneurs: The Establishment of International Agribusiness During the Spanish Pork and Poultry Boom, 1950–2000," *Agricultural History* 84 (Spring 2010): 176–94.

5. Senate Committee on Agriculture and Forestry, *U.S. Foreign Agricultural Trade Policy, Hearing,* 93d Cong., 1st sess., March 23, April 4, 5, 16, 30, 1973, 75.

6. Geoffrey Barraclough, "Wealth and Power: The Politics of Food and Oil," *New York Review of Books,* Aug. 7, 1975, 25, 29; Central Intelligence Agency, Office of Political Research, *Potential Implications of Trends in World Population, Food Production, and Climate* (Washington, D.C.: Office of Political Research, 1974), 2, 3; "U.S. Food Power: Ultimate Weapon in World Politics?" *Business Week,* Dec. 15, 1975, 54.

7. Anthony Lewis, "The Cold Warrior," *New York Times,* March 7, 1976, 24; Norman Podhoretz, "Making the World Safe for Communism," *Commentary,* April 1976, 35.

8. Lewis, "The Cold Warrior," 24.

9. Ibid.; Emma Rothschild, "Food Politics," *Foreign Affairs* 54 (Jan. 1976): 285, 286; Robert L. Paarlberg, "Food, Oil, and Coercive Resource Power," *International Security* 3 (Autumn 1978): 4.

10. William Robbins, "High Cost of the Grain Halt," *New York Times,* Jan. 14, 1980, D1; Senate Committee on Banking, Housing, and Urban Affairs, *U.S. Embargo of Food and Technology to the Soviet Union, Hearings,* 96th Cong., 2d sess., Jan. 22, March 24, 1980; Roger B. Porter, *The U.S.-U.S.S.R. Grain Agreement* (Cambridge: Cambridge University Press, 1984). Dwayne Andreas, head of the Archer Daniels Midland Company, went even further, suggesting that Americans had actually "shot ourselves in the foot" by allowing the Soviets to cultivate trade relations with U.S. competitors; James B. Lieber, *Rats in the Grain: The Dirty Tricks and Trials of Archer Daniels Midland* (New York: Four Walls Eight Windows, 2000), 95; "U.N. Group Urges World Food Plan," *New York Times,* Nov. 24, 1980, D7.

11. William S. Gaud, "The Green Revolution: Accomplishments and Apprehensions," speech, March 8, 1968, Washington, D.C., AgBioWorld, http://www.agbioworld.org/biotech-info/topics/borlaug/borlaug-green.html (accessed September 17, 2014); Norman E. Borlaug, "Green Revolution: For Bread and Peace," *Bulletin of the Atomic Scientists* 27 (June 1971): 6–9, 42–48; Nick Cullather, *The Hungry World: America's Cold War Battle Against Poverty in Asia* (Cambridge: Harvard University Press, 2010), 232–62; Michael Goldman, *Imperial Nature: The World Bank and Struggles for Justice in the Age of Globalization* (New Haven: Yale University Press, 2005); Akhil Gupta, *Postcolonial Developments: Agriculture in the Making of Modern India* (Durham, N.C.: Duke University Press, 1998); Vandana Shiva, "The Green Revolution in the Punjab," *Ecologist* 21, no. 2 (March 1991); Raj Patel, *Stuffed and Starved: The Hidden Battle for the World Food System* (Brooklyn, N.Y.: Melville House, 2007); Edward C. Wolf, *Beyond the Green Revolution: New Approaches for Third World Agriculture,* Worldwatch Paper 73 (Washington, D.C.: Worldwatch Institute, 1986).

12. "IBEC & AA Farms Background," n.d. (Feb. 1963?), Microfilm Reel J-78, IBEC-J, RAC; "Birds All Over the Bush," *Connecticut Life,* May 2, 1963, Microfilm Reel J-79, ibid.

13. "Arbor Acres' Breeding Program," Feb. 27, 1963, Microfilm Reel J-78, IBEC-J, RAC. On the broader consequences of "biological locks," see Jack R. Kloppenburg, Jr., *First the Seed: The Political Economy of Plant Biotechnology, 1492–2000,* 2d ed. (Madison: University of Wisconsin Press, 2004); William Boyd and Michael Watts, "Agro-Industrial Just-in-Time," in *Globalising Food: Agrarian Questions and Global Restructuring,* ed. David Goodman and Michael Watts (London: Routledge, 1997), 192–223.

14. "IBEC & AA Farms Background," 1, 4.

15. "Birds All Over the Bush," 18, 1; Kenneth D. Durr, *A Company with a Mission: Rodman Rockefeller and the International Basic Economy Corporation, 1947–1985* (Rockville, Md.: Montrose, 2006), 57–69; Stephen J. La Perla to W. Todd Parsons, July 7, 1966, Microfilm Reel J-43, IBEC-J, RAC.

16. Ernani Correa to Willis C. Arndt, Feb. 1, 1962, Microfilm Reel J-57, IBEC-J, RAC; J. E. Hinshaw to Henry Saglio, April 29, 1963, ibid.; Henry Saglio to Rodman C. Rockefeller, Sept. 5, 1969, ibid.; "History of Arbor Acres," n.d. (Oct. 1963?), Microfilm Reel J-78, IBEC-J, RAC. IBEC's Food Group in 1966 explicitly declared that it would not enter countries without "reasonable prospects of fiscal and political stability," suggesting an unwillingness to work closely with government leaders the way VBEC had attempted in the late 1940s. W. Todd Parsons to A. J. Kimmick, Aug. 2, 1966, Microfilm Reel J-43, IBEC-J, RAC.

17. John W. Uhlein to V. Peter Mortensen, May 1, 1967, Microfilm Reel J-79, IBEC-J, RAC; V. Peter Mortensen to John W. Uhlein, May 8, 1967, ibid.; Steve Striffler, *Chicken: The Dangerous Transformation of America's Favorite Food* (New Haven: Yale University Press, 2005), 21–30.

18. "Farm Bureau Unit Pushes U.S. Items in Western Europe," *New York Times,* Aug. 20, 1961, F1; Kevin Danaher, "U.S. Food Power in the 1990s," *Race & Class* 30, no. 3 (1989): 31; Lester R. Brown, "Implications of Changing Trade Programs to U.S. Agriculture," address at the National Agricultural Policy Conference, Allerton Park, Ill., Sept. 15, 1965, Box 2, Folder 3, Mordecai Ezekiel Papers, Franklin D. Roosevelt Presidential Library and Museum, Hyde Park, N.Y.; James J. Nagle, "Food Giant Sees Further Growth," *New York Times,* June 6, 1971, F15; Joint Economic Committee, *Food Retailing and Processing Practices, Hearing,* 93d Cong., 2d sess., May 21, 1974, 55, 152.

19. Dennis Henderson, Ian Sheldon, and Daniel H. Pick, "International Commerce in Processed Foods: Patterns and Curiosities," in *Global Markets for Processed Foods: Theoretical and Practical Issues,* ed. Daniel H. Pick et al. (Boulder, Col.: Westview, 1998), 7, 12, 29; Thomas Horst, *At Home Abroad: A Study of the Domestic and Foreign Operations of the American Food-Processing Industry* (Cambridge, Mass.: Ballinger, 1974).

20. Eric Pianin, "Meet the Master of (Risk) Free Enterprise," *Washington Monthly,* April 1981, 33–38. The libertarian Cato Institute has labeled ADM a "case study in corporate welfare" for its remarkable lobbying success: James Bovard, "Archer Daniels Midland: A Case Study in Corporate Welfare," Sept. 25, 1995, Cato Institute, https://www.cato.org/publications/policy-analysis/archer-daniels-midland-case-study-corporate-welfare (accessed November 14, 2017); Alessandro Bonanno, Douglas H. Constance, and Heather Lorenz, "Powers and Limits of Transnational Corporations: The Case of ADM," *Rural Sociology* 65 (Sept. 2000): 440–60; Lieber, *Rats in the Grain,* 77–78; E. J. Kahn, Jr., *Supermarketer to the World: The Story of Dwayne Andreas, CEO of Archer Daniels Midland* (New York: Warner Books, 1991), 4.

21. International Basic Economy Corporation, Annual Report, 1968, Microfiche 0700-20-01, IBEC-J, RAC; International Basic Economy Corporation, Annual Report, 1969, ibid.; International Basic Economy Corporation, Annual Report, 1971, ibid; Arieh Goldman, "Stages in the Development of the Supermarket," *Journal of Retailing* 51 (Winter 1975): 50.

22. Roger Clarke, Stephen Davies, Paul Dobson, and Michael Waterson, *Buyer Power and Competition in European Food Retailing* (Northampton, Mass.: Edward Elgar, 2002), 106–7; Andrew Seth and Geoffrey Randall, *Supermarket Wars: Global Strategies for Food Retailers* (New York: Palgrave Macmillan, 2005), 39–40; Haiming Hang and Andrew Godley, "Revisiting the Psychic Distance Paradox: International Retailing in China in the Long Run (1840–2005)," *Business History* 51 (June 2009): 393.

23. Thomas Reardon and Julio A. Berdegué, "The Rapid Rise of Supermarkets in Latin America: Challenges and Opportunities for Development," *Development Policy Review* 20 (Sept. 2002): 371–88; William I. Robinson, *Latin America and Global Capitalism: A Critical Globalization Perspective* (Baltimore: Johns Hopkins University Press, 2008), 190–94; Richard Henry and Karl Voltaire, "Food Marketing in Transition in Eastern and Central Europe," *Agribusiness* 11 (May 1995): 273–80; Liesbeth Dries, Thomas Reardon, and Johan F. M. Swinnen, "The Rapid Rise of Supermarkets in Central and Eastern Europe: Implications for the Agrifood Sector and Rural Development," *Development Policy Review* 22 (Sept. 2004): 525–56.

24. Jennifer Clapp and Doris Fuchs, "Agrifood Corporations, Global Governance, and Sustainability: A Framework for Analysis," in *Corporate Power in Global Agrifood Governance,* ed. Jennifer Clapp and Doris Fuchs (Cambridge: MIT Press, 2009), 1–25.

25. Nelson Lichtenstein, *The Retail Revolution: How Wal-Mart Created a Brave New World of Business* (New York: Metropolitan Books, 2009), 35–44; Ray A. Goldberg, "A Global Agribusiness Market Revolution: Marketing U.S. Agriculture," in U.S. Department of Agriculture, *Yearbook of Agriculture, 1988: Marketing* (Washington, D.C.: GPO, 1988), 21–22; Bob Ortega, *In Sam We Trust: The Untold Story of Sam Walton and Wal-Mart, the World's Most Powerful Retailer* (New York: Times Business, 2000), 78.

26. Senate Committee on Commerce, Science, and Transportation, *Universal Product Coding System, Hearing,* 93d Cong., 2d sess., Dec. 11, 1974, 2, 26, 62.

27. Ortega, *In Sam We Trust,* 149–50; Jean Kinsey, "The New Food Economy: Consumers, Farms, Pharms, and Science," *American Journal of Agricultural Economics* 83 (Dec. 2001): 1122–23.

28. Glass quoted in, and "organic outgrowth" from, Lichtenstein, *Retail Revolution,* 182; Bethany Moreton, *To Serve God and Wal-Mart: The Making of Christian Free Enterprise* (Cambridge: Harvard University Press, 2009); Stanley D. Brunn, ed., *Wal-Mart World: The World's Biggest Corporation in the Global Economy* (New York: Routledge, 2005); Alan Hallsworth et al., "The US Food Discounter's Invasion of Canada and Britain: A Power Perspective," *Agribusiness* 13 (March 1997): 227–35.

29. James Mammarella and Pete Hisey, "Wal-Mart International Reshapes the World Retailing Order," *Discount Store News* (Jan. 20, 1997): 21, 28; Lichtenstein, *Retail Revolution,* 184–97; Susan Christopherson, "Challenges Facing Wal-Mart in the German Market," 261–74, and Yuko Aoyama and Guido Schwarz, "The Myth of Wal-Martization: Retail Globalization and Local Competition in Japan," 275–92, and Chris Webster, "Supermarkets and the (M)art of *Ling Shou,*" 331–41, in *Wal-Mart World;* Russell Jay Hancock, "Grocers Against the State: The Politics of Retail Food Distribution in the United States and Japan" (Ph.D. diss., Stanford University, 1993).

30. Ray A. Goldberg, "The Role of New Technologies in Changing the Global Food System," in *The Emerging Global Food System: Public and Private Sector Issues,* ed. Gerald E. Gaull and Ray A. Goldberg (New York: Wiley, 1993), 13–22; William D. Heffernan and Douglas H. Constance, "Transnational Corporations and the Globalization of the Food System," in *From Columbus to ConAgra: The Globalization of Agriculture and Food,* ed. Alessandro Bonanno et al. (Lawrence: University Press of

Kansas, 1994), 29–51; Tim Lang, "Food Industrialisation and Food Power: Implications for Food Governance," *Development Policy Review* 21 (Sept. 2003): 555–68; Gary Gereffi, "The Organization of Buyer-Driven Global Commodity Chains: How U.S. Retailers Shape Overseas Production Networks," in *Commodity Chains and Global Capitalism,* ed. Gary Gereffi and Miguel Korzeniewicz (Westport, Conn.: Praeger, 1994), 97, 99; Jason Konefal, Michael Mascarenhas, and Maki Hatanaka, "Governance in the Global Agro-Food System: Backlighting the Role of Transnational Supermarket Chains," *Agriculture and Human Values* 22 (Sept. 2005): 291–302; Neils Fold and Bill Pritchard, eds., *Cross-Continental Food Chains* (New York: Routledge, 2005), 17. An exceptionally clear example of the construction of a transnational food-supply chain appears in Tore C. Olsson, "Peeling Back the Layers: Vidalia Onions and the Making of a Global Agribusiness," *Enterprise & Society* 13 (Dec. 2012): 832–61.

31. John Martin, *The Development of Modern Agriculture: British Farming Since 1931* (New York: St. Martin's, 2000), 67–93.

32. Terry Marsden and Neil Wrigley, "Retailing, the Food System, and the Regulatory State," in *Retailing, Consumption, and Capital: Towards the New Retail Geography,* ed. Neil Wrigley and Michelle Lowe (Harlow, U.K.: Longman, 1996), 33, 37, 38; Andrew Godley and Bridget Williams, "The Chicken, the Factory Farm, and the Supermarket: The Emergence of the Modern Poultry Industry in Britain," in *Food Chains: From Farmyard to Shopping Cart,* ed. Warren J. Belasco and Roger Horowitz (Philadelphia: University of Pennsylvania Press, 2009), 47–61; Marsden and Wrigley, "Retailing, the Food System, and the Regulatory State," 38; Susanne Freidberg, *French Beans and Food Scares: Culture and Commerce in an Anxious Age* (New York: Oxford University Press, 2004), 15, 21, 197, 194–210.

33. John A. Woodhouse, "Sourcing Fruits and Vegetables in a Global Food System," in *The Emerging Global Food System: Public and Private Sector Issues,* ed. Gerald E. Gaull and Ray A. Goldberg (New York: Wiley, 1993), 207–8.

34. Ian Cook, "New Fruits and Vanity: Symbolic Production in the Global Food Economy," in *From Columbus to ConAgra,* 232–48; Stephanie Barrientos et al., *Women and Agribusiness: Working Miracles in the Chilean Fruit Export Sector* (London: Macmillan, 1999), 79–85; Celia W. Dugger, "Supermarket Giants Crush Central American Farmers," *New York Times,* Dec. 28, 2004, A1, A10. See also Madelon Meijer et al., "Supermarkets and Small Farmers: The Case of Fresh Vegetables in Honduras," in *The Transformation of Agri-Food Systems: Globalization, Supply Chains, and Smallholder Farms,* ed. Ellen B. McCullough, Prabhu L. Pingali, and Kostas G. Stamoulis, 333–354 (Rome: Food and Agriculture Organization, 2008); Raquel Silva Gomes,

"Farming for Supermarkets: Its Collective Good Problems and What Brazilian Growers Have Done About Them" (Ph.D. diss., Massachusetts Institute of Technology, 2004); David Neven, "Three Essays on the Rise of Supermarkets and Their Impact on Fresh Fruits and Vegetables Supply Chains in Kenya" (Ph.D. diss., Michigan State University, 2004); Lori Ann Thrupp, *Bittersweet Harvests for Global Supermarkets: Challenges in Latin America's Agricultural Export Boom* (Washington, D.C.: World Resources Institute, 1995); Thomas Reardon and Julio A. Berdegué, "The Rapid Rise of Supermarkets in Latin America: Challenges and Opportunities for Development," *Development Policy Review* 20 (Sept. 2002): 371–88; Thomas Reardon et al., "The Rise of Supermarkets in Africa, Asia, and Latin America," *American Journal of Agricultural Economics* 85 (Dec. 2003): 1140–46.

35. Dugger, "Supermarket Giants," A10.

36. C. Peter Timmer, "Supermarkets, Modern Supply Chains, and the Changing Food Policy Agenda," Center for Global Development Working Paper 162, March 2009, www.cgdev.org/content/publications/detail/1421245 (accessed November 15, 2017), 1; Nick Cullather, "Miracles of Modernization: The Green Revolution and the Apotheosis of Technology," *Diplomatic History* (April 2004): 227–54, and Cullather, "The War on the Peasant," 192–207.

37. David Ekbladh, *The Great American Mission: Modernization and the Construction of an American World Order* (Princeton: Princeton University Press, 2009); Joel Isaac and Duncan Bell, eds., *Uncertain Empire: American History and the Idea of the Cold War* (New York: Oxford University Press, 2012); Alfred E. Eckes, Jr., and Thomas W. Zeiler, *Globalization and the American Century* (New York: Cambridge University Press, 2003).

Epilogue

1. Vikas Bajaj, "In India, Wal-Mart Goes to the Farm," *New York Times,* April 12, 2010; Vikas Bajaj, "Wal-Mart Debate Rages in India," *New York Times,* Dec. 6, 2011.

2. William J. Novak, "The Myth of the 'Weak' American State," *American Historical Review* 113 (June 2008): 752–72.

3. James Ferguson, *The Anti-Politics Machine: Development, Depoliticization, and Bureaucratic Power in Lesotho* (New York: Cambridge University Press, 1990).

4. Michael Conlon, "Venezuela Retail Food Sector, 2015 Annual Report," Global Agricultural Information Network, USDA Foreign Agricultural Service, December 30, 2015, https://gain.fas.usda.gov/Recent%20GAIN%20Publications/Retail%20Foods_Caracas_Venezuela_12-30-2015.pdf (accessed March 21, 2017); Food and

Agriculture Organization, "Venezuela and FAO Create SANA, a New Cooperation Programme to Eliminate Hunger," April 16, 2015, FAO, http://www.fao.org/ameri cas/noticias/ver/en/c/283757/ (accessed June 21, 2017); Christina M. Schiavoni, "The Contested Terrain of Food Sovereignty Construction: Toward a Historical, Relational and Interactive Approach," *Journal of Peasant Studies* 44 (Jan. 2017): 1–32.

5. International Markets Bureau, Agriculture and Agri-Food Canada, "Modern Grocery Retail Trends in Central and Eastern Europe," November 2012, Government of Canada Publications, http://publications.gc.ca/site/eng/9.579669/publication. html (accessed November 15, 2017); Andrea Felsted, "Aldi and Lidl Lead Charge of Discount Supermarkets," *Financial Times*, July 9, 2014; Jakob Hanke and Jan Cienski, "Store Wars: Brussels in Food Fight with Eastern Europe," Politico.eu, Sept. 20, 2016, http://www.politico.eu/article/store-wars-brussels-in-food-fight-with-eastern-europe-supermarket-poland/ (accessed June 21, 2017).

6. Jordan Kleiman, "Local Food and the Problem of Public Authority," *Technology and Culture* 50 (April 2009): 399–417; Julie Guthman, "Neoliberalism and the Making of Food Politics in California," *Geoforum* 39 (May 2008): 1171–83; Andrew Szasz, *Shopping Our Way to Safety: How We Changed from Protecting the Environment to Protecting Ourselves* (Minneapolis: University of Minnesota Press, 2009); Xaq Frohlich, "The Informational Turn in Food Politics: The US FDA's Nutrition Label as Information Infrastructure," *Social Studies of Science* 47, no. 2 (2017): 145–71; Bob Doherty, Iain A. Davies, and Sophi Tranchell, "Where Now for Fair Trade?" *Business History* 55 (March 2013): 161–89.

7. Mark Vandevelde, "Tesco Ditches Global Ambitions with Retreat to UK," *Financial Times*, June 21, 2016; Neil MacFarquhar, "Organic Farms Become a Winner in Putin's Feud with the West," *New York Times*, Nov. 18, 2014, A4; Jacob Sonenshine, "Amazon May Replace a Whole Lot of Whole Foods Cashiers with Robots," *New York Post*, June 19, 2017; Nick Wingfield and Michael J. de la Merced, "Amazon to Buy Whole Foods for $13.4 Billion," *New York Times*, June 16, 2017; Richard Kestenbaum, "Why Amazon Is Buying Whole Foods," *Forbes*, June 16, 2017; Allister Heath, "Amazon's Sparking a Grocery Revolution and Rivals Must Adapt or Die," *Telegraph*, June 16, 2017.

Index

Page numbers in *italics* indicate illustrations.